*South Asians and the shaping
of Britain, 1870–1950*

MANCHESTER
1824

Manchester University Press

South Asians and the shaping of Britain, 1870–1950

A sourcebook

Edited by
Ruvani Ranasinha with Rehana Ahmed,
Sumita Mukherjee and Florian Stadtler

Manchester University Press
Manchester and New York

Distributed in the United States exclusively
by Palgrave Macmillan

Published by Manchester University Press
Oxford Road, Manchester M13 9NR, UK
and Room 400, 175 Fifth Avenue, New York, NY 10010, USA
www.manchesteruniversitypress.co.uk

Distributed in the United States exclusively by
Palgrave Macmillan, 175 Fifth Avenue, New York,
NY 10010, USA

Distributed in Canada exclusively by
UBC Press, University of British Columbia, 2029 West Mall,
Vancouver, BC, Canada V6T 1Z2

British Library Cataloguing-in-Publication Data
A catalogue record for this book is available from the British Library

Library of Congress Cataloging-in-Publication Data applied for

ISBN   978 07190 8513 0 hardback
ISBN   978 07190 8514 7 paperback

First published 2012

The publisher has no responsibility for the persistence or accuracy of URLs for any external or third-party internet websites referred to in this book, and does not guarantee that any content on such websites is, or will remain, accurate or appropriate.

Typeset
by Action Publishing Technology Ltd, Gloucester
Printed in Great Britain
by Bell & Bain Ltd, Glasgow

Contents

List of figures

Acknowledgements

The contributors and the publishers wish to thank the following for permission to use copyright material. Every effort has been made to trace copyright holders, but if any have inadvertently been overlooked, the contributors and the publishers will be pleased to make the necessary arrangements at the first opportunity.

Anna Calder-Marshall for A.C. Marshall, 'Nurses of our Ocean Highways: The Fascinating Story of the Ayahs and Amahs who sail the Seven Seas', *Quiver*, 57, August 1922: 923–6.

Miss Elizabeth Carlile for the extract from Sudhindra Nath Ghose, 'War Diary', June/July 1942, MSS EUR F 153/19.

Getty Images for the use of photograph of protest march of Jamiat-ul-Muslimin, August 1938, image no 3351349; for the use of the photograph 'Meeting Bobby', October 1940, image no. 3242345; and the use of the photograph 'Rafiq Anwar's company of Indian dancers at the Ambassadors Theatre in London', May 1943, image no 3377259.

Houses of Parliament for an extract from Shapurji Saklatvala's maiden speech to House of Commons, HC Deb, 23 November 1922, Vol. 159, cols 115–17.

Kewal Anand and Lokayata Publishers for the use of Mulk Raj Anand's Review, *Indian Writing*, March 1941.

Mary Evans Picture Library for the use of the photograph of Uday Shankar in *Illustrated London News*, 20 March 1937, p. 480.

Richard Sorabji for an extract from Cornelia Sorabji's *India Calling: The Memories of Cornelia Sorabji* (London: Nisbet, 1934).

Satinder Pujji for permission to publish the interview with Squadron Leader Mahinder Singh Pujji.

Shakun Banfield for an extract from Savitri Chowdhary's *I Made My Home in England* (Laindon: printed by Grant-Best Ltd, n.d.).

Shakuntala Tambimuttu for an extract from M.J. Tambimuttu's First Letter, *Poetry London*, February, 1939; for permission to use photo of M.J. Tambimuttu at work at Manchester Square office of *Poetry London*; and for M.J. Tambimuttu's poem 'The Hero' from *Our War*.

The British Library for an extract from Immigration Officers' Report on Joffer Shah (Lascar deserter), 27 October 1930, IOR: L/PJ/9/962; for the use of 'Passport Facilities for Illiterate Indian British Subjects', Foreign Office Circular, 4 September 1931, IOR: L/E/9/954; for an extract from 'Unrest Among Indian Seamen', secret memo to Mr Silver, 16 November 1939, IOR: L/PJ/12/630; for extracts from Secret memo from the Indian Political Intelligence to Mr Silver on the Indian Workers' Association with dossiers on certain members, 1942, IOR: L/PJ/12/645; for extracts from Report on Swaraj House, 8 March 1944, IOR: L/PJ/12/646; for the use of photograph of Sophia Duleep Singh selling the *Suffragette* newspaper outside Hampton Court Palace, 1913, IOR: L/PS/11/52, image P1608; for an extract from petition of Jamiat-ul-Muslimin, August 1938, IOR: L/PJ/12/614; for the photograph of Highlander and Dogra soldiers in a trench with dugouts, August 1915, Photo 24/(294); for the use of cartoon 'Son of Ind wins Britain's most coveted Honour', *War Illustrated*, 13 February 1915; for the Open Letter by M.K. Gandhi to the India Office, 14 August 1914, MSS EUR F 170/8; for the Letter from Walter Lawrence to Lord Kitchener, 28 November 1914, MSS EUR F 143/65; for the Letter from 19 Ludder Singh to Raghubir Singh, 1 July 1915, MSS EUR F 143/84; for the extract of Report 'Operations in France', 19 July 1940, IOR: L/WS/1/355; for the extract from Indian Comforts Fund Progress Report, October 1941 to March 1942, IOR: L/Mil/17/5/2327.

The National Archives for the use of Special Restriction (Coloured Alien Seamen) Order, 1925; and letter from the Under-Secretary of

State to the Chief Constables of scheduled areas, 23 March 1925, HO 45/12314; extracts from the War Diaries of the Ferozepore Brigade, 12 March 1915, WO 9/3922.

The Tower Hamlets Local History Library and Archives for the use of Hindustan Community House: First Report, April 1940.

The Times for the use of the article 'A Princess Fined: Refusal to Pay Taxes', *The Times*, 30 December 1913.

Times Literary Supplement for the use of a review of Cornelia Sorabji, *India Calling: The Memories of Cornelia Sorabji, Times Literary Supplement*, 29 November 1934; and for the use of a review ' Tales of Indians', *Times Literary Supplement*, 7 December 1940; and for the use of the review of Anand's *The Sword and the Sickle'*, *Times Literary Supplement*, 2 April 1942.

We would like to thank Lyn Innes and Rozina Visram for their invaluable conceptual and factual contributions to this sourcebook.

We would also like to thank the Arts & Humanities Research Council (AHRC) for funding this research project (AH/E009859/1).

Contributors

Rehana Ahmed was a Post-Doctoral Research Associate on the three-year AHRC-funded research project *Making Britain: South Asian Visions of Home and Abroad 1870–1950*, based in the English Department at the Open University (2007–10). Her doctoral research was on representations of multicultural Britain in contemporary British Asian fiction, with a focus on class and Muslim identities. She has published articles on work by Moniza Alvi, Hanif Kureishi and Kamila Shamsie, and on the television film *Yasmin*. She is the editor of *Walking a Tightrope: New Writing from Asian Britain* (Macmillan, 2004). She is Senior Lecturer in English Studies at the University of Teesside. Her monograph on literary representations of British muslims will be published by MUP.

Elleke Boehmer was Co-Investigator on the *Making Britain* project. She is the Professor of World Literature in English at the University of Oxford. She has published four novels, *Screens again the Sky* (1990), *An Immaculate Figure* (1993), *Bloodlines* (2000), and *Nile Baby* (2008). She is the author of *Colonial and Postcolonial Literature: Migrant Metaphors* (1995, 2005), the monographs *Empire, the National and the Postcolonial, 1890–1920* (2002) and *Stories of Women* (2005), and of *Nelson Mandela* (2008). She has also produced an edition of Robert Baden-Powell's *Scouting for Boys* (2004).

Sumita Mukherjee was a Post-Doctoral Research Associate to the *Making Britain* project and based at the English Faculty in the University of Oxford (2007–10). She has written a number of articles and book reviews relating to nineteenth- and twentieth-century South Asian and British Imperial history. Her book *Nationalism,*

Education and Migrant Identities: The England-Returned was published by Routledge in 2009. She is Lecturer in Economic History at the University of Glasgow.

Susheila Nasta was the director of both projects: *Making Britain: South Asian Visions of Home and Abroad 1870–1950* and *Beyond the Frame: Indian-British Connections*. She is Professor of Modern Literature at the Open University and Editor of *Wasafiri*. She has written books on Sam Selvon and edited a collection of essays on women's writing, *Motherlands* (Women's Press; Rutgers University Press, 1991). Recent publications include: *Home Truths: Fictions of the South Asian Diaspora in Britain* (Palgrave, 2002) and (ed.) *Writing Across Worlds: Contemporary Writers Talk* (Routledge, 2004).

Ruvani Ranasinha was Co-Investigator on the project *Making Britain: South Asian Visions of Home and Abroad 1870–1950*. She is Senior Lecturer in Modern Literary Studies at King's College London. Her publications include *Hanif Kureishi: Writers and their Works Series* (Northcote House in association with The British Council, 2002) and *South Asian Writers in Twentieth-Century Britain: Culture in Translation* (Oxford University Press, 2007).

Florian Stadtler was a Post-Doctoral Research Associate to the *Making Britain* project based at the Open University. He is Research Associate on *Beyond the Frame: Indian British Connections, 1850–1950*. His PhD research was on the novels of Salman Rushdie and Indian Popular Cinema, and his book on the subject is under preparation with Routledge.

Rozina Visram is a historian and educationalist, and was a consultant on the *Making Britain* project. Her publications include *Asians in Britain: 400 Years of History* (Pluto, 2002) and *Ayahs, Lascars and Princes: Indians in Britain 1700–1947* (Pluto, 1986), as well as a number of books for schools on British Asian history. She is also a contributor to the *Oxford Dictionary of National Biography*. She has worked both in schools and in higher education and contributed to several museum projects. In 2006 Rozina Visram was awarded an Honorary Doctorate by the Open University.

Preface

Elleke Boehmer and Susheila Nasta

It is difficult when we imagine the past to hear the tenor of individual voices or fully feel the texture of public debates that inspired the
cultural, political and intellectual dialogues of those living alongside
each other in a different era. This has certainly been the case with the
often eclipsed narratives, untidy histories and surviving testimonies
of a mixed South Asian community who have been present in Britain
for over 400 years. It is only by entering the archives of individual
writers, or trawling the minutes and memos of political meetings
written soon after specific events, that a reader begins to get a more
nuanced sense of the complex layers of interaction and debate, the
specific moments that drove political action, the prejudices that
created fear-induced propaganda or stereotypes, the conflicted
passions that inspired literary works as well as the many sometimes
imposed silences that surround them.

This sourcebook stems from the collaborative research of a major
three-year interdisciplinary project funded by the Arts and Humanities
Research Council, 'Making Britain: South Asian Visions of Home and
Abroad 1870–1950', which set out to examine, analyse and showcase
the many ways in which South Asians contributed to, interrogated and
helped to diversify British culture between 1870 and 1950. Originally
conceived in 2006 by Susheila Nasta and Elleke Boehmer along with
Rozina Visram, the pioneering historian and author of the Afterword,
the research has benefitted greatly from the expertise and generous
intellectual insights of a large network of internationally distinguished
scholars and curators, many of them leading experts in the field:
among them, Antoinette Burton, Michael Fisher, Lyn Innes, Partha

Mitter, Deborah Swallow, and our partners at the British Library and SALIDAA (South Asian Literature, Diaspora and Arts Archive). Both the concept and the compilation of the material for this book has also been much enhanced by the commitment, rigour and exchange of ideas among the project's core research team (Elleke Boehmer, Rozina Visram, Ruvani Ranasinha, Rehana Ahmed, Sumita Mukherjee and Florian Stadtler, and Principal Investigator of the project Susheila Nasta). Designed as a valuable and useful tool to re-examine, re-contextualize and scrutinize the representation of the history of the South Asian presence in Britain, this book began life as one of several project outputs seeking to raise public and academic awareness of the significant roles that South Asians have played in the shaping and making of Britain. As such, it draws on a carefully selected grouping of archival sources which pinpoint a number of key areas of engagement, designed to enable readers to look both backward and forward in time and to respond through a variety of disciplinary and theoretical spectacles to a sample of the wide-ranging material resources opened up by the project.

Challenging some still surprisingly prevalent thinking that continues to position India's long history in Britain and British Asians firmly outside the nation's frame, the project's general aim was to interrogate familiar top-down models of colonial relations to explore lateral, transverse and often significantly differentiated responses among various displaced, travelling and migrated South Asian individuals, groups and networks across the class, race, gender divide. Taking the zenith of empire 1870 as the starting-point and traversing across eighty years to 1950 – a period which witnessed two world wars, the decline of empire, the fight for Indian Independence and the further unsettling of Partition – we were aware from the outset of the ambitious scope of our task as well as the fact that we could only ever begin to touch the silent edges of several much bigger stories.

There is no doubt that *Making Britain* was partially influenced by imperatives deriving from the theoretical preoccupations of contem-porary postcolonial, diaspora and cultural studies. Humanities scholarship has certainly now begun to focus its attention (belatedly) on the rich sources of Britain's long multicultural past, attempting to unravel diverse histories which are often too large, too conflicted and

too diverse to be neatly organized or shaped into an easily compre-
hensible and thus easily dismissed sequence of cause, effect and
consequence. Such disciplinary directives have frequently been
driven by present-day political concerns, by an increasingly urgent
need to direct our intellectual and ethical energies towards a fuller
understanding of the troubled histories of settlement and continuing
politics of inequality amongst Britain's contemporary migrant
communities – concerns currently prioritized in valuable ways by
funding bodies such as the Arts and Humanities Research Council,
Leverhulme, the ESRC and others. While much recent emphasis has
been placed on the notion of globalization and travel, on the hybrid
deterritorialized migrant as 'everyman' of the contemporary global
world, surprisingly little research has sought to look within, shift the
angle of vision and examine the extent to which Britain's own South
Asian population has long been a part of the formation of the
colonial and postcolonial nation; an integral element, as the well-
known historian of empire Antoinette Burton once put it in a
different context, of a long and troubled 'history-in-the-making'.[1]

In 2007, when we commenced our research into this little known
period of South Asian settlement, we realized that to examine the
underexposed sides of the nation's history through a systematic exca-
vation and interdisciplinary analysis of the available archives was
going to be a daunting task. For while the work of imperial cultural
historians and recent literary and cultural scholarship on history of
the black imperial metropolis has been enabling in many respects, it
has not yet resulted in creating the pedagogical, institutional and
social changes it ideally implies. There are of course many reasons for
this which it is not possible to detail here, but a key one is perhaps to
do with the way one looks, what one is looking for and how we as
critics find new ways of enabling such narratives to emerge more
fully into the field of vision. In consulting the numerous available
archives, we were looking for signs of significant presence, for
impact, for the emotional, psychological, political and cultural
remnants of relationships formed, broken or continued, for evidence

1 A. Burton, *Dwelling in the Archive: Women Writing House, Home and History
  in Late Colonial India* (Oxford: Oxford University Press, 2003), pp. 4–30, in
  particular p. 26.

of cross-cultural exchange, Indian-British friendships and interactions, so creating the base for a narrative which would help to expose lost heritages and influences. In many ways, our searches supplemented the already pioneering work in the period covered by many earlier historians and cultural critics. Yet the process of doing this work also created new and in some ways more intriguing points of departure, raising a series of not only difficult but uncomfortable epistemological, pedagogical and political questions, questions also raised by the gaps between archival traces rather than only by their startling connections.

As this implies, the discursive implications of investigating the South Asian presence in Britain, as in this sourcebook, reach far further than finding new content within that archive, or suggesting alternative ways of approaching it. What the variegated migrant textures of British social, cultural and political life rather suggest is that received ideas of Britishness and belonging, of centre and periphery, of citizenship and the cosmopolitan, need to be rethought in a fundamental way, from the ground up. Moreover, while the process of cultural retrieval is without question a vital one, it is also important to see in what ways these archives anticipate and generate more complicated versions of what today we might call cross-cultural or cosmopolitan global identities, definitions of an already migrant and culturally mixed Britain born on British soil.

The specific sources examined in this collection – sources which, it must be emphasized, form tasters only of the rich materials tracing early Indian pathways through Britain – might be seen as emergent points of light within the migrant archive, points of light that illuminate that palimpsest of documents and historical traces in diverse new ways. Differently put, the diverse texts, advertisements, voice traces, and images gathered here, including the mere smudges of an otherwise unrecorded life left, for example, on an official form, impel us to interrogate existing regimes of knowledge about the migrant and the colonial other. These documents ask us in insistent and compelling ways to return to our received knowledge of migrant histories, and to re-examine our settled understanding both of what it was to be British and what it was to belong to the subcontinent and to the rest of the empire, in the century leading from Queen Victoria's youth to the Second World War.

By looking at the different items selected, we need to ask a series of additional questions and consider their material and epistemological recalcitrance, to borrow a richly resonant term from the work of David Lloyd.[2] We also need to be aware of how they operate as catalysts or even goads to rereading, as engines generating new or revised perceptions of what we thought we already knew about South Asian migrant lives and histories. For it is important to recognize that these sources and traces, these to date forgotten or elided sediments of history, would have been retrieved and collected to no constructive effect if all they did, or invited us as their readers to do, was to enlist and even co-opt early migrant South Asians to the overarching and ultimately triumphalist narrative of Britain, of the tolerant nation coming into its own through absorbing, yet again, as has often been the case, allegedly from Anglo-Saxon times, the stranger from without.[3] Rather than seeing these South Asian-British sources as forming a seamless part of an archive that was already large and expanded, but to date not perceived as such, that was obscured by time or simple neglect, let us ask what the epistemological consequences are of retrieving eclipsed or occluded traces. Once the sources we see here are allowed to ask the questions of the one-time metropolitan centre they have to date silently but insistently posed, under what kinds of pressure are centre-and-periphery models, and of colonialism as outward-directed, from metropole to margin, placed?

To extend the remit of this interrogation a little further, it is worth also considering the significance of occluded and obscured traces; that is, the dangers of over-reading them, not only of overlooking them. When we observe the sometimes faint and seemingly slight, sometimes bold yet marginalized signs and markings left by South Asian migratory crossings to Britain, we must pause to ask, what are we in fact looking at, what are we looking for? To ask such questions implies considering not only what it is to trace networks of travel and connection, but also what is involved when we juxtapose and network traces, as we do within the very structure of this source-

---

2 See D. Lloyd, *Anomalous States* (Dublin: Lilliput Press, 1993).
3 See for example J. Bate, *English Literature: A Very Short Introduction* (Oxford: Oxford University Press, 2010).

book? In other words, does the task of networking traces not also imply thinking about the degree of elaboration and interpretation that traces either invite or permit? As interpreters of migratory texts and texts of migration we need to be careful as to the seductions of incompletion, the spaces around the marks on the page and the indistinctness of the marks themselves that seem to prompt or at least not to prevent speculation. We need to be both accessible to, yet at the same time wary of, their suggestibility.

Trace, Derrida reminds us, designates the shadow of something meaningful that remains after the word has overwhelmed the thing.[4] Though the traces, the faint tracks, the marks in margins, left by Indians in Britain in the late nineteenth and early twentieth centuries, especially by those who were not literate, yet were numerous, such as ayahs, lascars and convalescing soldiers, obviously are not of the same order of meaning as Derrida's trace, a link comes from that connotation of equivocation and indeterminacy in the concept of trace. As Amitav Ghosh also reminds us in *In an Antique Land*, the trace not only records the faint mark of the human on the torn and fragmentary page, it also points to the contingency involved in its discovery or rediscovery, as well as in its interpretation.[5]

But the questions that these documents ask of us do not of course relate only to the past, or to reshaping the prevailing historiography. They also, and with equal insistence, invite us to look at how we perceive multicultural Britain today – where the we refers not only to the wider public, but also to students of multicultural Britain in the academy, to whom this sourcebook is also directed. How do new generations of Britons, both those of recent and those of more long-standing migrant origin, approach the historically diverse make-up of the nation today? These documents suggest one certain answer to that question. In the light of the archive presented here, the relationship of all readers to the community from which they rise must be read in a different way from before.

---

4   J. Derrida, *Acts of Literature*, ed. Derek Attridge (London: Routledge, 1992), pp. 49–50, 61.
5   A. Ghosh, *In an Antique Land* (New Delhi: Seagull Press, 1992), pp. 161, 230.

Chronology of events

1857
Indian Rising
Strangers' Home for Asiatics, Asians and South Sea Islanders
founded in the East End of London

1858
Queen Victoria's Proclamation assuming the Government of India

1861
Religious Society of Zoroastrians founded in Kensington, London

1865
London India Society founded (becomes East India Association in
1866)

1869
Suez Canal opens

1870
National Indian Association set up by Mary Carpenter and Keshub
Chunder Sen
Dutt Family Album (poems by Toru Dutt's father and family)
published by Longmans

1875
Theosophical Society founded in New York

1876

Toru Dutt's *A Sheaf Gleaned in French Fields* published in Calcutta and reviewed by Edmund Gosse in London

1877

Queen Victoria becomes Empress of India

Arrival of Abdul Karim and other Indian servants in Royal Household

1882

Toru Dutt's *Ancient Ballads and Legends of Hindustan* published posthumously by Kegan Paul, Trench & Co, with an introduction by Edmund Gosse.

1883

Edinburgh Indian Association founded

Indian Institute in Oxford built

1885

Indian National Congress founded in India

Liberty's and Co. hold living 'village' display in Battersea

1886

Colonial and Indian Exhibition held in South Kensington

Lal Mohun Ghose stands as Liberal MP at Deptford in General Election, but is defeated. Dadabhai Naoroji is also defeated in Holborn.

1887

Queen Victoria's Golden Jubilee

1888

Glasgow International Exhibition

1889

Shah Jahan Mosque, Woking, built by Dr Gottlieb Leitner (following the establishment of the Woking Oriental Institute in 1883)

1890
Manmohan Ghose poems published in *Primavera* (edited by Laurence Binyon)

1891
Cambridge Majlis founded

1892
Dadabhai Naoroji elected as Liberal MP for Central Finsbury (until 1895)

1893
Independent Labour Party in Britain founded (to become Labour Party in 1906)
Imperial Institute opened in Kensington
Malabari's *Indian Eye on English Life* published in London by Constable

1894
Merchant Shipping Act passed (deters the settlement in Britain of South Asian seamen)

1895
Mancherjee Merwanjee Bhownaggree elected as Conservative MP for Bethnal Green (re-elected 1900 and serves till 1906)
Empire of India Exhibition at Earls Court

1896
K.S. Ranjitsinhji begins to play cricket for the England national side
Oxford Majlis founded

1897
Queen Victoria's Diamond Jubilee
Rev. T. Pandian's (of Madras) *England to an Indian Eye, or English Pictures from an Indian Camera*, published by Elliot Stock

1899
Boer War begins (ends in 1902)

1900
London City Mission opens Ayahs' Home in Hackney

1901
Queen Victoria dies
Naoroji's *Poverty and Un-British Rule* published by Swan Sonnenschein

1905
Partition of Bengal
Aliens Act
India House set up in Highgate by Shyamaji Krishnavarma and begins producing *The Indian Sociologist*
Sarojini Naidu's *The Golden Threshold* published by Heinemann, with an introduction by Arthur Symons

1906
Manmath Mallik stands as a Liberal at St Georges Hanover Square and is defeated. (Also unsuccessful in 1910 at Uxbridge)
Samuel Rahamin exhibits at the Royal Academy

1907
London Muslim League set up by Syed Ameer Ali

1908
Franco-British Exhibition held in London

1909
Curzon-Wyllie assassinated by Madan Lal Dhingra in London
Savarkar's *The Indian War of Independence* published in London

1910
India Society is formed in London

1911
Coronation of George V; Delhi Durbar
Festival of Empire in London
Bhupindra Dharamsala (Sikh Gurdwara) opens at Shepherd's Bush

1912
Sarojini Naidu's *The Bird of Time* published by Heinemann, with an
  introduction by Edmund Gosse

1913
Tagore awarded Nobel Prize

1914
First World War begins; Indian troops arrive on the Western Front
Khudadad Khan first South Asian soldier to be awarded the Victoria
  Cross
Indian Military Hospitals, including Pavilion Hospital, open in
  Brighton
Patcham crematorium for Hindu and Sikh soldiers established
Ramanujan at Cambridge (1914–1918) and elected Fellow of Royal
  Society

1915
Battle of Neuve Chappelle, with a high number of South Asian
  casualties
Horsell Common burial ground for Muslim soldiers built
Indian Political Intelligence unit begins monitoring South Asians in
  Britain (until 1945)

1916
Indian troops are withdrawn from France and redeployed to
  Messopotamia

1917
Indra Lal Roy, a student at St Paul's, joins Royal Flying Corps

1918
Armistice Day – end of First World War
British women win the right to vote

1919
Treaty of Versailles
Government of India Act

Amritsar Massacre following imposition of Rowlatt Act
Alien Restrictions Act
'Race riots' break out in Cardiff and other major seaports;
    repatriation attempts follow
YMCA found Indian Students' Union in Gower Street
Ayub Ali arrives in London and sets up the Shah Jolal Restaurant in
    the East End

1920
Aliens Order

1921
Further attempts to repatriate South Asian seamen
Sunity Devee's *The Autobiography of an Indian Princess* published
    (John Murray)

1922
Irish Free State established
Saklatvala elected MP for Battersea North (re-elected 1924)
Niranjan Pal's play 'The Goddess' performed in London theatres

1923
Uday Shankar and Anna Pavlova perform together at the Royal
    Opera House

1924
Wembley Empire Exhibition

1925
Special Restriction (Coloured Alien Seamen) Order (remains in force
    until 1942)
Indian Seamen's Union founded (with Saklatvala as president,
    Clemens Palme Dutt as coordinator, and N.J. Upadhyaya as
    secretary-organizer)
Indian Freedom Association inaugurated (becomes Indian Home
    Rule League then Indian Freedom League in 1928)

1926

General strike

Special Certificate of Identity and Nationality issued to South Asian seamen registered as 'aliens'

Coloured Men's Institute established in East London, with Kamal Chunchie as pastor/warden (closes 1930, re-launches 1933)

Anagarika Dharmapala, Buddhist teacher, addresses audiences in London

1928

Simon Commission to India and Indian protest against it

V.K. Krishna Menon becomes secretary of the Commonwealth of India League (later India League)

1930

World economic depression

Gandhi's salt march

1931

Special Certificate of Identity and Nationality issued to all South Asian seamen

1934

Modern Indian art exhibition at New Burlington Galleries, London

Hindustani Social Club established (1934/35), with Surat Alley as honorary secretary

Jamiat-ul-Muslimin (charitable society for the promotion of Islam) founded

Menon elected Labour councillor for Ward 4 in the Borough of St Pancras (serves for 14 years)

C. Sorabji's *India Calling* published (Nisbet & Co.)

1935

British Shipping (Assistance) Act passed (lifted in 1936)

Colonial Seamen's Association (CSA) formed, with Surat Alley as secretary

Penguin Books founded by Allen Lane, with Menon as founding editor of non-fiction imprint Pelican (first title published 1937)

Bibliophile bookshop, run by Sasadhar Sinha, opens in Little Russell
    Street
Anand helps found the All-India Progressive Writers' Union in
    London
Anand's *Untouchable* published (Lawrence & Wishart)
J. Vijayatunge's *Grass For My Feet* published (Edwin Arnold)

1936
Death of George V, accession and abdication of Edward VIII,
    accession of George VI
Spanish Civil War begins
Dr Jainti Saggar becomes the first Indian to be elected councillor in
    Scotland (Dundee, Labour)
Anand's *Coolie* published (Lawrence & Wishart)

1937
Sabu stars in *The Elephant Boy*
Indian Workers' Association (originally Indian Workers' Union)
    founded
All-India Seamen's Federation founded, with Aftab Ali as president
Federation of Indian Student Societies in Great Britain founded
Hindustan Community House established, with Kundan Lal Jalie as
    warden
Anand's *Two Leaves and a Bud* published (Lawrence & Wishart)
Cedric Dover's *Half-Caste* published (Secker & Warburg)

1938
Dr Chuni Lal Katial elected Mayor of Finsbury (Britain's first Asian
    mayor)
Akbar Ali Khan and Surat Alley set up the Oriental Film Artistes'
    Union

1939
Germany invades Poland, Britain and France declare war on
    Germany
Animal Transport Companies from the Royal Indian Army Service
    Corps sent to France
Indian Comforts Fund founded

South Asian seamen across Britain strike for better pay and working
conditions
Tambimuttu's magazine *Poetry London* inaugurated

1940

Udham Singh assassinates Michael O'Dwyer at a meeting of the East
India Association, Caxton Hall, London, and is subsequently
hanged
Noor Inayat Khan evacuated to England from France and joins the
Women's Auxiliary Air Force
Indian troops evacuated at Dunkirk
Indian Army divisions fight in North and East African campaigns
24 Indian pilots arrive in the UK to fly with the Royal Air Force
Anand's *Across the Black Waters* published (Lawrence & Wishart)
Ahmed Ali's *Twilight in Delhi* published (Hogarth)

1941

East London Mosque and Islamic Centre open on Commercial Road
Tambimuttu's *Out of this War* published (The Fortune Press)
Noor Inayat Khan recruited into F Section of the Special Operations
Executive

1942

Cripps mission to India
Indian National Congress makes 'Quit India' resolution
Swaraj House formed
Anand (and others) begin contributing to BBC radio programmes
Talking to India and *Voice*
Anand's *The Sword and the Sickle* published (J. Cape)
Anand's *Letters on India* published (Labour Book Service, introduc-
tion by Leonard Woolf)
Tambimuttu's anthology *Poetry in Wartime* published (Faber &
Faber)

1943

Indian Seamen's Welfare League established by Shah Abdul Majid
Qureshi and Ayub Ali
Indian Workers' Association joins Swaraj House to form Federation

of Indian Associations in Great Britain, with Surat Alley as
president and V.S. Sastrya as secretary
Noor Inayat Khan infiltrated into France to work as wireless operator
and later arrested
Indian Army regiments fight in Italian campaign

1944

Menon establishes St Pancras Arts and Civic Council which leads to
inauguration of St Pancras Arts Festival
Indian Army fights in battles of Imphal and Kohima; re-conquest of
Burma begins
Noor Inayat Khan executed at Dachau concentration camp

1945

Germany surrenders; atom bombing of Hiroshima and Nagasaki
Anti-Colonial People's Conference held in London
Pan-African Congress held in Manchester (T. Subasinghe is one of
the organizers)
Rajani Dutt contests Sparkbrook, Birmingham, as CPGB candidate
against Leo Amery

1947

Independence and partition of India, formation of Pakistan
Menon becomes India's High Commissioner in London

1948

Independence of Ceylon (becomes Republic of Sri Lanka in 1972)
British Empire becomes British Commonwealth
SS *Empire Windrush* brings 492 West Indians to Britain

1951
Festival of Britain

Introduction

Ruvani Ranasinha[1]

This anthology of primary material offers a revised narrative of the making of modern Britain. It aims to document, analyse and highlight the remarkable, yet still overlooked, formative contributions made by South Asians[2] to British culture, politics, and identity during the key period 1870 and 1950. A period bounded by imperial confidence (albeit punctuated with moments of crisis), and the dawn of decolonization. Our focus on the years preceding the influx of post-1945 colonial immigrants shows that British culture and history has a much longer and more complex multicultural heritage than is usually acknowledged, and that South Asian migrancy and acculturation have been experienced and conceptualized diversely at different historical moments. This volume engages implicitly with current debates on citizenship rights, migration policy, what constitutes 'Englishness' and multiculturalism, by illustrating how these questions were prompted and anticipated by the presence of South Asians (among other colonial subjects from overseas) within Britain over a century ago. Showing how the source materials can be read as

1 I would like to thank Lyn Innes and Rozina Visram for their comments on this introduction, and also Rehana Ahmed, Elleke Boehmer, Sumita Mukherjee, Susheila Nasta and Florian Stadtler for their input on earlier drafts.
2 Throughout this book the term 'South Asian' is used to denote peoples originating from the Indian subcontinent and Sri Lanka and their diasporas. For the main portion of the period under scrutiny (1870–1947) pre-partition India included the present-day nations of Pakistan and Bangladesh. Sri Lanka was known as Ceylon until 1972. The focus is on South Asians based in Britain either temporarily or permanently.

exemplary precursors to contemporary debates, the book argues that Britain was always 'multi-cultural' even before multiculturalism was theorized.[3]

Rather than simply illustrating the early presence of South Asians in Britain, this collection focuses on four key areas of South Asian *impact* on British society: namely, South Asian participation and attempts to influence minority rights, war, culture and reception, and representation so that they can be more fully understood. The source materials reveal how South Asians influenced public discourse on issues of empire and race (through the India League and other political organizations), but also intervened in the global war effort against fascism, and in the broader political and social reforms of their times, including women's suffrage (with for example, the involvement of the Indian princess Sophia Duleep Singh), international socialism (Communist MP Shapurji Saklatvala) and workers' rights. This range of topics also allows for a broad but deep understanding of the involvement of different classes and groups (including royalty, intellectuals, politicians, writers, journalists and suffragettes, alongside non-elite soldiers, activists, lascars) of South Asians in the complex shaping of Britain's history, cultural heritage, and identity.[4]

The collection as a whole considers Britain as a contested space for political and cultural inclusion. The sources in the first chapter, 'Equality of Citizenship' (Ahmed) position South Asian individuals at the heart of some of Britain's key political and social reforms, alongside groups that countered oppression in Britain through organizations such as the Indian Workers' Association. Ahmed's chapter highlights the pioneering nature of these embryonic

---

3 This book defines multiculturalism in terms of a sense of (un)belonging, a re-drawing of culturally and racially defined borders and re-mapping of British identities.

4 Complete coverage of the entire demographic of South Asians who made an impact on Britain including students, doctors, traders, pedlars, maritime workers, domestic servants and the petitioner class is not possible in one volume. For information on these groups, see R.Visram, *Asians in Britain: 400 Years of History* (London: Pluto, 2002) and M. Fisher, S. Lahiri and S. Thandi, *A South Asian History of Britain* (Oxford: Greenwood World, 2007).

communities' struggles as precursors to the campaigns for 'minority rights' by their successors of the post-war period. The second chapter, 'Britain's Forgotten Volunteers: South Asian Contributions to the Two World Wars' (Stadtler), documents South Asian contributions as soldiers, politicians, journalists and commentators to the cataclysmic 'national' and global events of the First and Second World Wars. Stadtler highlights how both wars shaped South Asian views of Britain, and the manner in which perceptions of South Asians by Britons changed as they were fighting side-by-side, alongside the complexities of the relations between the soldiers. The third chapter, 'Textual Culture and Reception' (Ranasinha), illustrates the role of South Asians writers, editors and reviewers in shaping Britain's cultural landscape, and their various kinds of literary interactions with their British counterparts. Investigating the shifting historical and cultural contexts of the production and critical reception of South Asian literary and non-fictional texts, the chapter assesses their impact on the cultural attitudes of white Britons. The final chapter, 'Representations and Display' (Mukherjee), examines portrayals of South Asians (and other colonial subjects) in exhibitions, the media and official documents, contrasting these with South Asian representations of themselves, focusing on the varying degrees to which a South Asian presence in Britain challenged Orientalist perceptions of South Asian culture.

This sourcebook is inspired by the pioneering scholarship of Peter Fryer and Rozina Visram:[5] the first books to disrupt the still persistent myth of a homogenous ethnically exclusive Britain prior to the Second World War, and to recover South Asian and black contributions to national history. It is indebted to the growing body of related research emerging in the wake of Visram and Fryer's publications, in the field of history and literature on South Asian travel and migration, that similarly imagines a different history of Britain, especially work by Antoinette Burton,[6] Michael H. Fisher, Shompa Lahiri,

5 P. Fryer, *Staying Power* (London: Pluto, 1984); R.Visram, *Ayahs, Lascars and Princes* (London: Pluto, 1986).
6 A. Burton (ed.), *Politics and Empire in Victorian Britain: A Reader* (Basingstoke: Palgrave, 2001) provided a model for this sourcebook. See also

Satadru Sen and Tim Smith.[7] Stimulated by new directions in recent scholarship, the sourcebook similarly aims to engage with the multiple vectors of place, race, class,[8] gender[9] and religion.[10] At the same time, this interdisciplinary volume draws on and extends the literary focus of studies on South Asian writers in Britain by Elleke Boehmer, C.L. Innes, Susheila Nasta, Ruvani Ranasinha and Sukhdev Sandhu.[11]

This sourcebook's unique contribution to this developing area of scholarship lies in its contextualized reproduction of primary sources and documentary material, which expresses *the voices and views* of South Asians from their British location and perspective at this time. Collating and interrogating a range of narratives, stories and fragments of lives tells us more about how South Asians have shaped the fabric of Britain's political and cultural life than we can

---

Burton's gendered accounts of Indian travel and migration. A. Burton, *At the Heart of Empire: Indians and the Colonial Encounter in Late-Victorian Britain* (Berkeley: University of California Press, 1998) and *Dwelling in the Archive: Women Writing House, Home and History in Late Colonial India* (Oxford: Oxford University Press, 2003).

7 S. Sen, *Migrant Races: Empire Identity and K.S Ranjitsinhji* (Manchester: Manchester University Press, 2004); M. Fisher, S. Lahiri and S. Thandi *A South Asian History of Britain* (Oxford: Greenwood World, 2007); T. Smith *Asians in Britain* (London: Dewi Lewis, 2003).

8 A. Martin Wainwright, *'The Better Class' of Indians: Social Rank, Imperial Identity, and South Asians in Britain, 1858–1914* (Manchester: Manchester University Press, 2008).

9 S. Lahiri, *Indian Mobilities in the West, 1900–1947: Gender, Performance, Embodiment* (Basingstoke: Palgrave, 2010); S. Lambert-Hurley and S. Sharma, *Atiya's Journeys: A Muslim Woman from Colonial Bombay to Edwardian Britain* (Delhi: Oxford University Press, forthcoming).

10 H. Ansari, *'The Infidel Within': Muslims in Britain since 1800* (London: Hurst, 2004).

11 Elleke Boehmer, *Empire, the National and the Postcolonial, 1890–1920* (Oxford: Oxford University Press, 2002); C.L. Innes, *A History of Black and Asian Writing in Britain, 1700–2000* (Cambridge: Cambridge University Press, 2000), Susheila Nasta, *Home Truths: Fictions of the South Asian Diaspora in Britain* (Basingstoke: Palgrave, 2002), Ruvani Ranasinha, *South Asians in Britain: Culture in Translation* (Oxford: Oxford University Press, 2007) and Sukhdev Sandhu, *London Calling: How Black and Asian Writers Imagined a City* (London: HarperPerennial, 2004).

glean from monographs and textbooks alone. Its uniqueness lies in
its provision of a different form of 'recovered histories', by enabling
its readers to access the period for themselves through these
documents and images. Readers are 'free' to interpret the sources
across disciplinary boundaries and theoretical perspectives within a
historical and biographical framework.

The collection draws on diverse archival forms including photographs, political journalism, literary texts, memoirs, private
correspondence, interviews, reviews and government documentation. The diversity testifies to the enormous range and vitality of
South Asian engagement. The volume juxtaposes South Asian voices
with white British governmental records, press coverage and reviews
to enable us to see the larger context within which South Asians were
viewed, and thus better assess the impact of their interventions.
Although minority voices are often difficult to trace in the archive,
this sourcebook counters those who explain the marginalized
presence of colonial and 'non-white' peoples in the metropole within
more conventional histories, as a result of the lack of archival documentation. Political agendas contribute to this erasure: the volume
unearths hitherto *overlooked* South Asian traces in standard sources
including the India Office Records, the BBC Written Archives Centre,
the Imperial War Museum, the National Archives; the British Library
Newspapers, and publishers' archives at Universities of Reading and
Bristol. It also draws on sources such as the Tower Hamlets' local
history archive. We are privileged to include the interview held with
Squadron leader Mahinder Pujji (Stadtler's Chapter 2) shortly prior
to his death in November 2010. Nevertheless, even this heterogeneous sample must be incomplete, relying as it does on traces
registered in the domain of the written record. Ayahs, one of the
largest group of South Asian visitors, leave no testimonials behind,
although as studies have shown, their traces can be gleaned from
photographs and advertisements, while some of the South Asian
soldiers' lives have entered oral narratives.

Furthermore, none of these voices comes to us unmediated, and
they cannot be taken at face value. Continuing the work of new
social historians, and the more recent trends in women's history
that re-conceptualize the archive and sources as 'a site for the
production of knowledge', rather than as 'immutable, neutral and

ahistorical',[12] this volume seeks not only to recover marginalized voices, but to find fresh ways of interpreting and illuminating this new material, which presents methodological challenges. Just as some of the activists in Chapter 1 (Ahmed) come into record in highly prejudicial historical accounts, certain soldiers' voices are mediated through censorship in Chapter 2 (Stadtler). In diverse ways, all four chapters unearth layers of state agenda from not only government records and official documents, but also from newspaper features, literary articles and reviews (Chapters 3 (Ranasinha) and 4 (Mukherjee)), while also considering the motivations of the South Asian contributions. Across the chapters, the sources are located in their historical moment, read against the grain for subtexts and silences, and with contextual knowledge of overarching power relations, and in relation to other relevant primary sources. Chapter 3 (Ranasinha) includes a diversity of sources around a key figure, the Indian writer Mulk Raj Anand. These discrepant responses to his work not only help us to evaluate his legacy more fully, but also make clear the reality of multiple narratives. Drawing on theoretical work on material culture in literature, notably Bill Brown's *A Sense of Things: The Object Matter in American Literature* (2003), the impact of South Asian presence in Britain is explored through a focus on each of the items selected for analysis – whether a review or a political tract – and the sedimentation of history and power relations within it. This book conceptualizes Britain temporally in terms of a palimpsest, a series of erasures, obliterations, and overwriting over time. It will unearth the buried layers of the nation's multicultural make-up from beneath its surface narrative of homogeneity, thereby re-mapping Britain and refracting its self-image.

This volume represents a further departure within existing scholarship with its emphasis on tracing and illustrating South Asian writers, soldiers or activists' *interaction* with their British counterparts, in both the framing essays and selection of material.

---

12 N. Chaudhuri, S.J. Katz and M.E. Perry (eds), *Contesting Archives: Finding Women in the Sources* (Urbana, IL: University of Illinois Press, 2010), p. xiii. This sourcebook is indebted to the conceptual framework and methodological terminology delineated in this collection.

Testimonies of contact reveal networks and relationships of creative exchange and collaboration, as well as at times fervent dissent. Our collection thus prompts a revision of national history through a re-imagining and re-mapping of the place of South Asians within it. This is not a solely ghettoized presence as it is often depicted in exhibitions, documentaries and museums, nor a separate, segregated history. While the focus is on reciprocal cultural and political British/South Asian networks, exchanges and alliances, we do not seek to promote a bicultural model. As far as possible, the chapters signal South Asian, African, Caribbean and other cross-cultural engagement, and the lateral relations between South Asians and other colonized communities within the context of empire and decolonization and the complex mix of British history during this period. Across the chapters we will see interracial and intra-racial solidarity, but also shifting sets of interracial and intra-racial hierarchies and entanglements.

Although this sourcebook reveals the British metropole's function as a centre for forging global networks of anti-colonial struggle and other forms of diasporic networking, it also regards Britain as just one nodal point or contact zone in the global vision of history, rather than *the* hub.[13] As far as possible the various chapters allude to diasporic South Asian networks in the rest of Europe, in North America and elsewhere in the empire, to the transnational nature of the political and literary process, alongside the transnational factors that influence the production of a sense of South Asian identity in Britain.

The collection as a whole aims to track moments of change in Britain's relationship with its South Asian colonies, the consequent shifts in perceptions of Britain among South Asians based here, alongside changing British views of South Asians. Given this intent, the experiences of South Asians in Britain need to be examined in relation to the wider developments taking place not only in Britain

---

13 See recent studies on the transnational and transcontinental movement of colonial subjects that cover a broad geographic scope of South Asian travel in North America and continental Europe as well as Britain, notably Lahiri, *Indian Mobilities*. See also the importance of travel to the autobiographies of leading male Indian nationalists in J. Majeed, *Autobiography, Travel and Postnational Identity: Gandhi, Nehru and Iqbal* (Basingstoke: Palgrave, 2007).

but also with regards to the nationalist discourses produced in the subcontinent. To this end, this introduction delineates a synoptic overview of these shifting transcontinental contexts insofar as one impinges on the other. This is to provide a chronological historical spine within which to locate the individual chapters that pursue their particular theme across the period, and to integrate the different themes covered in the chapters within a historical context. It serves as a kind of map and reference point for the changing conditions that shaped and were shaped by the South Asian groups and individual visitors, reformers and politicians who provided a conduit between Britain and the empire they straddled.

As Fisher and Visram[14] have shown, South Asian presence in Britain dates as far back as the beginning of the seventeenth century, with notable early settlers such as Sake Dean Mahomed (1759–1851), 'the shampooing surgeon'. However, it was during the nineteenth century that settler communities evolved. South Asian migrants varied in cultural, religious and socio-economic terms. With smaller numbers of traders, scholars and aristocrats scattered around Britain, the largest groups comprised of seamen (or lascars) and ayahs: one of the reasons behind the founding of the Ayahs' Home in around 1825, and later the Strangers' Home for Asiatics, Africans and South Sea Islanders (1857–1937). Prior to the period under scrutiny in this book, the bloody conflict of the Indian uprising of 1857–59 (sometimes called the Indian Mutiny or Sepoy Rebellion) marked a significant shift in Indo-British relations, and in the attitudes towards India and Indians in both the subcontinent and Britain. The 1857 uprising convinced British officials in London that a more direct hand was needed in governing India. In 1858 India was transferred from the East India Company to the British crown rule, marking a new era of the British Raj. (However, Queen Victoria's 1858 proclamation granting equality of citizenship remained illusory as Ahmed explores in Chapter 1.) Prior to this in the 1830s and 1840s, British Evangelicals and Utilitarians believed that their missionaries could re-structure and 'rescue' Indian society. After

14 Visram, *Asians in Britain*; M. Fisher, *Counterflows of Colonialism: Indian Travellers and Settlers in Britain, 1600–1857* (New Delhi: Permanent Black, 2004).

1857, with the focus on the Indian soldiers' offended religious and caste sensibilities, rather than on their wider aim of ending British rule, and the biased British reports and press coverage that condemned Indian violence, but not the harsh British reprisals, most officials concluded that Indians were too fanatical and superstitious to assimilate Western cultural values. The publication of Charles Darwin's *Origin of Species* in 1859 reified notions of difference and racial superiority. The impact of social Darwinism impinged on the increasingly negative way South Asians were perceived in Britain. At the same time, as Humayan Ansari has argued, the crushing of the Rebellion of 1857 convinced many Indian elites of the permanency of British rule, and of the superiority of the British educational system to which they attributed British power, and that Western education was the best way of achieving their social and economic aspirations. This encouraged the trickle of Indian students who had begun arriving at English and Scottish Universities somewhat earlier in the context of Macaulay's Minute on Education (1835) on creating 'Brown Englishmen'.[15] It was these anglicized, Western-educated 'moderate' Indian elites, notably W.C. Bonnerjee (alongside a few British and Scottish civil servants), who went on to found the Indian National Congress in Bombay in 1885 asking for basic rights.

As Visram and others have detailed, the construction of the Suez Canal in 1869 and the consequent reduced travelling time from the subcontinent, encouraged South Asian travel to Britain in the late nineteenth century.[16] Indian Royalty attended the celebration in Britain of Queen Victoria becoming Empress of India in 1876. But South Asian presence in Victorian Britain *ranged* from writers and social reformers (who published their views on Britain), politicians (notably Dadabhai Naoroji (1825–1917) who was eventually elected to parliament in 1892 and used his platform to critique colonial rule) to the largest groups comprising of seamen and traders shaping Britain's economic landscape as Ahmed details in Chapter 1.

---

15 H. Ansari, 'Mapping the Colonial: South Asians in Britain', in N. Ali, V.S. Kalra and S. Sayyid (eds), *A Postcolonial People: South Asians in Britain* (London: Hurst, 2006), p. 144.

16 Visram, *Asians in Britain*.

1870–1901

Intersecting concerns with socialism, Indian and Irish Home rule, Theosophy[17] and suffrage, provided contact zones for South Asian visitors and their British peers. Mohandas Karamchand Gandhi arrived in London in 1888 to study at the Bar (and stayed until 1891) where he met Annie Besant (a critic of British imperial policy in Ireland, Africa, Egypt as well as India) and came into contact with Theosophy in Britain, and Irish Home Rule with all its possibilities for India. The Indian poet-politician Sarojini Naidu (a product of the nationalist movement in Bengal from the 1880s) arrived in London for the first time in April 1895, and would stay until 1898. She travelled to London with Annie Besant with whom she went on to work closely, and became part of the networks of late Victorian London literary society, turn-of-the century occultisms, and cultural nationalists who emphasized the role of women in sustaining cultural nationalism in Ireland and India.

During the 1880s and 1890s Indian nationalists and Irish radicals forged political alliances to secure Home rule from the imperial parliament at Westminster. The Irish Home Rule league was founded Dublin in 1873: the bill for Irish Home Rule was defeated at Westminster in 1886. The place of religious minorities in Ireland and India provided another commonality. Pan-Islamism and the interests of Muslim minorities animated Indian Muslim nationalist discussions in Britain, most notably in the debates of Syed Ameer Ali[18] published in the influential *Nineteenth Century* magazine, in Britain in 1880s. Alarmed at the rise of the Hindu majority, Ali lobbied for Indian Muslims to claim rights from the colonial administration through the London branch of the All India Muslim League that he founded in 1908.

The *fin de siècle* – a time of economic downturn – prompted investigations into British social inequality. In Chapters 3 and 4,

---

17 Theosophy connected Indians and British, professionals, students, visiting scholars, travelling gurus in Britain in this period primarily via the impact of Madame Blavatsky's Theosophical society founded in New York in 1875 with its headquarters in Adyar in 1882, and centres in London and other European cities.

18 Ali (1849–1928): the barrister who settled in Britain with his English wife.

Ranasinha and Mukherjee allude to the intertextual relationships between the late Victorian South Asian and British ethnographies of the urban poor. The Dock Strike of 1889 and further industrial unrest saw the emergence of 'anti-alien' discourse focused at this juncture on the figure of the East European Jew intruding on labour markets, and the 'problem' of Jewish emigration culminating in the Alien Immigration Act of 1905 explored in Ahmed's Chapter 1. This period saw threats to Britain's role as an imperial power in Africa, Ireland, Australia, East Asia and Egypt: the First South African war of 1881, the Arabi uprising and British occupation of Egypt in 1882, the Sudanese rebellion and siege of Khartoum in 1884. Rivalry between Western colonial powers during 1890 to 1914 focused on 'the scramble for Africa': Joseph Conrad's *Heart of Darkness* (1899) and Rudyard Kipling's *Kim* (1901) map and interrogate this era of global empires. The celebration of empire via Queen Victoria's Jubilee in 1897 stood in marked contrast to the second Anglo-Boer War (1899–1902) that erupted just two years later. Notable figures, including Emmeline Pankhurst, George Bernard Shaw and J.A. Hobson, interpreted Britain's role in South Africa as an act of imperial aggression. The war prompted intellectuals to reconsider Britain's role in India, and eventually marked a shift in British policy from isolation to seeking allies and improving world relations.

1901–1914

Emerging socialism in Britain led to the formation of the Labour Party in 1900. During the first decades of the twentieth century London functioned as a global centre for various strands of Indian nationalism and the international suffragette activist movement, facilitating the meeting and forging of interracial, but also intra-racial alliances not always possible in the subcontinental country of origin. In 1905 Shyamji Krishnavarma founded the India Home Rule Society and a hostel for Indian students, India House, in Highgate in London, which became a centre for radical nationalist activism. Krishnavarma's links to the Irish Republican Party (Sinn Fein was formed in 1905), and his journal *The Indian Sociologist* considered inflammatory by the British Government, made him a target for arrest. He fled to Paris in 1907 and continued his journal from

Geneva. Other former India House members moved to New York, another centre of the global Indian nationalist movement, where they continued to circulate *The Indian Sociologist* and other nationalist literature. These revolutionary activities of the early 1900s – for example Sarvakar and Madame Cama's advocacy of violence and Madan Lal Dhingra's assassination of Sir William Curzon Wylie (the civil servant policing British-based Indian students' political agitation) in London in 1909, alongside the militant nationalist Ghadr party in the US – arose in part out of opposition to the Partition of Bengal (1905–08) and impatience with the constitutional path adopted by Indian Home Rulers. The limited constitutional concessions in the Morely-Minto reforms of 1909 increased Indian political representation, but British officials retained a majority on all legislative councils and refused to surrender their monopoly on Indian politics. Shortly before the First World War, a legislative council of anglicized, middle-class Ceylonese was formed.

In the first decade of the twentieth century the suffrage movement (first established in 1869) was at its height in Britain. As Ahmed explores in the first chapter, Princesses Sophia and Catherine Duleep Singh of mixed descent were prominent suffragettes: Sophia Duleep Singh marched with Emmeline Pankhurst on Black Friday in 1910. This movement needs to be seen in the context of a global International Women's movement, with the International Women's Suffrage Conference in Washington in 1902, and the International Women's Suffrage Alliance held in Geneva attended by Naidu during her second visit to London in 1912–14, when she also visited Ireland. During this, and her later extended stays in London, Naidu collaborated with British feminists, but like other early twentieth-century South Asian feminist campaigners, notably Pandita Ramabai,[19] Naidu focused on the position of Indian women. Naidu placed Indian women's suffrage and rights at the centre of the move towards increased Indian autonomy. She later reported to the Joint Committee on Indian Reforms (1919) and campaigned against the Montague-Chelmsford reforms, which ignored the question of

19 Ramabai (1858–1922): the Hindu widow who converted to Christianity shortly before arrival in Britain; like Naidu she visited America.

franchise for Indian women. It was in London that Naidu first met Gandhi on the eve of the First World War and went on to work with him on the 1919 campaigns. She had already entered national politics through her meetings with Gopal Krishna Gokhale[20] in London 1912–14.

The First World War: 1914–1918

As Stadtler explores in Chapter 2, Britain's deployment of Indian soldiers in the First World War provoked national debates and calls for greater political independence in both India and Britain. In the light of the role of Indian soldiers in the First World War, the British government (with a new Liberal Secretary of State for India, Edwin Montagu) conceded the possibility of home rule in 1917. Modelled on the Irish Home Rule League,[21] the founding of the Home Rule for India League in 1916 by Annie Besant further strengthened the hand of Indian nationalists. Violent rather than non-violent opposition to British rule influenced a future opponent of British imperialism, the young Jawaharlal Nehru training as a lawyer in London. Nehru was moved by Irish patriot, revolutionary and poet Roger Casement's speech on Ireland's right to self-government prior to his execution in 1916.[22]

The First World War shattered Britain's century-long dominance dating from the end of the Napoleonic Wars (the period referred to as *Pax Britannia*), and marked the beginning of Britain's declining status as a global empire. The bolstering of Empire through the new media, schools and to the millions attending the colonial exhibitions during the years after the First World War (Wembley 1924/25) has been seen as evidence of the case for colonialism having to be made more strongly because of increasing doubts about the imperial

20 Gokhale (1866–1915): the leader of the moderates in the Congress party (and its president in 1905) was Gandhi's political guru.
21 Although the heroic 1916 Irish Easter Rising against the British failed, it nevertheless kindled the struggle for secession: Britain partitioned Ireland into the Northern counties and the Irish Free State in the Anglo-Irish Treaty of 1921.
22 Cited in A. Marr, *The Making of Modern Britain* (Basingstoke: Palgrave, 2009), p. 162.

project.[23] The First World War constituted a watershed in the imperial relationship between Britain and India because India had contributed so heavily in both men and taxation. But as Stadtler elaborates in Chapter 2, the First World War also marked a turning point in the perceptions of South Asians living in Britain. South Asian efforts and sacrifices commanded respect and appreciation, although the segregation of soldiers suggests the persistence of notions of racial superiority. As Ansari has shown, meeting the demands of the war effort acted as a catalyst in stimulating the migration of maritime South Asian workers (as well as soldiers) required to man the merchant ships and sustain Britain's industrialized economy.[24] As Ahmed explores in Chapter 1, racially motivated attacks by white British seamen against 'coloured' seamen across Britain in 1919 culminated in the Coloured Alien Seamen Order. By the end of the First World War South Asians started to form a significant part of the visible migrant population. Economic stagnation and high levels of unemployment during the inter-war years acted as a brake inhibiting large numbers of arrivals from South Asia.

While India's mainstream political leadership and sections of the South Asian community in Britain had supported Britain during the First World War, the Ghadr party orchestrated by expatriate Indians in collaboration with Germany had attempted to trigger a mutiny within the Indian Army. This had resulted in the Defence of India Act in 1915, which increased the British Colonial government's powers of containing political unrest and rooting out conspiracy in India. The extension of these repressive measures during peacetime by the Rowlatt Act of 1919 marked a particularly brutal period of British rule, and caused outrage and Gandhi-led campaigns to repeal it. Protest against the Rowlatt Act sparked off the Jallianwala Bagh massacre (also known as the Amritsar massacre), which had significant repercussions in Britain as well as in India.

---

23 H.J. Booth and N. Rigby (eds), Introduction, *Modernism and Empire* (Manchester: Manchester University Press, 2000), p. 3.
24 Ansari, 'Mapping the colonial', 143.

1919–1939: the Jallianwala Bagh massacre and its aftermath in London

Anti-British nationalist sentiment intensified following the Jallianwala Bagh massacre in the Punjab in April 1919, when General Dyer ordered his army to shoot to kill an unarmed political meeting that assembled alongside crowds gathered on Baisaki Festival Day. The massacre led the Indian Congress to adopt the non-cooperation movement against the British proposed by Gandhi, and brought Gandhi to the forefront of Indian nationalist politics.

The massacre marked a turning point in the attitudes of key Indian figures at the interface of Indo-British relations. In protest, the Indian poet and Nobel Prize winner (1913) Rabindranath Tagore returned the knighthood he had received from the British government in 1915, and his nationalism contributed to a fall in his standing among some of his European supporters and interlocutors. While the British colonial government attempted to suppress news of the carnage reaching Britain, Naidu used her visit to Britain (1919–21) to denounce the massacre, especially the mistreatment of Indian women during the period of martial law in the Punjab that followed the Jallianwala Bagh massacre. Naidu's evidence proved controversial and was disputed in parliament by the Secretary of State for India, Edwin Montagu. On 31 July 1920 Naidu spoke at a public protest meeting at Kingsway Hall organized by the British Committee of the Indian National Congress to protest against the Hunter Commission's mild censure of Michael O'Dwyer[25] and General Dyer responsible for the slaughter. Krishna Menon and the India League similarly publicized the atrocities. In response to the massacre, Gandhi and Naidu went on to launch the non-violent, non-cooperation movement in India. By incorporating peasant, labour and other urban groups, this movement transformed the Indian Congress from an elite political organization into a mass nationalist, anti-colonial movement.

25 In 1940, two decades after Jallianwala Bagh, a witness and casualty of the massacre, Udham Singh assassinated Michael O'Dwyer, the British Lieutenant Governor of the Punjab whom Singh held responsible for the massacre. Singh was subsequently sentenced to death and hanged.

In Britain, nationalist and other kinds of activism also extended beyond elite social formations, as Ahmed makes clear in Chapter 1. The Commonwealth of India League (established in 1922), which had lobbied British MPs in support of self-government within India, was radicalized and renamed the India League in 1928 by Krishna Menon (who represented St Pancras as a local Labour councillor). Activists within the India League worked closely with the Ceylon Students' Association (established in 1920) and with Ceylonese Marxists who went on to found the Lanka Sama Samaja Party. In 1926 Mulk Raj Anand participated in the General Strike. Broader networks forged connections between the injustices of British rule in Africa and India, with London providing an intellectual space for nationalism for people throughout the colonies. Saklatvala addressed the second Pan African Conference held in London in 1921. The League of Coloured Peoples and the Anti-colonial People's conference held in Manchester in the 1940s followed.

The British Government sent the Simon Commission (1928–29) to India to review the Government of India Act, and to explore constitutional reform in India. In protest at the exclusion of Indians from the Commission, Congress set up its own committee under Motilal Nehru to formulate an Indian constitution. The 1927 Nehru report proposed a strong central government rather than separate electorates at a national level. This prompted M.A. Jinnah (a former student of law in Britain in the 1890s, working as a barrister in Britain in the 1930s) to join and revitalize the somewhat moribund Muslim League out of concern for the position of Muslims in a new India, after trying unsuccessfully to bring the Congress and League together. The poet Muhammad Iqbal promoted the notion of a Muslim state in the early 1930s. The Simon Commission report published in 1930 was opposed in both India and Britain, where the Indian Workers' Welfare League and London Branch of Indian National Congress held protests.

As a result of the failure of the Simon Commission, between 1930 and 1932 three Round Table Conferences between British politicians and key Indians were held in London to discuss India's new Constitution, Dominion status and the creation of separate provinces. At the Second Round Table Conference in 1931, Gandhi represented the Indian National Congress with Naidu speaking on behalf of Indian women. The conference exacerbated communal tensions with British officials pitting Hindus against Muslim communities. The resulting Government of India Act (1935) giving Congress its first measure of power was criticized in India and Britain. Between 1932 and 1939 the *Indian Bulletin* monthly, published in Britain by the Friends of India Association, sought to persuade British readers of the inevitability of Indian self-governance, by charting the civil disobedience movement launched by Gandhi in the 1930s, and by drawing attention to the colonial government's repressive measures erased from most mainstream British newspapers. It also covered Gandhi's resignation from Congress in 1934, and Nehru's visit to London in 1936.

The first real elections at state level in India in 1937 delivered an overwhelming Congress success, further alarming the Muslim League distressed by the communal logic of 'Hindu-plus' notions of Indian identity and even Nehruvian syncretism, and the idea of Pakistan developed. These debates played out in the British press and in the critical reception of Nehru's publications as Ranasinha discusses in Chapter 3. Indian nationalists' increasingly vociferous demands for independence alongside the Muslim question caused rifts between former left-wing, anti-imperialist allies Leonard Woolf and Mulk Raj Anand. Repudiating Anand's nationalism, comparing it to Irish nationalism and arguing that it distorts British involvement in India and marginalizes the Muslim position, Woolf went on to introduce Anand's *Letters on India* with a serious indictment. This is akin to the way in which the British focused on the Muslim question, and built up Jinnah whom they saw as the only effective counter to Gandhi's broad appeal and widespread support.

The Second World War (1939–1945)

The outbreak of the Second World War had an impact on South Asian patterns of migration to Britain. During the late 1930s, scores of South Asians migrated to the Midlands and the north of England to work in the factories manufacturing wartime products. As Stadtler (Chapter 2) and Ranasinha (Chapter 3) discuss, the Indian nationalists' (especially the two million soldiers') support for the war, in the fraught context of the independent struggles of the early 1940s, was crucial. During the period 1941–43 palpable tensions between Indian nationalism and anti-fascism and anti-imperialism emerged, embodied by Mulk Raj Anand among other anti-colonial Indian nationalists in London. These nationalists questioned the morality of Indian soldiers fighting a war for a British Empire that claimed them as their colonial subjects, while also recognizing the threat of the Japanese and German armies in view of the successes achieved between 1939 and 1943.

Emphasizing the systematic brutality of Nazi troops and the particular threat of Hitler's fascism to the subcontinent, the BBC Indian service (organized by George Orwell and Z.A. Bokhari with several South Asian participants including Anand, Tambimuttu and Venu Chitale based in Britain) aimed at India's opinion-forming intelligentsia and students, in the hope of maintaining the conditional allegiance of the Indian nationalists, and to counter Subhas Chandra Bose's anti-British rhetoric wooing anti-colonial nationalists to join the Axis side. In March 1942 Stafford Cripps was sent to India to secure Congress support for the war effort. This discussion of India's new constitution and self-government was also prompted by Chinese and American pressure on Britain to decolonize. The talks known as the Cripps' Mission failed over questions of India's control of its own defence. Emboldened by the fall of Singapore, the Congress rejected the proposals because they did not amount to complete independence, but continued to cooperate with Britain in the war effort, despite the failure of the Cripps' Mission.

Nonetheless, the actions of the British government during the Second World War hastened the movement towards Indian Independence. Disillusioned by the colonial government's ruthless and systematic suppression and imprisonment of Jawaharlal Nehru and other Indian nationalists, and by the British government's evasion of the question of India's independence promised before the war, and finally the failure of the Cripps' mission in April 1942, the Congress passed the Quit India resolution in August 1942. This led to further imprisonment of its leading figures and a mass civilian uprising inspired by the resolution that made clear the degree to which British political control had been undermined.

Throughout the 1940s, South Asian writers and commentators in Britain attempted to counter and complement the mainstream

British Press that 'gives so little news of India and so little account of different Indian political views'.[26] Bhattacharya wrote *So Many Hungers* to inform the British public about the Bengal famine (1943–44) during which almost four million died, as scarce food supplies were diverted to British troops and urban industrial areas, rather than to the rural poor. The Progressive Writers' Association was established in London in 1935 by Indian writers including Anand, Ahmed Ali and Sajjad Zaheer with the encouragement of some British literary figures. Its motivating aim was 'that the new literature of India must deal with the basic problems of our existence today – the problems of hunger and poverty, social backwardness, and political subjection'.[27]

Post-war and post-imperial Britain (1945–1950)

By 1946, India's political instability, Britain's parlous economic standing and pressure from the USA to decolonize motivated Britain's new post-war Labour Government led by Attlee to expedite a swift transition to Indian self-rule. In March 1946, Labour sent a Cabinet mission to negotiate the constitution of a free India. In February 1947, Prime Minister Attlee announced that India would be independent by June 1948. A month later, Mountbatten was appointed as the last Viceroy to oversee the final year of British rule. In March 1947, Nehru acknowledged the possibility of the partition of Punjab and Bengal. The division of India was deemed preferable by Congress to the British proposal of allowing all provinces to opt in or out of an Indian union, if no agreement on its future had been reached by mid-1948. Jinnah and the Muslim League followed fearing an undivided India with few guarantees over power-sharing. On 3 June 1947, the partition plan was agreed officially and announced to the nation. The date of Independence was brought forward to 15 August 1947, leaving the civil servant Sir Cyril Radcliffe little time to draw the new national boundaries of India and

---

26 V. Chitale, An interview with Kingsley Martin in 'The Man in the Street', broadcast 15 May 1942, Contributors Talks File 1, BBC WAC, transcript, p. 1.
27 Progressive Writers' Association, Manifesto.

Pakistan created from parts of Punjab and Bengal, and to address the questions of the large Sikh population in the Punjab. Nehru became first prime minister of independent India in 1947. The extreme haste and Britain's failure to organize a peaceful independence led to the horrific violence that accompanied the largest internal migration. Ceylon's initially more peaceful move to independence followed in February 1948.

In the wake of Indian independence, the Nationality Act of 1948 gave citizens of the former colonies rights of residence in Britain. Perceived links to the 'mother country' made Britain with its open-door policy, fuelled by its need for labour, a natural choice for migrants: not just the 492 'West Indian' arrivals on the *Empire Windrush*, but also many South Asians fleeing from the turmoil of partition. Riots in London, Liverpool and Birmingham against the newly arrived 'coloured' immigrants followed. This period marked the establishment of black and Asian populations and marked an important shift particularly in British identity. Received ideas on race, citizenship and nationality were dismantled and documented anew by the next wave of Caribbean, African and South Asian writers to arrive in Britain.

Overall, our collection aims to problematize this still ongoing, unfolding 'grand narrative' of public figures and large-scale events delineated above, and to raise questions about how we conceptualize the relationship between such events that frame, but also sometimes obscure, the lives of some of the individuals represented within the sources. In diverse ways, the sources collated complicate, interrupt or challenge the broad narrative outlined here by tracing the impact of these events on the everyday lives of South Asians and Britons, shaking out the human stories hidden in the folds of these documents, thereby illuminating dimensions of British race and class formations hitherto overlooked. In this way our volume plays a key role in shaping the conceptual framework of minority history. If some of the broader challenges of moving beyond 'retrieval' in recovered histories include how to suture the private and the public, how to map the individual onto the larger narrative, and the individual journey or migration in relation to wider global movements, we hope that this volume goes some way towards both enacting and addressing this problematic.

1

Equality of citizenship

Rehana Ahmed[1]

This chapter explores the position of South Asians in Britain and their struggle for equal rights as British citizens during the period 1870 to 1950. It focuses both on official and public attitudes to their settlement in Britain and on their involvement in a range of campaigns for equality. In doing so, it considers Britain as a contested space, shaped by boundaries of exclusion and by their subversion as South Asians journeyed from the peripheries of Britain towards its centre. Through readings of a variety of sources, including photographs, newspaper and journal articles, legislative acts and government surveillance reports, the chapter approaches its subject from three angles. First, it focuses on the boundaries, both physical and ideological, that obstructed South Asians' access to Britain and to an equal British citizenship. State discourses deployed to represent South Asians in Britain are considered, as is the strategic adaption and distortion of the category of Britishness according to political interests. Second, the chapter explores tactics of resistance by South Asians against structures of oppression in Britain through organizations and in the form of strikes and riots. It further excavates the ways in which South Asians engaged with and influenced alternative struggles for equality of citizenship beyond their immediate interests as South Asians in Britain, campaigning, for example, for the rights of women, workers and other minorities. Finally, it considers the imprint of South Asian cultures – particularly religious cultures – on

1 I am very grateful to Laura Tabili for her helpful comments on an earlier draft of this chapter.

British space, domestic and public, and addresses pioneering mobilization by South Asians for the right to practise their culture and religion within the public sphere. Throughout, the chapter emphasizes the role of class as well as race in shaping both the exclusionary boundaries to Britishness and the tactics of resistance against these.

Given the complexity and breadth of its subject as well as its coverage of eighty years, the chapter is necessarily selective in its focus and aims to suggest a framework for reading and approaches to the source material rather than offering a comprehensive historical account. Recognizing the primacy of anti-colonial mobilization for South Asians during this period, the chapter focuses rather on structures of inequality as they operated *within Britain* and South Asians' manifold resistances against these – while also acknowledging the problematic nature of separating these two struggles from one another.[2] With this focus on Britain, it seeks to sketch out a history of the campaigns for equal rights of the post-independence period and reconfigure these early migrants as pioneering precursors to later generations of British Asians.

The shifting boundaries of Britishness

In his powerful 1896 challenge to the exclusion of Indians from the commissioned ranks of the army, the politician Dadabhai Naoroji quotes at length from Queen Victoria's Proclamations of 1858 and 1887 to support his case [Source 1]. These assert that 'subjects of whatever race or creed, be freely and impartially admitted to Offices in our Service, the duties of which they may be qualified by their education, ability, and integrity duly to discharge'. They profess a colour-blind meritocracy, placing Indian subjects of the British Empire on 'exactly the same footing as all Her Majesty's other subjects'. Twelve years later, judge and activist Syed Ameer Ali, writing for the periodical *The Nineteenth Century*, similarly highlights the empire's pledge of

2 The chapter does not therefore include in its remit the India-focused activism of India House, or the mobilization for independence by the India League and other organizations. Similarly it does not consider the two assassinations of government officials on British soil by Madan Lal Dhingra (1909) and Udham Singh (1940), which are, however, noted in the introduction to this volume.

'equal rights for all races and creeds under its sway' in his article decrying the detainment of Indians seeking to enter Canada, a British dominion [Source 2]. Despite this declaration of equality, however, and as is evident from the War Office's stipulation that 'Candidates for Commissions in the British Army must be of pure European descent', hierarchies of 'race', 'creed', 'religion, place of birth and descent' frequently positioned South Asians beneath their white British counterparts in the metropolis, denying them full access to Britain and to the Britishness that was formally bestowed on them. This opening section of the chapter explores the tension between the notion of a singular imperial subject-hood that encompassed all peoples of the empire, including South Asians, and the exclusions that actually operated in Britain.[3] Modifying the title of Ali's 1908 essay 'Anomalies of Civilisation', it considers the 'anomalies of *citizenship*' for South Asians in Britain between 1870 and 1950, focusing on not just the role of race but also that of class in determining their access, or lack thereof, to the heart of the metropolis.

In his essay on the threatened deportation of Indians by the Canadian authorities, Ali makes the point that 'many of [the Indians barred or detained] have served their Sovereign *in the profession to which civilization accords the foremost place of honour:* they possess the insignia of bravery and good conduct' [Source 2]. He refers to their service in the British Army and the hypocrisy of debarring subjects who had risked their lives for Britain from access to the nation or its dominions. Indeed, it was against the backdrop of the two World Wars that the selective deployment of the category of Britishness – its distortion to fit political and economic interests – became particularly stark. Its inclusivity during wartime, when South Asian men were needed to fight Britain's battles, contrasted with its exclusivity during peacetime, particularly in periods of high unemployment and depression when minority workers were considered a threat to the welfare of their white counterparts.[4] Further, the notions of 'civilization', 'democracy', 'universalism' and 'freedom' that

3 For an analysis of this tension, see A.M. Wainwright, *'The Better Class' of Indians: Social Rank, Imperial Identity, and South Asians in Britain, 1858–1914* (Manchester: Manchester University Press, 2008), Ch. 5.

4 R. Visram, *Asians in Britain: 400 Years of History* (London: Pluto, 2002), pp. 196–205; L. Tabili, *'We Ask for British Justice': Workers and Racial Difference*

Britain purported to be struggling for during the World Wars influenced and infiltrated the thought of its South Asian subjects, thereby facilitating their criticism of the partial application, or paradoxical exclusions, of these ideals in the case of India. In his speech at PEN's international conference in 1942, in the context of the Second World War, the writer Mulk Raj Anand declared:

> If the ideals of Freedom and Democracy are good enough for the ninety million Czechs, Poles, Dutchmen, Belgians, Norwegians and the other conquered people of Europe, why is it not thought fit to apply them to the four hundred odd million peoples of India? Why is it that Mr Wells' Declaration of the Rights of Man passes India by? And how can any charter of freedom and human rights escape the test of India without becoming the rankest hypocrisy?[5]

In his speech, Anand emphasizes the cultural exchange and interdependence of India and Britain, their shared openness and rejection of racism and Fascism, in order to critique and ironize the divisions of empire which subordinated the one to the other. Ali adopts a different strategy of critique: by attributing the egregious treatment of Indians simply to their 'accident of birth in one continent', he subtly undermines the credibility of 'race' as rationale for imperial hierarchies. But particularly in the early decades of the twentieth century racial difference was very real in its material impact on South Asians in Britain as it was mobilized increasingly to justify their subordination and to manage their encroachment on national space. In the period immediately following the First World War race- and class-based hostility to

---

in *Late Imperial Britain* (Ithaca, NY: Cornell University Press, 1994), pp. 123, 161; S. Lahiri, *Indians in Britain: Anglo-Indian Encounters, Race, and Identity, 1880–1930* (London: Frank Cass, 2000), p. 134.

5 M.R. Anand, 'The Place of India', in H. Ould (ed.), *Writers in Freedom* (London: Hutchinson, 1942), pp. 127–32 (p. 131). PEN was founded in 1921 'to promote literature as a means of greater understanding between cultures' (see the English PEN website www.englishpen.org/). The final version of H.G. Wells' Declaration of the Rights of Man was published in the *Herald* in February 1940 (F. Klug, 'In the Footsteps of H.G. Wells', *New Statesman*, 9 October 2000, www.newstatesman.com/200010090006 [accessed 20 August 2011]).

non-white workers in Britain manifested itself starkly in the form of race riots in port cities. Between January and August 1919, minorities were targeted because of the competitive nature of the job market and the perception that they were 'stealing' the jobs of white indigenous British workers, as well as the housing shortage. South Asians suffered less than black, Arab or Chinese workers as they were not regarded as such direct competition for jobs and housing; most remained within the navy and in subsidized housing rather than seeking alternative employment and accommodation.[6] However, a number of incidents involving South Asians have been traced. In May 1919, a hostile crowd targeted the Strangers' Home for Asiatic Seamen in West India Dock Road shouting abuse at 'any coloured man who appeared'.[7] Newspapers of the time also report the devastation of a Malay boarding house and the shop of one Abdul Satar in Cardiff.[8]

Public hostility towards minorities mirrored official attitudes. In police reports on the 1919 events, the racialization of the minority rioters is striking. In an account of the events in South Wales, we are told, for example, that 'there is a readiness on the part of the coloured race to use firearms, razors and knives immediately a brawl commences'; by contrast the anger of the white rioters is constructed as a reaction to this 'unlawful and highly dangerous practice'.[9] Resonances with constructions of contemporary racial tensions can be traced here: critical analysis of the July 2001 race riots in Britain's northern cities reveals a similar racialization of South Asian British Muslims but articulated along the lines of culture rather than colour; aspects of their culture, including a reputed 'toleration of certain types of criminality', were cited as a cause of the conflict in official

---

6 For an analysis of the causes of the riots, see J. Jenkinson, *Black 1919: Riots, Racism and Resistance in Imperial Britain* (Liverpool: Liverpool University Press, 2009), Ch. 1.

7 *The Times*, 30 May 1919; cited in Visram, *Asians*, p. 199.

8 Visram, *Asians*, p. 199.

9 National Archives, CO 323/816, letter on 'Colour Riots' from Cardiff City Police to Director of Intelligence, Scotland House, Westminster, 9 October 1919. The term 'coloured', recurrent in documentation of the riots, is generally used to include West Indians, Africans, Arabs and South Asians, *inter alios*.

reports.[10] In the wake of the 1919 riots, police successfully called for paid repatriation schemes, and a series of subsequent legislative acts targeted minority seamen and workers, impeding their freedom of entry into and movement within Britain, and obstructing their access to full citizenship.[11]

Perhaps most notorious among these was the 1925 Coloured Alien Seamen Order, described by Laura Tabili as 'the first instance of state-sanctioned racial subordination inside Britain to come to widespread notice' [Source 5].[12] Issued by the Conservative minister William Joynson-Hicks under Article II of the Aliens Order of 1920, the 1925 Order required all 'coloured' seamen who were unable to produce 'documentary evidence of British nationality to register with the police as aliens'. Constitutionally South Asians were not 'aliens' but citizens of the British Empire. However, it was not easy for them to prove this. Sailors were not required to carry passports, and 'coloured' seamen's discharge certificates – unlike those of their white counterparts, British or 'alien' – were discredited as proof of nationality on the spurious grounds of alleged trafficking in these papers.[13] Connotations of criminality combine with racial 'otherness' to stigmatize minority seamen in the wording of the Order and the letter to chief constables. In the latter, the vagueness of the words 'problem' and 'difficulties' fails to obscure the racism underpinning the legislation which emerges clearly when the seamen's 'racial resemblance' is cited as a justification for its enforcement [Source 5].[14] In the wake of the Order, under pressure from the India Office who received numerous complaints from 'coloured' seamen forced to

---

10 P. Bagguley and Y. Hussain, 'Flying the Flag for England: Citizenship, Religion and Cultural Identity among British Pakistani Muslims', in T. Abbas (ed.), *Muslim Britain: Communities Under Pressure* (London and New York: Zed Books, 2005), pp. 208–21 (p. 211).
11 For a discussion of the repatriation schemes that followed the riots, see Jenkinson, *Black 1919*, Ch. 5.
12 Tabili, '*British Justice*', p. 114.
13 Visram, *Asians*, p. 206.
14 There were other racially discriminatory immigration acts preceding and following the 1925 Order. For details of these, see *Making Britain Database* www.open.ac.uk/makingbritain

register as 'alien', the Home Office agreed to allow the seamen to apply for a Special Certificate of Nationality. This cancelled their registration and proved their Britishness. In 1931, all 'coloured' British seamen were issued with these five-year certificates in lieu of passports.[15] With this, the boundaries of exclusion shifted from the borders of Britain to within the nation as the British citizenship of the seamen was acknowledged but degraded to a subordinate, temporary racialized category of national 'belonging'.[16]

While in the case of the discrimination in the higher ranks of the Army highlighted by Naoroji 'race' trumped class in shaping the contours of exclusion, here class combined with race to play a highly significant role in restricting the entry into or settlement within Britain of South Asians. It was not just seamen who were targeted; officials erroneously (but often knowingly so) applied the rules to other working-class South Asians, for example registering 63 Glasgow-based Indian pedlars and labourers as 'aliens' in 1926.[17] Thus, the apparent targeting of a specific category of newcomer (i.e., seamen) no longer obscured the broader class- and race-based prejudice that underpinned it. The 1931 Foreign Office Circular on 'Passport Facilities for Illiterate Indian British Subjects' makes class-based distinctions between 'Indian British subjects of ... established position' and those with rudimentary English, 'a low standard of education and limited means' in delineating the boundaries of Britishness, foreshadowing more recent immigration legislation [Source 7].[18] It is notable, too, that the interventions made by the India Office against the 1925 Order were motivated by a fear of dissent among their *elite* counterparts in India

---

15 Tabili, 'British Justice', pp. 129, 131; Visram, *Asians*, pp. 214–17.

16 Tabili, 'British Justice', p. 131.

17 Ibid., pp. 127–8; Visram, *Asians*, pp. 212–14.

18 For example the recently implemented points system which places non-EU would-be immigrants into 'tiers' according to skills, education and capital, currently barring the low-skilled from entry (Anon., 'Immigration Points System Begins', BBC News, 29 February 2008, http://bbc.co.uk/1/hi/7269790.stm [accessed 31 January 2011]; see also www.workpermit.com/uk/uk-immigration-tier-system.htm); or the need to pass an English test to acquire citizenship – a skill that is rooted in class for applicants from the Indian subcontinent (Home Office, Life in the UK Test, www.lifeintheuktest.gov.uk [accessed 31 January 2011]).

and consequent threat to the credibility of empire, rather than by a desire to support working-class seamen.[19]

The intersection of race and class in shaping the boundaries of Britishness is also visible in perceptions of mixed-raced relationships and identities in late nineteenth- and early twentieth-century Britain. It was when racial categories broke down, disturbing the hierarchies on which empire was founded as well as threatening racial boundaries within the nation, that anxieties about 'otherness' manifested themselves most starkly. Even within the context of the First World War, when Britain sought to appease its South Asian subjects, concerns about racial mixing resulted in a curtailment of the freedom of movement of South Asian soldiers recuperating in Britain's hospitals.[20] Further, the threat of miscegenation was a significant trigger of the race riots of 1919: a police report on the riots in South Wales traces the violence in Cardiff to the passage through the city of 'a brake containing a number of coloured men and white women'.[21] The Welsh city's chief constable went as far as calling for the illegalization of sexual relations between white women and 'coloured' seamen.[22]

In a pamphlet on the 'Conditions of the Coloured Population in a Stepney Area', authored by Phyllis Young in 1944, on the cusp of the demise of empire [Source 12], it is clearly racial *inter-mixing*, rather than racial *otherness*, that is considered most detrimental. While the report covers areas such as housing, health and employment, it dedicates a disproportionate amount of space to interracial relationships. In the division of the 'coloured' children of Stepney into categories of risk (categories which might represent an attempt to

---

19 Tabili, *'British Justice'*, pp. 122, 125, 133. The India Office, a government department, was responsible for the administration of all of Britain's South Asian territories, including India. The Judicial and Public Department and the Political and Secret Department were two key sub-departments concerned with Indians in Britain.

20 See D. Omissi, *Indian Voices of the Great War: Soldiers' Letters, 1914–18* (Basingstoke: Palgrave Macmillan, 1999).

21 CO 323/816, letter on 'Colour Riots'.

22 H. Ansari, *'The Infidel Within': Muslims in Britain since 1800* (London: Hurst, 2004), p. 98. See also B. Maan, *The New Scots: The Story of Asians in Scotland* (Edinburgh: Donald, 1992), pp. 110–14.

compensate for the breakdown of categories triggered by interracial relationships), mixed-race children rank lower than the children of two 'coloured' parents: whereas the homes of the latter have a 'natural tone', in those of the former 'the conditions ... are very rarely satisfactory and the home atmosphere is affected by the strain under which they are living'. A threat to racial hierarchies is combined with a threat to gender hierarchies: the white woman frequently assumes the dominant (masculine) position of sexual predator (while also remaining a victim), whereas the Indian man assumes the subordinate role of victim (simultaneously to that of predator or aggressor). This partial inversion of normative gender hierarchies suggests an anxious need to manage the transgression of race hierarchies present in such relationships while simultaneously maintaining constructions of Indian men as volatile and brutal – and thus in need of 'civilizing'.[23]

A 1943 police report on a Birmingham conference on 'Indian seamen deserters' echoes the Young report in its equation of interracial relationships with poverty, prostitution, disease, illegitimacy, stupidity and criminality, but goes further to overtly link them with the desertion of ships and uncontrolled influx into Britain – the transgression of the spatial boundaries that keep the racial 'other' at bay.[24] In an earlier police report, dating from 1930, Ethel Mohamed, the English wife of Noah Mohamed who runs a boarding house, is named as a key facilitator of deserter seamen, an example of the 'evil' discussed in the immigration officers' report on the 'lascar deserter' Joffer Shah [Source 6]. She fills in the forms needed to enable seamen to stay on British soil, and 'in this way', we are told, 'entices them to patronise her business'.[25] The language constructs her not just as a canny businesswoman, but also, implicitly, as a temptress, and an interracial relationship is again aligned with the subversion of boundaries of nation: a

---

23 In the report, whereas the mothers of the children of Category C are 'neglectful' and lacking in 'real affection and care' (characteristics normatively constructed as male), the 'coloured' men 'instinctively love children'.

24 British Library, L/PJ/12/645, 'Conference on Indian Seamen Deserters', 2 March 1943, p. 106.

25 British Library, L/E/9/962, Report by Sergeant Lawson of CID Special Branch, 26 November 1930, p. 126.

boarding-house run by a racially transgressive couple enables working-class South Asians to transgress the physical boundaries that separate India and Britain.

The philanthropic guise of Young's report, as well as its paradoxical combination of an apparent advocacy of racial integration – visible in the denunciation of the 'colour bar' as a cause of the deprivation and moral turpitude of the Stepney community – with an unease with mixed-race relationships, can be traced to the anomalies of citizenship for Britain's South Asian subjects resident in the imperial motherland: the tension between the inclusive concept of imperial subject-hood and empire's need for the racial hierarchies which demoted its 'coloured' minorities, especially the working class, to the status of second-class citizens.

Transgressing the boundaries of Britishness

In her discussion of early twentieth-century multi-ethnic communities in Britain's port cities, Laura Tabili argues that the 'persistence of ... interracial settlements posed a tacit challenge to the racial divisions in the maritime workforce and in the empire as a whole'.[26] In the face of the hostility with which they were received, then, interracial relationships and children enacted and embodied a transgression of the boundaries of Britishness. This section will consider how the 'anomalies of citizenship' discussed above also opened up opportunities for the subversion of structures of race and empire, as well as class and gender, by South Asians in Britain, both elite and working-class. While the metropole, as the centre of imperial power, was the source of the oppression of India and its peoples, its contradictory – and of course partial – commitment to the 'ideals of Freedom of Democracy' cited by Anand meant that it was also, paradoxically, a space of relative freedom to mobilize and protest against this very oppression.

In contrast to the construction of the 'coloured' children of Stepney in Young's report, representations of the suffragette Sophia Duleep Singh, daughter of Duleep Singh, deposed Maharajah of the Punjab, and his German–Ethiopian wife Bamba Müller, do not tend

26 Tabili, *'British Justice'*, p. 135.

to draw attention to her mixed-race heritage. At first glance, racial difference, or 'Indianness', is curiously absent from both the 1913 *Times* article on Sophia Duleep Singh's refusal to pay taxes and the contemporaneous photograph of her selling the *Suffragette* newspaper outside Hampton Court Palace [Source 3, Figure 1.1]. In the former, the only indication of her South Asian identity is the familiar Sikh surname 'Singh' which jars with the quintessentially English first name 'Sophie'. Sophia Duleep Singh's 'race' is almost erased too, in the photograph; her light skin, combined with her English dress, enables her to 'pass' for an Englishwoman. The title 'Princess', which recurs several times in the space of the short article, screens her racial difference behind her elite class status while simultaneously exoticizing her racial 'otherness', thereby rendering it palatable.[27] Arguably, Sophia's class status combined with her Western roots enabled her to gain full access to Britishness. Indeed, the content of her speech at the police court, reported in the newspaper article, locates her squarely within the nation: the emphasis on the marginalization she experiences because of her gender and the consequent erosion of her status as citizen positions her among 'the women of England' and deflects the focus away from her 'Indianness'. It is perhaps by virtue of her elite status that Sophia is able to see and be seen beyond her position as a colonial subject in Britain and thus to mobilize on behalf of another minority struggle; she is not defined primarily by her 'Indianness', even though, as others have shown, it continued to be an important part of her identity and influenced her social and political concerns and activities.[28]

Other South Asians looked further than the immediate struggle for

27 For an illuminating discussion of the 'exotic', albeit in the context of post-colonial culture, see G. Huggan, *The Postcolonial Exotic: Marketing the Margins* (London: Routledge, 2001), Preface. For an account of another exoticized mixed-race Indian in Britain – singer, writer and photojournalist Olive Christian Malvery, known as the 'little princess' – see S. Lahiri, *Indian Mobilities in the West, 1900–1947* (Basingstoke: Palgrave, 2010), Ch. 1. While no suffragette, Malvery also focused her concern on women – specifically the plight of London's poor working women which she recounted in *The Soul Market* (London: Hutchinson, 1907).

28 S. Mukherjee, 'Herabai Tata and Sophia Duleep Singh: Suffragette Resistances for India and Britain, 1910–1920', in R. Ahmed and S. Mukherjee (eds), *South Asian Resistances in Britain, 1858–1947* (London:

Indian independence by mobilizing for the rights of white working-class Britons; thus, they can be said to have reversed hierarchies of empire, which placed white Britons in the superior role of benefactor.[29] V.K. Krishna Menon, best known for his leadership of the India League, showed his commitment to Britain's white working class in his role as Labour councillor in the impoverished London borough of Camden as well as by co-founding Penguin's non-fiction, educational imprint, Pelican Books, which sought to democratize knowledge by bringing it to the masses.[30] Several years before Menon's interventions into British political life, the Communist MP Shapurji Saklatvala was engaged in a similar transgression of boundaries of race, nation and class through his vociferous and provocative advocacy of the Irish Republican cause both inside and outside Parliament, as well as through his commitment to the predominantly working-class and substantially Irish electorate of Battersea. In his maiden speech to the House of Commons, he spoke at length about the Irish Treaty of 1922, describing it as a 'forced freedom' and highlighting its incompatibility with the Labour movement [Source 4].[31]

Continuum, 2011); Visram, *Asians*, pp. 164–8. Mukherjee also discusses the contribution of Herabai Tata to the struggle for women's rights. While Tata spent time in Britain, continuing her work there, her main focus was on the Indian context. Other South Asian women, notably Dhanvanthi Rama Rau and Avabai Wadia, also participated in women's organizations in early twentieth-century Britain (see D. Rama Rau, *An Inheritance: The Memoirs of Dhanvanthi Rama Rau* (London: Heinemann, 1977); A. Wadia, *The Light is Ours: Memoirs and Movements* (International Planned Parenthood Federation, 2001)).

29 See also note 27 on Malvery. If read alongside the Phyllis Young report [Source 12], the concern of Malvery, a mixed-race woman, for Britain's indigenous poor ironizes the philanthropic concern with interracial relationships articulated in the former decades later.

30 T.G.S. George, *Krishna Menon: A Biography* (London: Jonathan Cape. 1964), Ch. 11. See also Chapter 3 in this volume.

31 The extraordinary geographical range of Saklatvala's speech in its entirety, which takes in India, the Middle and Far East and Russia, as well as South Africa, Ireland and Britain, is indicative of the global reach of South Asian political engagement and activism in Britain during this period. Syed Ameer Ali's focus on Canada is similarly suggestive of this internationalist perspective [Source 2].

Newspaper reports, particularly from the right-wing press, frequently racialize Saklatvala: in one article the charismatic appeal of his speeches is likened to the 'black magic' of an 'Indian fakir', and in another we are told that 'Mr S made a speech full of curry, real hot stuff, charging the Govt with causing death, insanity and worse kind of poverty among Indians'.[32] While his class privilege facilitated his political career, Saklatvala's subordinate and outsider status as an Indian in Britain arguably enabled mutual identification between him and his working-class and largely Irish constituents, and motivated his engagement with another minority's struggle for equal rights. An article in the *British Weekly* implies this, claiming that '[h]is colour, just because it was a handicap, made the contradictory Battersea public rally to him more strongly'.[33] If for his detractors his racialization reinforced the 'otherness' of Communism, keeping it on the periphery of Britishness, for Saklatvala, the exclusions he experienced as an Indian migrant may have pushed him further into the margins of parliamentary politics, sharpening his critical gaze on the shortcomings of both the Labour Party and, for its lukewarm attitude to the anti-imperial struggle, the Communist Party, and aligning his sympathies with radical extra-parliamentary political movements such as Sinn Fein.[34]

Saklatvala's radical connections caused the India Office to place him under surveillance. While his political activities can be excavated through a range of archival sources, those of his working-class South Asian counterparts, struggling for equality of citizenship in Britain in the 1930s and 1940s, are traceable primarily – and at times uniquely – from government or police surveillance reports, which must be read with a degree of scepticism, or brushed against the grain, as noted in the introduction.[35] Unlike Saklatvala's or Sophia Duleep Singh's, their dissent was enacted from a position of relative power-

32 Anon., 'It's the Man that Matters', *Daily Graphic* (30 October 1924), n.p.; W. McCartney and 'Poy', *Evening News* (6 July 1923), n.p.

33 M.M. Thomson, 'A Pilgrimage to Battersea', *British Weekly* (11 December 1924), n.p.

34 For Saklatvala's connections to Irish radicals, see K. O'Malley, *Ireland, India and Empire: Indo-Irish Radical Connections, 1919–64* (Manchester: Manchester University Press, 2008), pp. 23–9.

35 W. Benjamin, 'Theses on the Philosophy of History', in *Illuminations*, ed. and intro. Hannah Arendt (London: Fontana, 1992 [1973]), pp. 245–55 (p.

lessness. Akin to the 'tactics' described by Michel de Certeau in his
The Practice of Everyday Life, it took place in the 'space of the other'.
Often lacking the ability to plan their resistance to the hardship
imposed on them by shipping companies and government officials,
they had to 'make use of the cracks that particular conjunctions
[opened] in the surveillance of the proprietary powers' or '[take]
advantage of "opportunities"' that arose unexpectedly, seizing them
'on the wing'.[36] Thus seamen capitalized on gaps in their surveillance
to 'jump ship', often failing at first.[37] Once on British soil, like Joffer
Shah, the subject of an immigration officer's report, they were able to
accrue Britishness by claiming certificates of nationality. These
enabled them to circumvent the Indian and British Merchant
Shipping Acts, either by signing on to British Articles rather than the
inferior Asiatic Articles, or by seeking alternative employment as
pedlars or labourers [Source 6].[38]

As the narrative of Shah Abdul Majid Qureshi illustrates, having
crossed Britain's borders they frequently continued their journeys,
both geographical and social, travelling from Tilbury to London, or
covering vast swathes of the country as pedlars or in their quest for
work, and sometimes eventually progressing to better jobs in the
restaurant trade or in other businesses.[39] Their frequent displace-
ment is again redolent of de Certeau's 'walker' whose 'placelessness'
necessitates a mobility, which while symptomatic of disempower-
ment, nevertheless creates its own possibilities for transgressive
practices.[40] Thus former sepoy and activist Thakur Singh's
movement across a range of towns and cities enabled him to spread
the Indian nationalist message among the British people, much to
the dismay of the authorities [Source 10]. But combined with this

---

248). The Indian Political Intelligence was formed in 1909 in response to an
increase in Indian nationalist activities throughout Europe. It closed in 1947
(O'Malley, *Ireland, India and Empire*, pp. 5–8).

36 M. de Certeau, *The Practice of Everyday Life* (Berkeley: University of
California Press, 1987), pp. 371, xix.

37 C. Adams (ed.) *Across Seven Seas and Thirteen Rivers: Life Stories of Pioneer
Sylheti Settlers in Britain* (London: THAP, 1987), p. 149.

38 Visram, *Asians*, pp. 215–18.

39 Adams, *Across Seven Seas*, pp. 149–67.

40 de Certeau, *Practice of Everyday Life*, pp. 92–3.

mobility was the creation and deployment of networks among working-class South Asians in Britain, which laid the foundation for the more entrenched communities that developed subsequently. The 'evil' manipulation of seamen by 'coloured' boarding-house keepers mentioned in the 1930 immigration officer's report can be read, against the grain, as evidence of such a network, both economically and socially supportive, as well as of a developing shrewdness and entrepreneurialism on the part of some migrants who seized an opportunity to turn the lascars' search for a better standard of living to their own economic advantage [Source 6].

There is a tendency in government surveillance reports to represent South Asian workers involved in dissenting organizations or events as simultaneously passive and threatening; their activities are often constructed as either irrational or self-interested and are thereby shorn of political validity or even significance.[41] Organized resistance, such as the lascar strikes in 1939 for better pay and working conditions, is frequently attributed to manipulative leaders rather than to the majority of the dissenters who are divested of agency. For example the strike on the SS *Oxfordshire*, we are told, was 'in large measure due to the activities of two agitators'; the spread of the strike from one ship to another is described as 'strike fever', a phrase which has connotations of irrational, hot-headed behaviour [Source 8]. Several historians have countered this depoliticizing interpretation by emphasizing the agency and resourcefulness of South Asian seamen and workers in Britain.[42] Reading archival documents together often yields contradictory evidence, which high-

41 For a detailed discussion of this tendency, see R. Ahmed, 'Networks of Resistance: Krishna Menon and Working-Class South Asians in Interwar Britain', in R. Ahmed and S. Mukherjee (eds), *South Asian Resistances in Britain, 1858–1947* (London: Continuum, 2011). See also G. Wemyss, *The Invisible Empire: White Discourse, Tolerance and Belonging* (Farnham: Ashgate, 2009), Ch. 3, for a similar argument about contemporary Bangladeshis being constructed as politically passive but manipulated by 'extremists'.

42 G. Balachandran, 'Cultures of Protest in Transnational Contexts: Indian Seamen Abroad, 1886–1945', *Transforming Cultures* e-journal, 3:2 (2008), http://epress.lib.uts.edu.au.ojs/index.php/TfC/ (accessed 20 December 2010); Wemyss, *Invisible Empire*; Visram, *Asians*, Ch. 8.

lights and undermines depoliticizing stereotypes of passivity. The helpless, near-destitute Indians represented in the paternalistic First Report of the Hindustan Community House are reconfigured not just as social subjects but as activists when read alongside a Scotland Yard report claiming that the House in fact harbours radical 'propagandists': twelve unemployed Indians, two of whom are 'out-and-out revolutionaries' [Source 9]. This assertion is, however, closely followed by the claim that these men were 'encouraged by Kundan Lal JALIE ... who looks upon himself as a protector of working-class Indians', thereby partly undermining the political agency of the working-class men.[43]

South Asian workers' struggle for equality tended to have a more localized focus on their immediate material conditions – made pressing by their poverty and disenfranchisement – than did that of their elite counterparts. The boundaries they circumvented or transgressed were frequently tangible, literally delimiting their own movement and obstructing their access to British space. This physical curtailment of mobility is evident during the lascar strikes in 1939 when dissenting crewmembers were arrested and sometimes imprisoned. The refusal of the lascar members of the crew of SS *City of Manchester* to board their ship and leave British soil during the 1939 strikes in turn makes physical their claim to being British and to the rights that this entailed, as does their rejection of post-First and Second World War repatriation schemes [Source 8].[44] But the struggle for access to better conditions within Britain intersected and overlapped with nationalist struggles for Indian independence, as is evident in several of the examples cited above. The Indian Workers' Association (IWA) focused their concern on both the welfare of Indians in Britain, and the fight for an independent India. Thakur Singh, a key player in this organization, is denounced for his bid to progress from working as a bench-hand to machine work; while this is an attempt to improve his own material conditions, which is of course a profoundly political act in itself, when read alongside other documents it can also be perceived as an intervention in the Indian

---

43 British Library, L/PJ/12/630, 'Communist and Anti-British Propaganda amongst East End Indians', 13 December 1939, p. 59.
44 Visram, *Asians*, pp. 201–5.

nationalist struggle. The government was allegedly attempting to prevent South Asians in Britain from acquiring factory skills for fear that they would take these skills back to India, thereby undermining a rationale for imperial rule [Source 10].[45]

As well as connecting a local British focus and a nationalist Indian one through their acts of dissent, working-class South Asians in Britain also, on occasion, subverted boundaries of ethnicity in a shared struggle against subordination. While South Asians remained largely on the periphery of the race riots of 1919, as mentioned above (p. 25), instances of their involvement and collaboration with other minorities have been recorded; one such example recounts the fining of Essup Mohammed, a South Asian seaman, and the West Indian ship's fireman Richard Jones for causing a disturbance at a café which was probably provoked by their confrontation by a crowd of white men.[46] The immigration legislation that followed the riots entrenched this collaboration, eventually precipitating the inauguration of the Coloured Colonial Seamen's Association, which comprised 'Negroes, Arabs, Somalis, Malays and Chinese', as well as South Asians.[47] In this context, Tabili describes the formation of a 'multicultural Black political identity', thereby tracing the better-known and more explicit anti-racist deployment of such an identity in the 1970s and 1980s back to this earlier period of empire.[48]

Reshaping Britishness

Alongside their interactions with other minority communities as well as the white British, many South Asians in Britain continued to prioritize their own distinct cultural and religious concerns and practices. As sociologists have demonstrated, the erosion of the term 'black' as a catch-all for Britain's minority groups in the 1990s and 2000s stems in part from a marginalization of South Asians

45 British Library, L/PJ/12/645, 'Indian Workers Union', 22 February 1942, p. 9.
46 *South Shields Gazette*, 13 February 1919; cited in J. Jenkinson, 'On the Margins? South Asians in Britain during the 1919 Seaport Riots', unpublished paper presented at the 'Making Britain: South Asian Resistances, 1870–1950' Inter-University Postcolonial Seminar Series, spring 2009.
47 Tabili, *'British Justice'*, pp. 158–9.
48 Ibid., p. 159.

(as well as other minorities) within this broad category and their consequent assertion of a way – or ways – of 'being British' distinct to them.[49] The final section of the chapter will consider some early examples of South Asian 'cultural assertiveness' in Britain, and the beginnings of a mobilization for what might be termed 'minority cultural rights', focusing in particular on minority religious rights.[50]

In the report on the IWA, we are told that Thakur Singh advised Indians to refuse national service on the grounds that 'it was against their religious scruples to take part in military training' [Source 10]. Given his political activism, it is possible that he suggested this as a cover and that Thakur Singh's refusal of national service, and that of his fellow Indians, was motivated in part by a nationalist, anti-imperialist rejection of the deployment of Indians in Britain's battles. There was a significant anti-conscription movement among South Asians in Britain during the Second World War. It was a focus of both the IWA, who 'objected to service in the armed forces both on political and economic grounds ... arguing that the war was not their business and that calling-up would involve a considerable drop in the money which they were earning',[51] and the organization Swaraj House. The latter issued a statement in February 1944 declaring that 'owing to the persistent refusal of the British Government to grant freedom to India, no self-respecting Indian can accept its orders [to join up] as in any sense morally binding' [Source 11]. Against this, Krishna Menon argued that 'if Indians were to be exempted from

---

49 See for example T. Modood, '"Difference", Cultural Racism and Anti-Racism', in *Multicultural Politics: Racism, Ethnicity and Muslims in Britain* (Edinburgh: Edinburgh University Press, 2005), pp. 27–46. H. Kureishi, *Dreaming and Scheming: Reflections on Writing and Politics* (London: Faber, 2002), p. 55.

50 For an argument for a notion of equality that goes beyond 'individualism and cultural assimilation' to a 'politics of recognition' of cultural difference, see Modood, *Multicultural Politics*, p. 134. For an argument for the importance of a notion of 'collective rights', see B. Parekh, *Rethinking Multiculturalism: Cultural Diversity and Political Theory* (Basingstoke: Macmillan, 2006 [2000]), pp. 215–19.

51 British Library, L/PJ/12/645, 'The Indian Workers' Association', 14 April 1942, p. 30.

conscription it would amount to definite racial discrimination against them' on the part of the government. Thus, like Naoroji and Ali decades earlier, he alludes to the pledge of equality for all subjects of empire [Sources 1 and 2]. Whereas Menon's interpretation of the issue situates South Asians within Britishness but demands parity for them, the rejection by Swaraj House of imperial citizenship in favour of citizenship of a new, independent India locates South Asians outside the boundaries of Britain. But Swaraj House's position could, alternatively or additionally, be interpreted as hinting at a move beyond equality as assimilation to assert the right of a minority to be different *within* Britain.

Further, especially when read through the lens of contemporary multicultural politics in Britain, citing minority religious beliefs as a reason for exemption from the duties of citizenship – which government officials implied was a mere strategy of evasion – can be seen as cultural assertiveness, a demand for the legitimization of a minority culture and its associated practices within the boundaries of Britain. Indeed, Thakur Singh's citation of religion as a reason for non-conscription could, alternatively, be interpreted simply as such – and, moreover, as an example of an early assertion of a minority religious identity. South Asians expressed their commitment to the practice of their religions in Britain's public sphere by the establishment of mosques, gurdwaras and temples, as well as religious organizations, from the nineteenth century. Thus they imprinted their cultures on British soil. The first purpose-built mosque, the Shah Jahan Mosque in Woking, was completed in 1889. The Religious Society of Zoroastrians was founded in Kensington as early as 1861,[52] and in 1927 Saklatvala had his five children initiated into the Parsee faith in Caxton Hall, Westminster. Said to be only the third such ceremony to have taken place in Britain, it was widely reported by the press.[53] The west-London-based Bhupindra Dharamsala, Britain's first Sikh gurdwara, was established in 1911, three years after the first Sikh society in Britain.[54] The Sikh pedlar Anant Ram's first destination on

52 Visram, *Asians*, p. 298.
53 Anon., 'The Mark of their Caste', *Daily News* (23 July 1927), n.p.; Visram, *Asians*, p. 319.
54 Visram, *Asians*, p. 298.

his arrival in Britain in 1936 was a gurdwara.[55] In his account he describes it as much more than a place of worship. For him, and others like him – as for later generations – religious buildings were sites of community support and therefore of enablement and resistance against structures of exclusion, not unlike their secular counterparts such as the Hindustan Community House and the Hindustani Social Club [Source 9].[56]

South Asians established restaurants and cafés as well as political, religious and social organizations. These too served as a hub for an embryonic British South Asian community, and made their mark on the culinary landscape of the nation. The writer Attia Hosain describes Shafi's restaurant in London, founded in the 1920s by two Indian brothers, as a 'rendez-vous for Indians – visitors, expatriates and students alike'. D.P. Chaudhuri, owner of another central London restaurant, Rajah, is said to have initiated the social 'Indian Centre' there in 1945; while former seamen Ayub Ali's East End restaurant, Shah Jolal, was a focal point for the community of workers who inhabited the area, and location of the East End branch of Krishna Menon's India League.[57] If restaurants were public sites of the dissemination of cultural difference and gradual diversification of Britain, the ostensibly 'private' spaces of domesticity also housed the enactment of South Asian cultures which quietly permeated national life, penetrating the boundaries of a normative Britishness.[58] The memoir of Savitri

55 A. Ram, 'This Is My Home Now: Reminiscences of a Panjabi Migrant in Coventry', unpublished interview, p. 4 of typescript. I am grateful to Rozina Visram for giving me access to this document.

56 See 'Hindustani Social Club', *Making Britain Database* www.open.ac.uk /makingbritain/content/hindustani-social-club

57 A. Hosain, 'Of Memories and Meals', in Antonia Till (ed.), *Loaves and Wishes, Writers Writing on Food* (London: Virago, 1992), pp. 141–6; British Library, L/PJ/12/646, p. 122; British Library, L/PJ/12/455, 'India League', 23 June 1943. p. 80; for information on Ayub Ali, see also Adams, *Across Seven Seas.*

58 Antoinette Burton, among others, has rescued the domestic sphere from the margins of history, demonstrating the political significance of house and home through her readings of Indian women's memoirs in the context of late colonialism. See *Dwelling in the Archive: Women Writing House, Home and History in Late Colonial India* (Oxford: Oxford University Press, 2003).

Chowdhary, the wife of an Essex medical doctor, Dharm Sheel Chowdhary, offers a rare window into the home and life of an Indian woman in early twentieth-century provincial Britain [Source 13].[59] In fact, Savitri Chowdhary's engagement with British life extended beyond the domestic: as well as helping with the smooth running of her husband's surgery, she wrote one of the first British Indian cookery books and gave talks and presented television programmes on the subject. She also participated in cultural and political associations in London, including Krishna Menon's India League.[60] Her account of the creation of a family home in Britain – and concomitant reimagining of Britain as her home – is, however, no less politically significant. In many ways, Chowdhary assimilated into conventional British life, exchanging her saris for dresses for everyday living and cutting her hair short in line with her husband's wishes.[61] And yet she combined a self-consciously anglicized and 'modern' public persona with the maintenance of certain Hindu Indian cultural practices and traditions, donning saris as evening wear in Laindon and when visiting Indian friends in London, and cooking curries for her family as well as for English friends.[62] The memoir conveys a strong feeling of a local British female collectivity, forged through the shared

59 For other South Asian women's accounts of early twentieth-century Britain, see for example Rama Rau, *Memoirs*; and Wadia, *The Light*. While these two women returned to South Asia after periods in Britain, Chowdhary settled in Britain, making it her home.

60 S. Chowdhary, *Indian Cookery* (London: Andre Deutsch, 1954). Interestingly, Mulk Raj Anand published a cookery book, *Curries and Other Indian Dishes*, even earlier, in 1932, which was aimed at English housewives (Desmond Hamsworth). Although Indian women were a minority in the India League, others were involved, including Bhicoo Batlivala and Mrs J. Handoo (see British Library, L/PJ/12/448–54).

61 In the light of Savitri Chowdhary's husband's apparent wish for her to assimilate, it is interesting to consider how gender might shape opinions on the desirability of cultural assimilation among immigrants or minorities.

62 Some of this detail was provided in an unpublished interview with Chowdhary's daughter, Shakun Banfield, 17 March 2008, Bromley. Cf. Wadia's account of wearing a sari to her English school in the late 1920s. Of particular interest is her claim that this assertion of her cultural identity won her respect (*The Light*, pp. 34–5).

experience of having children as well as of undergoing the traumas of the Second World War. But this sense of community is combined with a borderline perspective that yields an empathic 'othering' of the British and their culture and customs. As well as working to subtly destabilize the normativity of everyday British life, Chowdhary's narrative of self-formation, through its articulation of a balancing and accommodation of Indianness and Britishness, difference and assimilation, suggests a cultural duality that seems composed of two discrete strands but could nevertheless be read as a forerunner to more contemporary hybridized modes of British Asianness.

Chowdhary is well aware of her class privilege, explicitly suggesting that it was this that protected her from racism. Class hierarchies conflict with and subvert those of race in her account; domestic help is provided by a series of white British women, and a Sikh pedlar she encounters is apparently surprised to discover the Westernized doctor's wife is in fact a fellow Indian. It was a very different group of working-class Indian men – some of them, no doubt, also surviving by peddling, and all of them excluded from the relative privilege and acceptance experienced by the Chowdharys – that enacted one of the most striking examples of a demand for the public recognition of cultural difference within Britain during the period of empire. In August 1938, at a meeting at King's Hall, Commercial Road, of the Jamiat-ul-Muslimin, a Muslim organization affiliated to the East London Mosque,[63] a copy of H.G. Wells' *A Short History of the World* was 'ceremoniously committed to the flames by a party of Indian Mohammedans' because of references to the Prophet Mohammed which were perceived as offensive. These include a description of the Prophet Mohammed as 'a man ... of ... considerable vanity, greed, cunning and self-deception' as well as a challenge to the divine authority of the Quran.[64] This act was followed by a

---

63 For more information on the Jamiat-ul-Muslimin, see British Library, L/PJ/12/614, Report by Special Branch of Metropolitan Police, 17 August 1938, pp. 1–2.

64 L/PJ/12/614, Report by Special Branch of Metropolitan Police, 17 August 1938, p. 3; 'Mr. Wells and Mohammed', *Manchester Guardian* (13 August 1938), p. 5.

march of protest by members of the Jamiat to India House in Aldwych (Figure 1.3).[65] The deputation, met by the Indian High Commissioner Feroz Khan Noon (also a Muslim), requested that Wells retract his remarks and offer an apology, as well as that the book should be banned. While the Jamiat's protest failed in its aims, it remains a remarkable act of cultural assertiveness in the context of imperial Britain.[66] The fact that the protestors were working-class, evident from their petition which includes crosses in lieu of signatures, enhances its extraordinary nature, and disturbs hegemonic constructions of South Asian workers in Britain as passive pawns who become politicized only in response to the manipulation of their 'leaders' (Figure 1.2). Not only did a group of working-class South Asian Muslims march into central London, symbolically laying claim to the very heart of the imperial metropolis, but they did so to request public recognition of the sensitivities of Muslims within Britain, thereby bringing their religion out of the private domain into the British public sphere. Thus, their demand was not just for individual rights as British citizens, but for collective minority rights.

The Jamiat protest resonates with contemporary literary controversies involving religious minorities, in particular the 1989 protests by Bradford South Asian Muslims against Salman Rushdie's novel *The Satanic Verses*.[67] The significant and multifarious South Asian

65 The march began at Bank Station and proceeded through Fleet Street to Cannon Street then India House. (L/PJ/12/614, p. 13). The photograph of the march (Figure 1.3) is dated 1 January 1938 by Getty Images – but it is highly probable that this is in fact the march of August, documented in the India Office files. There is no record of any other march taking place earlier in the year.

66 While sympathetic with the protestors, Feroz Khan Noon explained to the deputation that 'in England only obscene or blasphemous books could be proscribed and blasphemy was only against the Christian religion', but agreed to transmit their grievances to the Secretary of State for India. The latter responded by asserting that 'having regard to the freedom permitted to the expression of views in this country', he had 'no power to secure a modification of the passage' (ibid., p. 15; letter to Feroz Khan Noon, 24 August 1938, p. 28).

67 For readings of the 'Rushdie affair', see, among several others, T. Modood, 'Reflections on the Rushdie Affair: Muslims, Race, and Equality in Britain', in *Multicultural Politics*, pp. 103–12; M. Ruthven, *A Satanic Affair: Salman*

mobilization for equality of citizenship in late nineteenth- and early twentieth-century Britain outlined in this chapter can be seen as a precursor to the better-known British Asian voices and acts of assertion and dissent of post-independence Britain – including the 1977 strike by female South Asian workers at the Grunwick Photographic Processing Plant, the 1979 anti-fascist protests in Southall and pioneering work of Southall Black Sisters, the 2001 race riots in Britain's northern cities, and the various campaigns led by Shami Chakrabarti on behalf of the pressure group Liberty, to name just a few.[68] The last twenty-five years have seen a gradual increase in the presence of Asians in Parliament, and South Asian cultures have permeated many other spheres of British life, including the arts, sport and of course the culinary. While the boundaries to an equal British citizenship and the focus of activism are continuously shifting, and while Asian voices, both historical and contemporary, are often contradictory and conflictual, all of these episodes nevertheless form a narrative that is reshaping the contours of the nation and the national imaginary.

Rushdie and the Rage of Islam (London: Chatto & Windus, 1990); L. Appignanesi and S. Maitland (eds), *The Rushdie File* (London: Fourth Estate, 1989).

68 On post-independence South Asian resistances, see A. Sivanandan, *A Different Hunger: Writings on Black Resistance* (London: Pluto Press, 1982); A. Brah, *Cartographies of Diaspora: Contesting Identities* (London: Routledge, 1996).

Source material for Chapter 1

1 *Letter from Dadabhai Naoroji to the War Office, 7 August 1896.*
[National Archives, Kew, WO 32/8651, pp. 87–8][69]

> Cambridge Lodge,
> West Hill Road,
> Southfields, S. W.
> 7th August, 1896.

Sir,

I thank you for your letter of 23rd Ultimo, (100/Candidates/1692) and I have obtained a copy of the Royal Warrant from Messrs Eyre and Spottiswoode.[70]

In your letter of 10th June last you were good enough to acquaint me 'that Candidates for Commissions in the British Army must be of

69 Naoroji was born in Bombay in 1925 and came to Britain in 1855. While in Britain, he campaigned tirelessly for freedom for India. In 1892, he won the Finsbury Central seat for the Liberal Party and became Britain's first South Asian Member of Parliament. See 'Dadabhai Naoroji', *Making Britain Database* www.open.ac.uk/makingbritain/content/dadabhai-naoroji; O. Ralph, *Naoroji, the First Asian MP: A Biography of Dadabhai Naoroji* (Antigua: Hansib, 1997).

70 This letter forms part of a substantial correspondence between Dadabhai Naoroji and the War Office between June 1896 and January 1897 in which Naoroji persistently questions the War Office for its exclusion of Indians from the commissioned ranks of the armed forces. Eyre & Spottiswoode was the Queen's printing company.

pure European descent, and are also required to be British-born or Naturalised British subjects'[.] In your letter of 18th July last (100/Candidates/1659) you inform me 'that the Conditions for admission to the Commissioned ranks of the Army are laid down by Regulations made by the Secretary of State for War under the Authority of Her Majesty the Queen as signified by Article I of the Royal Warrant for the pay, appointment, promotion and non effective pay of the Army'.

I need not say how very much obliged I feel to the Secretary of State for War for all your replies, and I now beg further indulgence and favour of His Lordship to give me some further explanation on the matter, that I need.

In 'Article I – First Appointments' I do not find a word to exclude British subjects like the Indian British subjects. The candidates are required to be 'persons duly qualified under Regulations approved by Our Secretary of State'[.]

Now I cannot suppose that any such Regulation can be made constitutionally under the Warrant by the Secretary of State as would supercede [*sic*] any Act of Parliament or any Proclamations of Her Majesty the Queen, but that such Regulations can only be made in accordance with Acts of Parliament, and Proclamations of the Sovereign. I desire to know whether I am right.

Under the Section I of the Warrant there is in Clause 1a 'To a duly qualified candidate from a University'[.] In the Regulations for such Candidates certain British Universities are specified. There are Indian British subjects who have graduated and are graduating almost every year in some of these Universities. There is not a word to exclude such Graduates. This would show that the Warrant did not mean to exclude Indians. Under Clause 3 there is 'By open Competition'[.] Here again no exclusion is made by the Warrant, of British Indian subjects.

And it stands to reason that it could not be otherwise. The Act of Parliament of 1833 enacted 'that no Native of the said territory (meaning India) nor any natural-born subject of His Majesty, resident therein shall, by reason only of his religion, place of birth, descent, or any of these, be disabled from holding any place, office, or employment under the said Company'[.]

Now, all the powers, duties and responsibilities of the Company are transferred to the Queen by another Act of Parliament of 1858,[71] and the entire exclusion of the consideration of religion, place of birth and descent has remained as binding now as it was by the Act of 1833, for any place, office, or employment under Her Majesty. Not only did Parliament, not repeal or amend the clause of the Act of 1833, but in far more emphatic and explicit terms, the Sovereign issued a Proclamation, strongly and explicitly confirming, and in the most solemn manner pledging before God and Man with an invokation [sic] of the blessing of God, placing Her Indian subjects on exactly the same footing as all Her Majesty's other subjects – in these clear words; –

'We hold ourselves bound to the Natives of our Indian territory by the same obligations of duty which bind us to all our other subjects, and these obligations by the blessing of Almighty God we shall faithfully and conscientiously fulfil'[.]

'And it is our further will that, so far as may be our subjects of whatever race or creed, be freely and impartially admitted to Offices in our Service, the duties of which they may be qualified by their education, ability, and integrity duly to discharge'.

'In their prosperity will be our strength, in their contentment our security, and in their gratitude our best reward. And may the God of all powers grant to us and to those in authority under us strength to carry out these our wishes for the good of our people'[.]

Nothing can be clearer than that British Indian subjects are most solemnly and honourably pledged to be exactly alike all other British subjects.

In 1887 on the occasion of the great Jubilee, the Queen and Empress of India again confirmed Her Proclamation of 1858 in these clear words; –

'It had always been, and will always be, Her earnest desire to maintain unswervingly the principles laid down in the proclamation

---

71 Founded in 1600, the East India Company was originally a British trading company which operated in Asia and the Middle East. In the mid-eighteenth century it began to assume administrative control over India. After the Indian Rebellion in 1857, the government of India was transferred from the East India Company to the British crown, and in 1877 Queen Victoria became Empress of India.

published on Her assumption of the direct control of the Government of India'.[72]

I do not see therefore, how it is possible that the Queen would intend in this Warrant any thing so contrary not only to Acts of Parliament but to Her own most gracious and explicit Proclamations of 1858 and 1887. That our gracious Sovereign and the British people whose voice and desire she represents, could have been anything but sincere in Her Proclamations cannot be admitted for a moment, and it is impossible to believe that Her Majesty's Warrant could have had the least intention of stultifying and superceding [*sic*] Acts of Parliament and falsifying Her Majesty's own great Proclamations, so seriously made to the World on two great and historical occasions.

There is this further indication. I find that in the spirit of and in accordance with the Acts of 1833 and 1858, and the Proclamations of 1858 and 1887, all the Civil Services of the United Kingdom in every Department, Civil, Military and Naval, are open to the British Indian Subjects. There are no doubt some flaws in the rules and their execution, which I cannot refer to in this letter, but the fact is there, that all the Civil Services of the United Kingdom are open to the Indian British Subjects to the same extent as to any other British subject, such as the British people.

There is one other explanation I feel necessary to ask as to the qualifications stated in your letter of 10th June 'that the Candidates must be of pure European descent, and are also required to be British-born or naturalized British subjects'[.]

This would mean that a Turk or a Russian, or a Bulgarian or a Spaniard or any other of European descent can have the qualifications of admission by being only naturalized while natural-born

72 Wainwright discusses the reasons for the transfer of rule to Queen Victoria and the ways in which this shift to imperial subject-hood affected the position of Indians: in the aftermath of the Rebellion of 1857, 'British authorities sought to legitimize their rule in terms of equality before the law and a common allegiance that transcended ethnic diversity. In order to achieve this goal, they perpetuated the dynastic concept of subjecthood to a monarch at the expense of the concept of citizenship of the state', *'The Better Class' of Indians* (Manchester: Manchester University Press, 2008), p. 99.

subjects of Her Majesty's own British dominions, and even after publicly pledged to be exactly like other British subjects, are to be excluded as only mere helots. Even those born in the Colonies would appear to be thus excluded.

You will easily see how puzzled I feel at your letter of 10th June last, and I shall feel exceedingly obliged to the Secretary of State for War to give me the necessary explanations.

I remain,
Your obedient servant,
(Sd) Dadabhoi Naoroji.

The Under Secretary of State
War Office,
Pall Mall,
London, S.W.

2 Extract from *Syed Ameer Ali*, 'Anomalies of Civilisation: A Peril to India', *The Nineteenth Century and After*,[73] April 1908, pp. 571–2.[74] [British Library shelfmark: P.P.5939.e]

A fortnight ago came the news from Vancouver that a number of British Indians, who had been passed by the Dominion authorities, were immediately informed by the provincial officials that they must be deported, and on their refusal to re-embark had been 'put to prison.'[75] The correspondent telegraphing the news added, 'it is now generally admitted that "the Natal Act" is *ultra vires* so far as the

73 The monthly periodical *The Nineteenth Century and After* (1877–1972) was founded by architect Sir James Knowles. Knowles was also founder of the Metaphysical Society which debated the relationship between science, religion and morality and whose membership comprised some of the leading intellectual figures of the day. Many of its members contributed to the periodical which aimed 'to provide a platform from which men of all parties and persuasions might address the public in their own names'. Knowles was particularly successful in encouraging his contributors 'to engage in controversy with one another … on matters of moment'. See S. Lee, 'Knowles, Sir James Thomas (1831–1908)', rev. H.C.G. Matthew, *Oxford Dictionary of National Biography* (Oxford University Press, 2004; on-line edn, Sept 2010, www.oxforddnb.com/view/article/34353 [accessed 5 August 2011]).

74 Syed Ameer Ali first arrived in England on a government scholarship in 1869 and was called to the Bar in 1873. In 1890, he became the first Muslim judge of the Calcutta High Court in India. On his retirement from this position, he returned to England where he settled. His political priority was to advance the position of Indian Muslims. He co-founded the London Branch of the All-India Muslim League in 1908. See 'Syed Ameer Ali', *Making Britain Database* www.open.ac.uk/makingbritain/content/syed-ameer-ali; Visram, *Asians*, pp. 146–9.

75 As a British dominion, Canada was a self-governing, semi-autonomous territory of the British Empire. As Wainwright notes, the dominions developed particularly harsh immigration restrictions to bar the entry of non-white imperial citizens. This was because their white inhabitants had gained ownership of their land precisely by expelling the non-white indigenous inhabitants from it; hence, to maintain justification of their dominance they had to exclude on the basis of race (*'The Better Class' of Indians*, p. 101).

Japanese or Chinese are concerned.[76] The Indians say they are loyal subjects of the King, and ask why if other Asiatics are allowed to land they should be forbidden to do so. Many other persons are asking the same question. A large proportion of the Indians arriving here have served the King in the Army, and the treatment to which they are being subjected shocks even exclusionists.'

As I write comes further news respecting a situation which is fast tending to develop into a crisis. This time the Dominion Government itself, taking its stand behind a legal quibble, has added to the gravity of the problem that faces the Empire, which is neither exclusively European nor exclusively Asiatic, but has to maintain, for its own sake, a just and equitable balance between the two component elements.

> In what even some opponents of Asiatic immigration admit [says the special correspondent of *The Times* (19th of March 1908)[77]] to be an arbitrary and indefensible manner, the Dominion Government has ordered the deportation of the Indians who were allowed to land from the *Monteagle*. ... It appears that seventy-eight of the Indians on arriving at Hong-kong from Calcutta were unable to obtain accommodation in the first steamer, as it was full, and they had to stay at Hong-kong for a month. The Dominion Government rules that these immigrants are not to be admitted, as they did not come direct from the land of their birth. One hundred and five Indians came by continuous passage from Calcutta, but the Ottawa authorities demand proof that they are the men who purchased the tickets, and of course this proof is impossible to furnish. ... I saw the Indians examined by the Federal immigration officer on Sunday. Many wore medals won in the Sudan and other campaigns, medals which a certain member of the British Columbian Legislature recently termed 'tinpot adornments.' ... There is in Vancouver a well-known Indian official who sails by the *Empress of Japan* tomorrow. He assumes that there will be grave danger of disaffection, even mutiny, among the native troops, if these men are deported. I can vouch for the fact that there is intense indignation among the Indians. The order spells

76 The Natal Act of 1897 required would-be immigrants to have knowledge of a European language and a sum of £25. Ostensibly colour blind, it was in fact aimed to limit Indian immigration into Natal.

77 This parenthesis is given as a footnote in the original document.

tragedy for them. 'We are subjects of the King,' they say, 'this is part of the King's dominions. Why do they keep us out?'

A more interesting or more deplorable commentary on the methods of civilized government could hardly be furnished by any other incident in recent times. Here are the subjects of the Empire which professes equal rights for all races and creeds under its sway, and which makes in theory equity and fair treatment the corner-stone of its policy, proceeding from one part of the King's dominions to the other. There is nothing against their conduct, many of them have served their Sovereign in the profession to which civilization accords the foremost place of honour: they possess the insignia of bravery and good conduct. And yet from accident of birth in one continent they are refused permission to abide on the soil of a British Colony and subjected to treatment which shocks even the advocates of exclusion. The feeling which these acts engender in British India can scarcely fail to cause some degree of concern among the responsible Ministers of the Crown. Nor are they likely to forget that the Indian subjects of the Sovereign cannot apprehend the reasons which stand in the way of England in securing for them equal rights in other parts of the Empire. To the people of India she owes special obligations, both by virtue of her pledges and their place in history. Naturally, when the Imperial Government acknowledges its inability to insist upon the same treatment being accorded to them in British Colonies as is accorded to the Colonials in India, it is regarded as a lamentable confession of weakness. So long as this idea does not take an articulate shape it may perhaps be ignored as a factor in Imperial policy, but once it gives rise to a comparison, as it has begun to do, between the power of Great Britain and that of other States to protect its subjects from humiliations and restrictions the matter assumes an aspect that needs serious reflection.

3 'A Princess Fined. Refusal to Pay Taxes', The Times, 30 December 1913, British Library Newspapers at Colindale, 1788–2010. [British Newspaper Library shelfmark: MLD1 NPL]

At the Feltham Police Court yesterday PRINCESS SOPHIE DULEEP SINGH [sic], of Faraday House, Hampton road, Hampton Court, was summoned for employing a male servant and keeping two dogs and a carriage without licences.[78]

The Princess, wearing the medal and badge of the Tax Resistance League, and accompanied by six other ladies, admitted the offences and made a statement which she read from a sheet of foolscap.[79] She could not, she said, conscientiously pay money to the State, as she was not allowed to exercise any control over its expenditure. She had no voice in the choosing of members of Parliament, whose salaries she had to help to pay. When the women of England were enfranchised, and her citizenship acknowledged, she would pay her share willingly. Taxation without representation was tyranny, and it was a great injustice that women should be called upon to pay these taxes.

When the Princess finished there was slight applause amongst her friends.

It was stated that the Princess had been fined before for a similar offence and the Bench imposed a fine of £5 each in respect of the carriage and the male servant, and 25s. in respect of each dog, making £12 10s., with costs in each case.

---

78 Sophia Duleep Singh was the youngest daughter of Maharaja Duleep Singh of the Punjab, who owned the Elveden estate in Norfolk. Sophia combined a privileged English lifestyle with an interest in her Indian Sikh heritage, and was active in the Women's Social and Political Union and its offshoot, the Women's Tax Resistance League. See 'Sophia Duleep Singh', *Making Britain Database* www.makingbritain/content/sophia-duleep-singh; Visram, *Asians*, pp. 164–8.

79 For more information on the Women's Tax Resistance League, see H. Frances, '"Pay the Piper, Call the tune!": The Women's Tax Resistance League', in M. Joannou and J. Purvis (eds), *The Women's Suffrage Movement* (Manchester: Manchester University Press, 1998), pp. 65–6.

The Princess said she wished it clearly understood that she would not pay these unjust taxes, and remarked that if she did not pay the fines she supposed a distress would be levied.[80]

The Chairman said that was the usual course.

---

80 To levy a distress, or 'distraint', was to seize property of sufficient value to cover the amount owed plus costs (ibid., p. 70).

4 *Extract from Saklatvala's maiden speech to House of Commons.*
[HC Deb 23 November 1922, Vol. 159, cols 115–17][81]

In reference to Ireland, I am afraid that I shall strike a jarring note in the hitherto harmonious music of this House. I am well disciplined and trained in the general principle of the Labour movement, namely, that the happiness of the world depends on international peace, and that international peace is possible only when the self-determined will of the people of each country prevails in each country. I deplore greatly those elements still existing in the Irish Treaty that are not compatible with that great and wholesome principle.[82] It is no use denying the fact, for we shall not in that way create peace in Ireland. As a House we say that we are giving this Irish Treaty with a view of bringing peace to Ireland, but we know that it is not bringing peace. Either we are actuated by the motive of restoring thorough peace in Ireland or we are doing it as partial conquerors in Ireland. Everyone knows that the Treaty has unfortunately gone forth as the only alternative to a new invasion of Ireland by British troops. As long as that element exists the people of Ireland have a right to say that the very narrow majority which in Ireland accepted the Treaty at the time, accepted it also on this understanding – that if they did not accept it the alternative was an invasion by the Black-and-Tans of this country.[83] The Irish Treaty all along

81 This is an extract from Saklatvala's maiden speech in the House of Commons. Shapurji Saklatvala arrived in England in 1905. A committed anti-imperialist and anti-capitalist, he joined the Independent Labour Party and later, on its formation, the Communist Party of Great Britain. In 1921, he was adopted as Labour candidate for Battersea North, winning the seat in the elections of 1922 and again (as a Communist) in 1924. See S. Saklatvala, *The Fifth Commandment: Biography of Shapurji Saklatvala* (Salford: Miranda Press, 1991); M. Squires, *Saklatvala: A Political Biography* (London: Lawrence & Wishart, 1990); M. Wadsworth, *Comrade Sak. Shapurji Saklatvala MP: A Political Biography* (Leeds: Peepal Tree, 1998).
82 The Irish Treaty established the Irish Free State as a self-governing dominion within the British Empire, granting Northern Ireland the right to opt out of the State.
83 The Black-and-Tans were mainly former soldiers sent by the British government to assist the Royal Irish Constabulary in Ireland. They were notorious for their brutal attacks on Irish civilians.

continues to suffer in Ireland from the fact that it is not a Treaty acceptable to the people as a whole.

If it were possible in some way in the preamble of the Treaty or by an Act of this House to allow the people of Ireland to understand that their country's constitution is to be framed by them as a majority may decide, and that the alternative would not be an invasion from this country, but that this country would shake hands with Ireland as a neighbour, whatever shape or form that Government took, it would be quite a different story. Otherwise, whatever we may do, however many treaties we may pass, however unanimous the British may be in their behaviour towards Ireland, Ireland will not be made a peaceful country. As in 1801 England gave them a forced Union, so in 1922 England is giving them a forced freedom.[84] We must remove that factor. Unless we do so we shall not be giving to the Irish the Treaty of freedom which we have all decided mentally that we are doing. When I say so, I put forward not my personal views but the views of 90 per cent of those Irishmen who are my electors. They have pointed out to me that, whereas under the threat of renewed invasion the Dail[85] only passed the Treaty by a majority of barely half a dozen votes, Irishmen who are not under that threat – Irishmen who are living in Great Britain – have, by a tremendous majority, voted against it. As long as those factors continue to exist, the Irish Treaty is not going to be what we – in a sort of silent conspiracy – have decided to name it. The reality will not be there. The reality is not there.

Before I conclude I wish to refer to one point which is conspicuous by its absence from the King's Speech. If in the Empire, this House and this Government is going to take the glory of the good, they will also have to take the ignominy of anything disgraceful which happens outside this country. This Government may not be responsible. This House may not be responsible. The people of this country may not be responsible. Yet there is something like a public voice and public prejudice, and if this Government and this House

---

84　The 1801 Act of Union stipulated that Ireland was to be joined to Great Britain.

85　Dail Eireann was the revolutionary parliament of the Irish Republic, formed in 1919.

are proud of their association with the Colonies and the Empire, this Government and this House will also have to satisfy this country as well as outside countries, why the policy of the South African Government, in hanging and shooting workers, was permitted and was kept quiet.[86] We are still calling Ireland a part of this Empire, and it is only last week that four young working-class lads, without an open trial and without even fair notice to their families, were shot dead.[87] Even on the night before, their families were told that every-thing was all right, but on the following morning, when the mother of one of them went to convey a bundle of laundry to her son, she was informed that the poor boys had been executed. These acts might be described as the acts of independent governments. Either these governments are independent or they are part of this Empire. If they are part of this Empire, then the Government in the centre of the Empire must see to it that a policy of this kind does not go without challenge and without, at least, protest from this House, if nothing else can be done.

86 Probably a reference to the 'Rand Rebellion', a 1922 armed uprising of white miners against their employers in Witwatersrand, South Africa, triggered in part by the lifting of the colour bar to enable the use of cheaper labour, and eventually crushed by the military. Over 200 people were killed.
87 Probably a reference to the Free State's execution by firing squad of four Republican men in Kilmainham Jail, 17 November 1922.

5 *Special Restriction (Coloured Alien Seamen) Order, 1925; and letter from the Under-Secretary of State to the Chief Constables of scheduled areas, 23 March 1925.*
[National Archives, Kew, HO 45/12314]

REGISTRATION OF COLOURED ALIEN SEAMEN

Notice is hereby given that, in accordance with the Special Restriction (Coloured Alien Seamen) Order, 1925, made by the Secretary of State for the Home Department, coloured alien seamen are required to register with the Police, whether or not they have been in the United Kingdom for more than two months since their last arrival.

Any coloured alien seaman who is not already registered should take steps to obtain a Certificate of Registration without delay.

Nearest Registration Office _____

BY ORDER.

HOME OFFICE,
WHITEHALL.

23 March, 1925.

REGISTRATION OF COLOURED ALIEN SEAMEN (OTHER THAN CHINESE AND JAPANESE).

Sir,

I am directed by the Secretary of State to inform you that he has recently had under consideration measures to facilitate the control of coloured alien seamen at present in this country and to prevent more effectively the entry of others into the United Kingdom without proper authority; and he has come to the conclusion that in order to deal with the problem presented by these aliens, – particularly those of them who are 'Arabs', – it is necessary that they should be required to register in all cases, including those where the alien has hitherto been exempt under Article 6(5) of the Aliens Order, 1920, by reason of the fact that less than two months has elapsed since his last arrival in the United Kingdom or that he is not resident in the United Kingdom.[88]

2. The difficulties of the present situation, which are doubtless well known to you, can, in the Secretary of State's opinion, be satisfactorily met by applying to coloured alien seamen the ordinary system of registration (Police Handbook, paragraphs 98 to 102), subject to certain modifications as regards the form of the Certificate of Registration. The difficulties arise mainly from the fact that the racial resemblance between many coloured seamen is such that there is no satisfactory means of identifying individuals; and the primary object which the Secretary of State has in view is to remedy this deficiency by requiring every coloured seaman (excluding Chinese and Japanese) unless he is able to show that he is a British subject, to provide himself immediately with a document by which he can be readily identified and on which his entry into the United Kingdom (if duly authorized by grant of leave to land) can be recorded.

3. In these circumstances the Secretary of State has made a special restriction Order under Article II of the Aliens Order, 1920, imposing an obligation to register upon all coloured seamen found in the United Kingdom on or after 6th April next. Copies of the order are enclosed herewith.

4. Full instructions as to carrying the Order into effect are set out in the accompanying memorandum. It will be observed in particular that the Registration Certificate to be used for the purpose of registration under the Order is the ordinary form of certificate, modified in certain particulars so as to enable a fuller description of the alien to be entered.

---

88 The 'problem' presented is articulated in a letter from the Under-Secretary of State in which he describes the demands made at the end of the First World War by the National Sailors and Fireman's Union that 'steps should be taken to restrict the admission to this country of coloured seamen who could not establish that they were British subjects, since they competed in the overstocked labour market for seamen and were a source of grave discontent among British sailors' (National Archives, HO 45/12314, 14 August 1926). For an analysis of the reasons for the 1925 Order which paints a much more complex picture than this, highlighting in particular the role of the state in initiating it, see Tabili, 'British Justice', Ch. 6.

5. Although the Order applies generally throughout the United Kingdom, it is intended that it shall be carried into effect only in the limited number of areas where the registration of coloured alien seamen is specially required. A list of these areas is appended.[89] If it should prove desirable to do so, steps will be taken as and when required to enforce the Order in other areas.

6. Copies of the new Order are being printed in poster form for display at seamen's boarding houses and a supply is being sent to the Chief Constables concerned under separate cover.

I am,
Sir,
Your obedient Servant,
John Pedder[90]

---

89 These areas were: Glamorgan, Cardiff, Newport, Swansea, Carmarthenshire, Liverpool, Salford, Newcastle-on-Tyne, South Shields, Middlesbrough, Hull. In January of the following year, it was extended throughout Britain (Visram, *Asians*, p. 205).

90 This name is signed in the original document.

6 *Immigration Officers' Report on Joffer Shah (lascar deserter), Port of Liverpool,* 27 *October* 1930.
[British Library, London, LE/9/962, pp. 129–30]

H.M. Inspector,
Liverpool.

The above named Lascar seaman reported at this office to-day, having been referred by the Liverpool Police with regard to the issue of a Pedlar's Certificate.

Cert. G.86.1.19/621 26/9/30. Br. Indian Seamen.
High Commissioner for India.
Coloured. Mohammedan. b. 1909. Seaman.

He produced a Pedlar's Certificate issued St. Helens 26/7/30 and stated that he originally deserted the s.s. 'MAIDAN' at Liverpool in May 1927 and had lived for some time in Glasgow. Obviously his application for a Pedlar's Certificate here in Liverpool <u>cannot be resisted</u>, but I am anxious to draw your attention to an evil that is rapidly growing throughout the U.K. and is, now that the C.A.S.O.[91] has thwarted them, being engineered by the coloured boarding-house keepers.

Numbers of Lascar seamen on arrival here are persuaded by the boarding-house keepers to desert their ships with the promise of lucrative employment as pedlars or seamen and are taken into their boarding houses. Application is then made to the India Office for a certificate of British nationality, and armed with this they endeavour to sign on British ships at the standard rate of wage, or alternatively when there is no seafaring employment, do hawking and peddling.

In some cases correspondence has been exhibited which shows the India Office were aware that these men were deserters from Asiatic Articles and in spite of this certificates have been issued to them, although under the Indian Merchant Shipping Act they must be maintained and repatriated by the shipping company concerned. Further the British Merchant Shipping Act requires the said owners

91 Coloured Alien Seamen Order.

to maintain and repatriate such men, and yet they are enabled by these means to be exploited by the boarding-house keepers and compete on the already over-crowded labour market.[92] I cannot of course speak from the political aspect, but certainly this type, who soon learn to speak good English, may prove to be a menace.

The numbers of Lascar deserters are growing daily but to the best of my knowledge there is no arrangement whereby the shipping company concerned is officially called upon to notify same either to the Board of Trade, India Office or this Department.

I respectfully submit that representation should be made to the India Office, who, by issuing certificates to these men, are assisting the Boarding-house keepers, burdening the ship owners and defeating the object of their own Merchant Shipping Act.

(Sgd.) P.R. FUDGE.
27.10.30.

H.M. Chief Inspector,
This shows that the evil discussed at the Conference held at the Board of Trade Offices in Liverpool on 4th December, 1929, and duly reported on to you by Mr. Cooper, is still continuing.

From what we see here it has indeed become worse during the present year. In all the villages and suburbs in this part one sees these coloured pedlars going from door to door, and I was told by a C.I.D. Officer the other day that some of them are rampant propagandists on the Indian question both by the remarks and innuendoes they make to the people on whom they call with their wares and occasionally by taking part in meetings, at which they are allowed to 'speak for India'.

(Sgd.) THOS. M. BLAGG.
28.10.30.

---

92 For information about the Merchant Shipping Acts and how they worked to restrict the entry and settlement in Britain of South Asians, see Wemyss, *Invisible Empire*, pp. 148–53.

7 *'Passport Facilities for Illiterate Indian British Subjects', Foreign Office Circular T 10179/6202/378, 4 September 1931.*
[British Library, London, L/E/9/954, p. 64 + verso]

Sir,
I AM directed by the Marquess of Reading to inform you that it is desired to modify the instructions contained in Foreign Office circular T 3491/144/378 of the 15th April, 1930, concerning the issue of passport facilities to Indian British subjects.[93]

2. In future Indian British subjects of good character and established position, who apply therefor, may be granted ordinary British passports of full validity and bearing the usual endorsement for the British Empire, in the absence of any special reasons which may make restriction desirable in individual cases.

3. Indian British subjects of a low standard of education and limited means, who wish to travel to the United Kingdom in search of employment or to engage in petty trade, should not be granted passports, or an endorsement on a passport, valid for the United Kingdom, unless they can produce evidence that they have a definite offer of employment or that they are unlikely to fall into a state of destitution in the event of their being unsuccessful in obtaining employment.

In considering the probability of employment in the United Kingdom being obtained by a particular applicant due weight should be given to the ability of the applicant to speak English.

Persons in this class who can produce evidence of a satisfactory reason for requiring passport facilities would generally be eligible only for passports available for India and such other countries, British and foreign, as they may actually have occasion to visit. The general endorsement for the British Empire should be omitted.

If an applicant is returning to India an emergency certificate, or, in default, a temporary passport available for the single journey only, should be granted.

A restricted passport so issued should bear a clear endorsement

---

93 Foreign Office circular T 3491/144/378 can be found in the British Library, L/E/9/954, p. 97. It was issued to 'His Majesty's Consular Officers authorized to issue and renew passports.'

that it is available only for the necessary period for the most conven-
ient or direct journey to India, and that application must be made by
the holder to the authorities in India for any further extension that
may be required.

4. To meet special local conditions, such as occur owing to the
traffic between the Netherlands East Indies and the Straits
Settlements,[94] Consular officers may, at their discretion, and
provided there is no local objection, grant extended emergency
certificates, available for one journey and return, to Indian British
subjects of a low standard of education and limited means residing
within their district who have occasion to make temporary visits to
India or other British territory from the foreign State in which they
reside.

5. Applications for endorsements or renewals from Indian British
subjects who are holders of passports issued in India, should be dealt
with under the general instructions given above. Cases of doubt
should be referred to the Government of India.

6. This circular supersedes the Foreign Office circular of the 15th
April, 1930, referred to above.

7. Additional copies of this circular are enclosed for distribution to
Consular officers under your superintendence who are authorized to
issue or renew passports.

I am,
Sir,
Your obedient Servant,
ROBERT VANSITTART.

---

94 The Netherlands East Indies became Indonesia. The Straits Settlement,
formerly a British territory, is modern-day Malaysia and Singapore.

8 'Unrest among Indian Seamen', secret memo to Mr Silver, 16 November 1939.
[British Library, London, L/PJ/12/630, pp. 21–3]

On the 17th October the lascar crew of the s.s. 'Oxfordshire', a Bibby Line steamer, which is being fitted out as a hospital ship in the King George V Dock, went on strike.[95] Of the large number of demands which they made, most were immediately sanctioned, but the crew stood out for an 8-hour day and a monthly ration of ½lb. tobacco, demands which the owners refused to grant.[96] The strike terminated on the 26th October when the men returned to work. Among the most important concessions granted were a £10 war bonus and a 100% increase in wages.

2. The prolongation of the strike on the s.s. 'Oxfordshire' was in large measure due to the activities of two agitators named SURAT ALI and TAHSIL MIYA. The former is Secretary of the COLONIAL SEAMEN'S ASSOCIATION: he is a Communist who for some time has been endeavouring to establish his influence among Oriental seamen in the East End of London. TAHSIL MIYA, whose real name is ABDUL ODOOT, is a lascar who deserted his ship at Liverpool in February 1938 and was undoubtedly sent to the East End to agitate among India seamen. He is the London representative of the INDIAN SEAMEN'S UNION, with headquarters at Calcutta.[97] A prosecution has been launched against him for deserting his ship and if convicted he will probably be shipped back to India. Standing behind these two men, but taking care not to appear in the open, was V. K. KRISHNA MENON of the INDIA LEAGUE, an extremist

95 The King George V Dock, the West India Dock and the Tilbury Dock were all located in the East End of London.

96 Contrary to the statements and suggestions in this report, Indian lascars suffered severe hardship and discrimination, receiving lower wages and enduring harsher working conditions than their white counterparts. See Visram, *Asians*, Ch. 8; Tabili, *'British Justice'*, Ch. 3.

97 The Indian Seamen's Union was, as the document states, based in Calcutta. There was also, however, an Indian Seamen's Union based in London which was active in mobilizing Indian seamen to protest against their conditions from the mid-1920s and had N.J. Upadhyaya at its helm. Saklatvala was involved with this organization (see Visram, *Asians*, pp. 231–4).

Indian who is interesting himself in the affairs of Indians in the East End of London, and is the prospective Labour candidate for Dundee.[98]

3. The strike fever proved contagious and spread to the s.s. 'Clan Alpine', berthed in the West India Dock. The pay of the crew had been raised by 100% but they demanded also a bonus of £10. Persisting in their refusal to return to work, they were arrested and prosecuted for disobedience of lawful orders, under Sec. 225 of the Merchant Shipping Act 1894. Sentence of two months' imprisonment was passed on the 44 accused on the 1st November. SURAT ALI was opposed to this strike and the responsibility must rest largely with TAHSIL MIYA, again backed, it is believed, by V.K.K. MENON. The latter has advised against a Court appeal, but wishes to present a petition to the Home Secretary. TAHSIL MIYA now feels that he has been very badly 'let down' by MENON.

4. On the 11th November the lascar members of the 'City of Manchester' (Ellerman Line), which was about to sail from Tilbury Dock, intimated their refusal to undertake the voyage and went ashore. A warrant was immediately applied for and 76 lascars were arrested and presented before a Bench of Justices later in the day, under Sec. 225 of the Merchant Shipping Act. The Court was informed that the crew had signed on at Colombo and had been given a 25% increase in pay, which had been incorporated in their Articles of Agreement. On arrival at Tilbury they heard that certain other ships had been given a 100% increase of pay and decided to put forward a similar demand, though their conditions of service were quite different. The court sentenced all the prisoners to one month's

---

98 Surat Ali (or Surat Alley) was a trade unionist and political activist who campaigned for the rights of South Asians – particularly seamen – in Britain in the 1930s and 1940s. He was also secretary of the Hindustani Social Club. The Colonial Seamen's Association was formed in response to the 1935 British Shipping (Assistance) Act which discriminated against non-British seamen. Shortly after his election as Labour candidate for Dundee in July 1939, Krishna Menon's candidature was cancelled by the Dundee Trades and Labour Council on the grounds that he had been speaking against official Labour Party policy. For information on these figures, see *Making Britain Database* www.open.ac.uk/makingbritain. Tahsil Miya was deported following the strikes (Visram, *Asians*, pp. 239–40).

imprisonment holding that their grievances should have been put forward in a constitutional manner. This strike appears to have been quite spontaneous but to have been encouraged by the strike on the s.s. 'Oxfordshire' and the large increase in wages which many lines have sanctioned.

9 *Hindustan Community House First Report, April 1940.*
[Tower Hamlets Local History Library and Archives, London]

Hindustan Community House has been formed to meet the needs of
Indians in East London. A few facts about the work of the House will
illustrate in which way it will try to meet some of these needs.[99]

FOOD, CLOTHING AND SHELTER
Since the completion of the House, fifty men have lived in it and
another fifty have taken meals in it. Indian or English food is
available for these men. To enable the fullest use to be made of the
House its charges for board or lodging are fixed at the lowest possible
figure.

The House has been able to accommodate shipwrecked sailors,
and Indians stranded in London.

Gifts of clothing have been received and distributed.

MEDICAL WORK
Two Indian doctors, who have returned to India, attended the weekly
clinic and gave free medical advice. The new surgery has been
equipped by an Indian doctor. It is open three nights a week for free
medical advice and attention. A fourth Indian doctor is in charge.

Indian patients have been visited in hospitals and sanatoria, and if
necessary an interpreter has been provided for them. Patients have
been assisted in gaining admittance to the hospitals, and in making
arrangements for operations.

Lectures have been given in First Aid and A.R.P. Nine students
passed the Air Raid Warden's Test.

EMPLOYMENT
The House is in touch with the Employment Exchange and serves to
remove differences between employers and employed, and to provide

99 The Hindustan Community House, located at 79 Lambeth Street, London,
    opened in 1937. Its warden, Kundan Lal Jalie, raised money by giving
    lectures about the plight of Indians in Britain across the country, and even-
    tually opened the HCH (B. Sokoloff, *Edith Ramsay: The Life of Edith Ramsey*
    (London: Stepney Books, 1987), pp. 155–8).

interpreters. Indians have been found employment in East London and the country. Through the High Commissioner the House assisted destitute Indians to return to India. Compensations and free passage to India have been obtained from Shipping Companies in some cases of disabled seamen.

EDUCATIONAL

Two classes in English with an average of fifteen to twenty students were held every week night. These were discontinued on account of the war, but have been since restarted.

A class in English and Urdu for Indian children was discontinued owing to the evacuation of the children.

SOCIAL

The House has a wireless set and gramophone with Indian records. Indian and English newspapers and periodicals are available. Indoor games, ping pong, darts, etc., have been provided. Outdoor games (volley ball, etc.) will be arranged in the summer.

The House is becoming a Social Centre for Indians. It is hoped to extend its influence throughout the Indian community in East London.

THANKS

To the public spirit of the friend who has made possible the existence of the House, and to all who have helped its indoor and outdoor activities, cordial and deep thanks are tendered.[100]

79 Lambeth Street, E.1   April, 1940

---

100 Sokoloff claims this 'friend' was a Cambridge undergraduate named Thomas Tufton who contributed £22,000 after hearing Jalie speak about the plight of Indians in Britain (ibid., p. 156).

10 *Extracts from secret memo from the Indian Political Intelligence to Mr Silver on the Indian Workers' Association, with dossiers on certain members, 2 April 1942.*[101]
[British Library, London, L/PJ/12/645, pp. 12, 14–15]

Immediately after the Indian Independence Day meeting held at Birmingham on 25.1.42, I received from the Security Service a memorandum suggesting that some action should be taken against disaffected Indians in the Midland Regional Area. The Chief Constable of Birmingham was reported to be feeling apprehensive about the extensive Indian colony engaged mainly in industrial work in his area, and to be afraid that under invasion conditions some of them, particularly the Sikhs, might present considerable danger. It was suggested that the worst of them might be included in the Regional Commissioner's Suspect List (i.e. might be earmarked for internment should there be an invasion). This involves a legal difficulty, as internment under 18-B of the Defence Regulations requires some evidence of enemy association; but it was thought that the difficulty might be overcome by treating Indians in the same way as Irish are treated in the Midland Area.[102] These latter do not fall within the terms of the Defence Regulations, but the Regional Commissioner is determined to run no risks and has expressed his readiness to give authority to Chief Constables to arrest suspected Irishmen if and when the signal is given for 'Action Stations'.

   2. After studying my records, I came to the conclusion that there were comparatively few Indians whose names I could recommend

---

101 The Indian Workers' Association is described as 'partly a mutual welfare society aimed at protecting the interests of the Indian worker in this country and partly an instrument for educating the Indian worker politically and utilizing him in the general struggle for India's political emancipation' (British Library, L/PJ/12/645, 'The Indian Workers' Association', 14 April 1942, p. 30).

102 Written in the context of the Second World War, the 'enemy' referred to in this memorandum is the Axis powers. During this period, there was an increase in the monitoring of Indian radicals, especially because a number of Indian nationalists had found safe haven in Germany (O'Malley, *Ireland, India and Empire*, p. 8).

for inclusion in the list. I did, however, submit four names (I attached summaries of the information on record about them) suggesting that, as far as disaffected and troublesome Indians were concerned, the best way to deal with them would be to make an example of the leading figures. The four men whose dossiers I sent up were (i) THAKUR SINGH BASRA, (ii) CHARAN SINGH CHIMA, (iii) KARM SINGH OVERSEER, and (iv) KARTAR SINGH NAGRA. The first three of these live at Coventry, the fourth at Stratford-on-Avon ...

THAKUR SINGH was formerly a sepoy in the 38th Rifles, Frontier Force. He joined up in 1917 and was demobilized in 1922. He arrived in the United Kingdom in 1935 and worked as a pedlar for some time before he came to notice. While at Broughton, near Kettering, he became a subscribing member of the 'Hindustan Ghadr'[103] ... In 1939, while living at Coventry, he remitted money to India for political purposes on behalf of the Indian Workers' Union,[104] of which he was then Secretary, though at that time it existed little more than in name. He was then employed as a labourer on the site of an aircraft factory. When the Caxton Hall affair (assassination of Sir Michael O'Dwyer) occurred in March 1940, THAKUR SINGH took a very prominent part in raising funds for the defence of the accused Udham Singh.[105] In November 1940 he made another remittance of £39 to India from the Indian Workers' Union to the Patriots' Relief Committee, Amritsar (an organization which cares for the dependents of Sikhs executed or imprisoned for terrorist crimes). In the course of the following year he was engaged in collecting further subscriptions for the same purpose, travelling as far afield as Southampton, and made substantial remittances to India. He took advantage of these visits to advise Indians to stand firm on the subject of national service and to claim that it was against their

---

103 The Ghadr Party is described as 'a notorious revolutionary Sikh society' which 'inspired many terrorist crimes in India and elsewhere' and was subsidized by Germany in the last war (L/PJ/12/645, p. 15). Its headquarters were in San Francisco and its figurehead Lala Har Dayal.
104 The original name of the Indian Workers' Association.
105 Udham Singh was a member of the Ghadr Party.

religious scruples to take part in military training. In 1941 he obtained work as a bench-hand with the firm of Clark Cluley & Co., Coventry, but left this employment without permission on the plea that he could not support numerous relatives on his pay and wanted machine work instead. Though this was an infringement of the Essential Work Orders 1941, the authorities decided not to prosecute and let him off with a warning. He is at present doing work as a labourer with peddling as a side-line: his house was searched on 26.2.42 on suspicion that he was connected with the Black Market and the case is still pending.

THAKUR SINGH BASRA is one of the most important figures in the movement known as the Indian Workers' Union and is the recognized leader of the disaffected Sikhs in Coventry. His views are those of the Ghadr Party (i.e. he believes in securing independence for India by force if necessary), but he is careful not to commit himself openly. In time of emergency or crisis he might well be dangerous.

11 *Extracts from report on Indian Activities in the United Kingdom, 8 March 1944 and 8 May 1944.*
[British Library, London, L/PJ/12/646, pp. 95, 110]

The Vaidya Case.[106] In spite of representations made to him by Sunder KABADI and others, that his non-espousal of Vaidya's case has identified him with the attacks made on Vaidya by Amiya Nath BOSE and the latter's organization,[107] MENON has declined to move from his position in the matter, which is doubtless dictated by the Communist Party's policy of full support for the War effort. His views are that if Vaidya had wished to evade conscription, he should have originally claimed to be a conscientious objector; that since he has a British domicile dating back ten years and has not pleaded as a C.O., the Government are perfectly within the law in the stand they have adopted. When confronted with the favourite argument of the 'sentimental Left', that it is not worth while for the Government to stir up additional bitterness for the sake of some 1500 Indians, at least a third of whom would be physically unfit, he has been known to make the very pertinent comment that if Indians were to be exempted from conscription it would amount to definite racial discrimination against them – and that this would not suit their book as they wanted to have Indians in the Army in India and therefore had no fight against the principle of Conscription as such.

(Vaidya elected to base his case on grounds of 'Indian Nationalism'. His cause has been wholeheartedly espoused by his own organizations, Swaraj House and the Federation of Indian Associations in Great Britain and by the 'Trotskyist' and Pacifist organizations which support them, (e.g. the I.L.P.,) which are opposed to any cooperation

106 Suresh Vaidya was a leading figure in Swaraj House.
107 Nephew of Subhas Chandra Bose, Amiya Nath Bose was an activist based in Britain in the 1930s and 1940s and co-founder of the Committee of Indian Congressmen which sought to promote the Indian National Congress and protected Indians in Britain from conscription during the Second World War (see entries in *Making Britain Database* www.open.ac.uk/makingbritain).
108 Swaraj House was a break-away group from the Committee of Indian Congressmen, alienated from the latter by the alleged pro-Axis leanings of Amiya Nath Bose and Pulin Behari Seal. The Federation of Indian

with the war effort.[108] It is understood that Vaidya's Court Martial was to be on March 8th and that he was permitted by the Military Authorities to spend some days unescorted in London so that he might arrange for his defence. It is further understood that Fenner Brockway has put him in touch with Stephen Murray, who will defend him.) . . .[109]

SWARAJ HOUSE is divided among itself on the VAIDYA issue, Drs D.N. DUTT and C.B. VAKIL having gone over to Amiya Nath BOSE's viewpoint. This is roughly to the effect that, so long as Vaidya adhered to a pledge given to Swaraj House that he would fight the case solely on the argument that he should not be expected to join the British Armed Forces while India remained enslaved, he deserved the moral and financial support of fellow Indians; when, however, he allowed his Counsel to seek exemption on the grounds of temporary residence in the United Kingdom, he lost face, and still more so when he made eulogistic comments on the treatment received while under detention. Although he was given the somewhat stiff sentence of 98 days hard labour, Vaidya seems to have lost the sympathy of his fellow countrymen here – with the exception of the Trotskyist faction; in fact he himself has now become a cipher in a case which has developed into a slanging match between the BOSE clique and the INDIAN FREEDOM CAMPAIGN, a quarrel between members of Swaraj House and an occasion of much satisfaction to MENON.[110]

Associations in Great Britain brought Swaraj House and the Indian Workers' Association together in 1943 (see entries in *Making Britain Database* www.open.ac.uk/makingbritain).

109 Fenner Brockway was a prominent member of the Independent Labour Party, leading the Party's opposition to the First World War and campaigning against military conscription (D. Howell, 'Brockway (Archibald) Fenner, Baron Brockway (1888–1988)', rev. *Oxford Dictionary of National Biography*, www.oxforddnb.com/view/article/39849 [accessed 30 January 2011]).

110 The Indian Freedom Campaign brought together members of the Independent Labour Party, pacifists and liberals in its campaign for independence. Brockway was its chair. The IFC, CIC and Swaraj House were all opposed to Menon's India League's pro-war stance (N. Owen, *The British Left and India: Metropolitan Anti-Imperialism 1885–1947* (Oxford: Oxford University Press, 2007), pp. 264–72).

12 Extract from Phyllis Young, *Report on Investigation into Conditions of the Coloured Population in a Stepney Area*, printed by 'The Hornsey Journal' Ltd, 1944, pp. 26–7.[111]
[British Library shelfmark: YD.2008.b.696]

Into this tragic corner of Stepney half-caste children are being born, at the best to begin life handicapped by the colour bar, at the worst to be dragged up in an atmosphere of prostitution and vice of all kinds ...[112]

The homes of these children may be classified in three categories:

A. Homes in which both parents are coloured.
B. Homes in which the parents are mixed (coloured father, white mother) but are not connected with the prostitution in the area.
C. Homes of mixed marriages but where the mother lives promiscuously (e.g., while the father is at sea) or where either parent or both are connected with the promiscuous living in the area.

The children whose homes fall into category A. are in a far happier position than the half-caste children. The parents are generally happy together and although the children may come into contact with, and in some instances live in, an immoral atmosphere (judged by British standards), the home itself has a natural tone. The child is wanted and is generally well cared for.

111 The Hornsey Journal, a local north London newspaper, was founded in 1879. While authored by Young, the research for the report was conducted by a committee. Its chairman was Reverend St John B. Groser, Rector, St George's, Stepney. Information was collected from 'local officials, welfare workers, hospitals, hostels and doctors' and by visits to cafés, public houses, and homes. Focusing on an area of 'just under a square mile of back-street slums', the report includes commentary on family life, employment, recreational facilities, accommodation and health. Notably, it includes chapters on 'The Coloured Man' (with a subsection entitled 'Attitude to the White Woman') and 'The White Woman' (with a subsection entitled 'Attitude to the Coloured Man').
112 The report includes in the category 'coloured' West Africans, West Indians, Ceylonese, Malayans, Adenese, Sudanese, South Africans, French West Africans, Egyptians, Maltese, 'Negro Americans', as well as Indians.

In category B. the conditions, for reasons given earlier in this Report, are very rarely satisfactory and the home atmosphere is affected by the strain under which they are living.[113] This seldom fails to influence the children to some degree and may in certain cases lead to divided loyalties as between father and mother.

Category C. unfortunately includes the larger number of children in the area; unfortunately, because the home atmosphere is bad. In many of these homes the children are regarded as a nuisance and the mother does not look after them properly. The coloured father, who instinctively loves children, will spoil them when he is at home and do his best for them in every way, but this only tends to make the children realize more poignantly the mother's lack of real affection and care.

---

113 The 'reasons given earlier' are, *inter alia*, that the 'coloured' man beats the white woman or rejects her for another woman 'if she displeases him' (p. 21), that 'coloured' men and white women rarely 'go about in the streets together' and lack 'the sense of companionship which is such an important factor in western marriages' (ibid.), and that the white woman does not consider the 'coloured' man to be her equal (p. 23).

13 Extract from Savitri Chowdhary, *I Made My Home in England*, Laindon: Grant-Best Ltd, n.d. [c.1957], pp. 63–6.[114]
[British Library shelfmark: 10712.i.20]

[W]e celebrated the V. Day with great rejoicing. We switched on all the lights we could find on that night. We tore down the blinds and the blackout curtains. It was hard to believe that we were free from the horrors of war once more.

There were long Parades and Thanksgiving Services during the morning and grand Dinners and Dances at night, but with all that we were fully aware of the lonely feelings of the parents, wives and even children whose dear ones had laid down their lives to make this day possible. Although their hearts must have been weeping, yet most of them had put on brave faces and tried to rejoice with the rest of the world.

Just at that time Sheel had to employ a new assistant, Dr. Madan.[115] He was tall, quite fair complexioned for an Indian, with jet-black wavy hair and dark penetrating eyes. The only thing which somehow marred his good looks was the roughness of the skin on both sides of his face.

By his appearance and mannerisms I guessed that Dr. Madan had been in this country for some years, and that he had become quite Anglicized. But I was shocked to hear from him that he couldn't even speak Punjabi, his mother-tongue, properly.

I felt like asking him so many questions, and yet I had to restrain myself until we became a little more familiar with each other. I found him very affable and ready to impart his knowledge and experience. In fact, he almost told me the story of his life without much persuasion on my part.

'I came to this country when I was barely nineteen,' he went on, 'and believe it or not, I was a Kattar (staunch) Sikh then, with my long hair under the turban, my luxuriant beard and an iron bangle on my arm.'

114 The book was self-published by Savitri Chowdhary.
115 For more information about Dharm Sheel Chowdhary, see 'Dharm Sheel Chowdhary', *Making Britain Database* www.open.ac.uk/makingbritain /content/dharm-sheel-chowdhary. Dr Madan was one of a series of South Asian assistant doctors at Chowdhary's surgery.

At that moment I watched his clear-cut features and fine build with a fresh interest, and decided that he must have been a very impressive looking Sikh, and now he was just an ordinary person.

'So you chose to reform yourself in this country, Dr. Madan?'

'Yes, because I didn't like to look conspicuous. I hated being stared at. But, believe me, it wasn't an easy task. In the first place I had to struggle with my own thoughts and beliefs ...'

[Madan continues] '... I never talk to [my children] about India. I want them to get thoroughly assimilated in this country. I don't believe that one can be loyal to two countries at the same time. I don't want them to be frustrated and belong to neither this country nor India. In fact, Mrs. Chowdhary, this is where we Indians make a mistake. We come to live in other countries, and yet we still dream of our Homeland – India. We never seem to get free of the old sentiments and ties.'

Dr. Madan then generally criticised what he called the 'Indian Mentality.' I listened for a while, and told him that there was some truth in what he said.

'But when we criticise Indians, Doctor, let us not forget that we are no different from our brothers and sisters in India. We have also got their weaknesses, you know. This question of assimilation in the country of your choice is rather a thought-provoking one,' I added. It certainly was. I couldn't get it out of my mind the whole day. I laid awake thinking about it.'

It wasn't easy to belong to two countries. What was the meaning of assimilation in the true sense of the word? The Oxford Dictionary gave the meaning as 'getting absorbed into a System or Country,' and I knew that Dr. Madan meant the same. Was it possible, or even wise for a person like myself, who had been born and brought up in India, a country which had its own strong culture and traditions, to get completely absorbed in this country, or in any other country, if it came to that? Was it wrong to dream of your old country and the dear ones you left behind: your parents who sacrificed their all for you and gave you a good start, and helped to build your character? Wasn't it your duty to be grateful and loving towards them for all your life?

They were your old and trusted friends, so why should you abandon them simply because you had preferred to settle down and start your working life in another country. Surely it was possible for you to have a big enough heart to make as many new friends and acquaintances as you could, and still keep your old ones? What a vast field of knowledge and interest was open to you. One could get accustomed to the divided loyalties to two countries, especially when they were friendly countries.[116]

I wondered whether Dr. Madan had in mind some of the Indian people, who, while living more or less permanently in this country, refused to mix with the British people. They even considered themselves superior to them. That is positively a wrong way of going on. That did not benefit anybody, and what lonely and uninteresting lives those people must lead through nobody's fault but their own.

No, I wouldn't like to live like that, I thought, and yet I was determined to keep in contact with my friends and the country.[117]

---

116 In her introduction to the book, Chowdhary describes one of its aims as to 'further the cause of peace and good will between the two countries'.

117 Immediately after this passage, Chowdary describes her decision to make a visit to India with her son. The last three chapters of the book record this visit, but it ends, significantly, with them on the ship heading back to their home in England.

2

Britain's forgotten volunteers: South Asian contributions to the two world wars

Florian Stadtler[1]

India and the two world wars: questions of commemoration and memorialization

The First World War and the Second World War were the two defining catastrophes of the twentieth century. Britain mobilized South Asian troops heavily in both world wars, marking a turning point in the history of the Indian Army.[2] As the generations who experienced these large-scale conflicts are passing away, European nations seek to commemorate adequately the contributions of these men and women. Yet some groups have been excluded from the frenzy of memorialization, marginalized in the processes of writing this history. In this context this chapter traces South Asian participation in both world wars and challenges certain Eurocentric and nationalistic assumptions.

---

1 I would like to thank Rozina Visram for her thoughtful guidance and advice during the development of this chapter, and Santanu Das and Ruvani Ranasinha for their helpful comments on earlier versions of this chapter.

2 The designation 'Indian' refers here to the historical term used for the army in pre-Partition India. Even in the pre-First World War context the term was inexact as many of its soldiers defined their identity by their region of origin or their religious identity, as a fledgling conceptualization of Indian identity was only in the process of being born.

Questions of commemoration preoccupied Britain immediately after the end of the First World War with some memorials erected soon after in numerous cemeteries across Flanders and Northern France, and the Menin Gates at Ypres (June 1927). The All India War Memorial (inaugurated 1921, unveiled 1931), now known as India Gate, in New Delhi, was designed by architect Edwin Lutyens, who became an instrumental figure in the planning of numerous monuments to the fallen in the First World War. However, there were fears that the sacrifices of South Asian soldiers would be forgotten all too soon after the conflict's end. General Sir James Willcocks, commander of the Indian Corps until 1915, raised the issue in his book *With the Indians in France*. While many historical accounts of Scottish, Irish and English battalions would be produced, Willcocks argued, 'it is not always so of Indian troops; their raconteurs are few and far between; the chief actors in the play, still living, will probably be counted in the tens not thousands. The rank and file will furnish no writers to thrill the generations to come'.[3] His poem 'Hurnam Singh', published in 1917 in *Blackwood Magazine* as a tribute to the common sepoy fighting in the trenches, marks his attempt to highlight South Asian soldiers' sacrifices in France for a wider British audience [Source 6]. Yet the 'rank and file' were not as voiceless as Willcocks assumed in 1920. In subsequent years, much archival evidence has been released and the extracts of censored letters available in the British Library's Asia Pacific and Africa collections, the recordings of Indian prisoners of war in the Berlin Lautarchiv, or the Diaries of Thakur Amar Singh at Nehru Memorial Library, Delhi, represent important first-hand accounts of South Asian soldiers' experiences [Source 4]. In this respect the challenge is to generate wider awareness of this material, a lack of which has meant that the recognition of the scale of South Asian soldiers' contributions has not been forthcoming until recently.[4] Archives of these first-hand accounts are sparse and their evaluation throws up several problems. Many soldiers were recruited from poor, semi-literate backgrounds.

---

3 J. Willcocks, *With the Indians in France* (London: Constable and Co., 1920), p. xviii.
4 See for example the work of pioneering historians Rozina Visram and David Omissi.

Many records, oral narratives and written outputs have not survived, while the items that remain, such as the censored mails, are mediated. The censored mails contain only selected translated extracts in English, presented without the context of the full letter. Some correspondence considered unsuitable or politically controversial was withheld, never reaching its intended reader. There is no evidence of how the letters were received by the wives and families of these soldiers with no available records of their experiences during and in the immediate aftermath of the war.

This chapter and the source materials outline the manifold South Asian contributions to both world wars, highlighting the First World War and the Second World War as engines and catalysts for change for local and global South Asian populations, and the impact both wars had on their perceptions of Britain. As Britain's population has diversified in the past decades, contemporary commemorations of the world wars need to develop more inclusive approaches, and there is an urgent need to acknowledge the vital involvement of the citizens of empire in these conflicts. Archival evidence highlights the large-scale contributions made by this earlier South Asian presence in Britain and in different theatres of war. Increasingly accessible in the archives, this material is only now being disseminated to a wider audience through books, exhibitions and television documentaries.[5] These materials demonstrate that these pivotal historical events, so often described as Britain's 'Finest Hour', form part of a common shared history that unearths the complex interactions between South Asians and Britons at home and abroad.

The Indian Army in the First World War

In the First World War, the Indian Army provided some 1.45 million men, serving in France, East Africa, Mesopotamia and Egypt.[6] For the first time, Indian troops fought in large numbers in a European

---

5 For many years, grass-roots community campaigners and historians in Britain and Europe have lobbied for a move away from parochial Eurocentric versions of history.

6 War Office, *Statistics of the Military Effort of the British Empire During the Great War, 1914–1920* (London: His Majesty's Stationery Office, 1922), p. 777.

theatre of war. Until then, the Indian Army's main role was to keep the peace internally. Indian troops had only been deployed overseas in small contingents in East Africa, Egypt and the Middle East and during the 1900 Boxer Uprising in China. Thus, the First World War marked an important watershed. India's contribution to Britain's war effort was vast. By 1918 India had provided the largest number of soldiers from any other colony in the British Empire. Indian Army contingents deployed in the First World War were largely a product of the large-scale reorganization in the aftermath of the 1857 Indian Uprising. In this period, the 'martial races' theory began to influence British commanding officers, impacting significantly on the recruitment of Indian soldiers. Lord Kitchener's 1885 and 1902 reorganizations, creating one unified Indian Army, favoured recruitment from the so-called 'martial races'. This increased disproportionally the number of soldiers from Punjab, especially Sikhs, Dogras, Jats and Punjabi Muslims, who were regarded as excellent soldiers. In conjunction with the Gurkhas and Pathans they constituted the majority of the Indian Expeditionary Force's infantry divisions at the outbreak of war. Although 'martial race' theory was scientifically dubious, it continually dominated the army's recruitment policy.[7] Discriminating against the peoples of southern India, many of whom had served the British well in past conflicts, race (referred to as class) and territory became overarching enlistment criteria. Consequently, this strategy narrowed the Indian Army's make-up to a small range of communities, leading to difficulties in recruitment during the war.[8] On top of these racial recruitment criteria, South Asians also featured in wider hierarchical division of race in comparison with colonial troops drawn from other parts of

7 Lieutenant General George MacMunn, Officer of the Royal Artillery, was a popularly recognized authority on 'martial races' theory. While the assertions in his book *The Martial Races of India* (London: Sampson Low, Marston & Co., 1930) are often naive and scientifically dubious, they reflect the opinions of the time and their impact on the army's recruitment policy. See also P.D. Bonnerjee, *A Handbook of the Fighting Races of India* (Calcutta: Thacker Spink and Co., 1899).

8 For further details, see D. Omissi, *The Sepoy and the Raj: The Indian Army, 1860–1940* (Basingstoke and London: Macmillan/King's College, London, 1994), pp. 10–43.

the empire, which had a bearing on their encounters with other ethnicities in the trenches.[9]

On the outbreak of war, India supported Britain in the name of imperial loyalty with offers of money and troops from all over India. The princely states made large contributions including cavalry, infantry, sappers and transport contingents, and money – the Maharaja of Mysore alone pledged 5,000,000.00 Rupees.[10] More surprisingly, nationalist leaders like Dadabhai Naoroji urged South Asians to support the empire in its hour of need. As S.L. Menezes explains, 'the Congress remained remarkably moderate and non-revolutionary throughout the First World War, in no way tampering with the Indian Army.'[11] M.K. Gandhi, in London at the time, also pledged his and the South Asian community's support, volunteering its services in an open letter to the India Office [Source 1]. The signatories were largely from a professional middle-class background, including lawyers, doctors and students. In his autobiography Gandhi rationalizes this decision: 'if we improved our status through the help and co-operation of the British, it was our duty to win their help by standing by them in their hour of need.'[12] Gandhi was instrumental in galvanizing South Asians in Britain, playing a key role in the formation of the Indian Field Ambulance Training Corps. Gandhi selected initial recruits, some 281 men, 198 of whom were employed subsequently. These volunteers, mainly students, worked as dressers assisting surgeons in operations, interpreters and clerks in the hospitals for wounded Indian soldiers along Britain's southern coast [Source 2]. Some were also sent to Calais, serving on hospital ships and ambulance trains in France.[13] Once numbers in London were exhausted, the corps

9 See D. Dendooven and P. Chielens (eds), *World War I: Five Continents in Flanders* (Tielt: Lannoo, 2008).

10 J.W.B. Merewether and F. Smith, *The Indian Corps in France* (London: John Murray, 1917), pp. 4–5.

11 S.L. Menezes, *Fidelity and Honour: The Indian Army from the Seventeenth to the Twenty-First Century* (New Delhi: Oxford University Press, 1999), p. 264–5.

12 M.K. Gandhi, *An Autobiography, or The Story of my Experiments with Truth*, trans. M. Desai (London: Penguin, 2001), pp. 316–17.

13 British Library, London, MSS Eur F 170/8, 'Letter to Lord Crewe', 4 January 1915, pp. 77–94.

recruited further students from Oxford and Edinburgh universities. Despite his initial reservations, Walter Roper Lawrence, responsible for the Indian hospitals, found that these students played an invaluable supporting role despite their differing political views on the question of India's status in the empire.[14]

On the Western Front, 1914–1918

The first Indian troops, two brigades from the Lahore Division, arrived in Marseilles on 26 September 1914.[15] After heavy losses suffered by the British Expeditionary Force, the British army was in desperate need of replacements. Britain was lacking in recruits and the required army of one million could not be deployed for another year. Consequently the 3rd and 7th Indian divisions renamed the Meerut and Lahore Divisions were sent to Europe and placed under the command of General Sir James Willcocks. The Lahore Division arrived in Flanders on 21 October and was immediately deployed to defend Ypres. The Meerut Division arrived on 29 October 1914. The desperate situation on the Western Front did not allow for the Indian Corps to be reconstituted as a separate army, nor did it allow for training with unfamiliar equipment. Instead, Indian Army divisions were placed under British Military authority. Indian Army battalions were either uniformly Indian, while some included Indian and soldiers of British origin. Each battalion had British and Indian officers, with British officers being of higher rank than Indians. These battalions were fed piecemeal into the line to bolster depleted British troops, outnumbered by the German army two to one, leading to Indian units fighting alongside British units [see Figure 2.2].[16] Throughout November 1914, the majority of Indian troops

14 British Library, London, MSS Eur F 143/73, 'Letter from Walter Roper Lawrence to Lord Hardinge', 18 March 1915, pp. 12–13.

15 Brigades usually consist of 4,000–6,000 men, led by a Brigadier General, with staff and two regiments. Divisions consist of 15,000–18,000 men. See Dendooven and Chielens, *World War I*, p. 9.

16 For a detailed list of the Indian Expeditionary Force 'A' and details of Indian and British units fighting together see British Library, MSS Eur F 170/8, 'Indian Expeditionary Force "A"', 3 September 1914, pp. 20–24 and 'Indian Expeditionary Force "A"', 24 September 1914, pp. 35–42.

were stationed in the area around Givenchy and Neuve Chapelle in Northern France, a bleak stretch of land of about seven miles where they would remain until their withdrawal at the end of 1915. Conditions in these trenches were atrocious, especially in autumn and winter, when it was difficult to dig deep because of the proximity of ground water to the surface. Inclement weather quickly transformed these trenches into waterlogged ditches.[17]

Between November and December 1914, the Indian divisions saw heavy fighting near Festubert and Givenchy. In the Battle of Givenchy, the Indian troops were outnumbered and, compared to their opponents, less well equipped. The German kit was technically far more advanced, leading to many casualties. On 19 and 20 December alone, the 1st Battalion of the 4th Gurkhas lost 302 men. The appalling conditions of trench warfare, heavy shelling and aerial bombardments resulted in high casualty numbers, affecting the morale of Indian troops, and incidents of alleged self-inflicted wounds were reported, sparking independent investigations and court martials.[18] In the period 10–12 March 1915, Indian troops and the British IV Corps fought in the battle of Neuve Chapelle, suffering 13,000 fatalities. The Ferozepore Brigade experienced the heavy fighting first hand [Source 3].[19] Nevertheless, Merewether and Smith note that 'the camaraderie existing between the British and Indian soldiers was very marked during the battle.'[20]

South Asian soldiers' experiences of mechanized warfare – including the use of poison gas – were horrific, as evidenced in extracts from the censored mails [Source 4]. On 25 April 1915, the Lahore Division was deployed for the second battle of Ypres, where Mir Dast of the 55th Coke's Rifles experienced the effects of chemical weapons first hand. He survived a gas attack by German forces that killed all his officers. During his retreat, he rescued several wounded British and Indian officers from different trenches, despite himself

17 Merewether and Smith, *The Indian Corps in France*, p. 68.
18 G.M. Jack, 'The Indian Army on the Western Front, 1914–1915: A Portrait of Collaboration', *War in History*, 13(3) (2006): 340–1.
19 Part of the Lahore Division, the Ferozepore Brigade comprised the 4th London Regiment, 57th Rifles, 129th Baluchis and a Divisional Battalion of the 9th Bhopal Infantry.
20 Merewether and Smith, *The Indian Corps in France*, p. 241.

being wounded. He was the fourth South Asian soldier to receive the V.C., conferred on him by King George V at the Brighton Hospital for wounded Indian soldiers [Source 5]. In a letter dated 12 July 1915 he commented: 'The Victoria Cross is a very fine thing, but this gas gives me no rest. It has done for me.'[21] Throughout the war, the Indian Army was highly decorated, winning 12,908 awards, including eleven Victoria Crosses.[22]

South Asian soldiers in Britain during the First World War

When plans for the provision of Indian hospitals in France and Egypt fell through, because the French government would not guarantee Indian soldiers' transport to Marseilles in less than seven days, hasty arrangements for Indian wounded had to be made in Britain.[23] Sir Walter Roper Lawrence acted as Kitchener's commissioner for the Indian hospitals in Britain from 19 November 1914 onward. The provisions initially consisted of two converted hotels near Brockenhurst in the New Forest. Given the large number of wounded and the remote nature of the hotels, it was deemed more suitable to find accommodation in Brighton. Brighton made available the Pavilion, a secondary school, converted into the York Place Hospital, and the infirmary and workhouse, accommodating some 1,500 patients and named the Kitchener Hospital. The two hotels near Brockenhurst, which had been initially converted into hospitals, subsequently became convalescent homes. Nearby the Lady Hardinge Hospital for Indian troops was opened at Brockenhurst Park. Indian soldiers were also accommodated at the Royal Victoria Hospital at Netley [Source 2]. Funded by the War Office, its proximity to Southampton, where the majority of wounded disembarked, was particularly useful. By March 1915, some 8,000 wounded had been treated in Britain and 1,068 of these had been returned to the front, a practice that caused huge resentment among the South

---

21 British Library, London, MSS Eur F 143/84, 'From Subedar Mir Dast, 55th Coke's Rifles, attached, now in the Pavilion Hospital in Brighton, to Subedar Khan of his own regiment at Kohat (Urdu, 12/7/15)', p. 76.
22 Willcocks, *With the Indians in France*, p. 347.
23 British Library, London, MSS Eur F 120/1, 'Indian Soldiers' Fund: proceedings of general committee, Book 1', 1914–15.

Asian troops. As David Omissi suggests, this was unprecedented in the recent history of the Indian Army [see Source 4].[24]

South Asian wounded would at first be treated in the clearing hospitals close to the front, then be transferred to one of three base hospitals in Boulogne, Hardelot and Montreuil, before being shipped to England. At the behest of the India Office and War Office the hospital authorities made provisions to respect the religious sensibilities of the troops, in particular in relation to food preparation, the distribution of meals, bathroom, kitchen and prayer room facilities, and cremation and burial procedures. Muslim soldiers were buried near the Woking Mosque and cremations were arranged on the South Downs near Patcham. The Indian Soldiers Fund distributed comforts for troops on the front as well as in hospitals.[25] Soldiers were taken on tours of London, and a newspaper in Hindustani and later in Gurmukhi, *Akhbar-i-Jang*, was published and later also available to soldiers on the front. The British government appeared to make every effort that Indian wounded and their British counterparts were treated equally to ensure the continuing loyalty of the troops and to retain the support of Indian nationalists in the war effort. However, equality only existed on the surface. While soldiers praised the medical treatment they received, they were critical of the manner in which their freedom of movement was severely restricted, with high walls and barbed wire surrounding hospital compounds and Indian soldiers chaperoned at every occasion. The authorities feared soldiers might form relationships with white British women, a perennial theme of the Raj. The authorities' heavy-handed measures made the soldiers de facto prisoners in the hospitals, segregated from the local communities for fear of any possible scandal that might impact on the manner in which South Asian subjects viewed their imperial masters.[26]

---

24 Omissi, *Sepoy and the Raj*, p. 118.
25 Largely funded by subscriptions and donations in Britain and India, the Indian Soldiers Fund provided comforts and clothing for Indian troops and prisoners of war in France and Mesopotamia, and ran the Lady Hardinge hospital near Brockenhurst. By the end of the war, the fund had collected £255,511.00. British Library, London, MSS Eur F 120/10, 'Fifth Report of the Indian Soldiers Fund, For the Period 1st January, 1918 to July, 1919'.
26 For further details, see Chapter 1.

The Indian Army after 1915

With the arrival of Kitchener's New Armies, the Indian Corps was redeployed to the Middle East in December 1915, to bolster Indian Army contingents in Mesopotamia. Two Indian cavalry divisions remained in France until March 1918 and saw action in the 1916 Battle of the Somme. The legacy of the Indian troops in France has generated controversy, their contributions evaluated in opposing ways. Jeffrey Greenhut has argued that the Indian Army was unfit and ill-prepared for modern warfare and that their deployment was a failure, blaming this on a narrow recruitment policy unsuitable for modern warfare.[27] George Morton Jack, however, on evaluation of a wider selection of available European and South Asian sources arrives at a different conclusion.[28] He convincingly counters claims, often repeated by Western historians, that the sepoys were unsuited to fight in the cold European climate. Medical statistics prove the contrary. He also disproves that the Corps needed to be dissolved because of low morale after heavy losses in the field. He further negates claims that they were exceptionally inadequate in battle because they were recruited from too narrow a pool of people, and that British Generals treated the Indian Corps more harshly. The high number of military awards and War Office statistics provide ample proof supporting Jack's assessment.

South Asian casualty numbers on the Western Front were high. According to War Office figures, 7,710 South Asians died in France alone. Entire battalions had been decimated, and had to fight on with insufficient numbers of officers. For example, the 59th Rifles arrived in France in 1914 with 13 British and 18 Indian officers and 810 troops; by November 1915, no British officer, and only 4 Indian officers and 75 troops remained.[29] However, the Indian Army suffered its heaviest losses in fighting in Mesopotamia, with 29,555

---

27 J. Greenhut, 'The Imperial Reserve: The Indian Corps on the Western Front, 1914–15', *The Journal of Imperial and Commonwealth History*, 12(1) (1983): 54–73.

28 Jack, 'The Indian Army on the Western Front', 329–62.

29 Merewether and Smith, *The Indian Corps in France*, p. 458.

fallen and 32,608 wounded. Throughout the conflict, the Indian Army suffered 53,486 casualties, 64,350 wounded, 2,937 missing.[30] The decision of sending Indian troops to relieve British troops until Kitchener's New Armies were ready resulted in a heavy toll for the Indian Army. The scale of the losses would lead to lasting changes in its organization, such as the process of Indianization of its officer cadre from the mid-1920s onward. The impact on the Punjab would also be long-lasting, especially after demobilization released thousands from well-remunerated employment. It also emboldened Indian nationalists to fight for greater autonomy. Indian nationalists hoped that Indian support in the war would convince Britain of its loyalty and win India Dominion status. As noted in the introduction, the disappointment of these hopes led to the push for complete independence, which was accelerated by the events of the Second World War.

South Asian Soldiers in the Second World War

The Indian Army in the Second World War differed from the one fighting in the First World War. The inter-war period saw tentative attempts at reform with Indian officers gradually replacing British officers, crucial in any provision for India's future self-government. The initial plans looked at Indianization over a thirty-year period from 1925 onward, with an increased intake of Indians at Sandhurst, until similar training was available in India.[31] Yet the pace of these reforms to increase the number of Indian officers in the Indian Army, leading to greater equality in its command structure, was slow. By 1939, political wrangling had greatly impeded modernization; just over sixty Indian officers had been trained. The Indian Army went to war when viceroy Linlithgow declared a state of war emergency on 3 September 1939, without consulting the Central Legislature, causing widespread resentment among nationalist leaders, such as Gandhi and Jawaharlal Nehru. While Indian princes pledged their support again, the Indian National Congress refused to cooperate with the war effort unless a settlement for post-war Indian independence

---

30 War Office, *Statistics of the Military Effort of the British Empire*, p. 778.
31 Menezes, *Fidelity and Honour*, p. 324.

could be reached, despite Gandhi and Nehru's opposition to fascism. The London-based political pressure group the India League, which had strong affiliations with Congress, did support the war effort on the home front and made judicious use of India's vital role in the war effort in its argument for support for post-war Indian independence in Britain.[32] The divisions within Congress led to a group around Subhas Chandra Bose to organize more radical opposition to British rule, collaborating with Nazi Germany and Japan. Bose would later help form the Indian National Army, recruited from Indian prisoners of war in South East Asia, fighting alongside the Japanese against the Allies. Mohamed Ali Jinnah's support for the war effort also led to further divisions among Indian nationalist leaders.

At the outbreak of war the Indian Army totalled some 194,373 soldiers, comprising 96 infantry battalions and 18 cavalry regiments. The period of the 'phoney war', 1940/41, was ill used as Linlithgow and the Indian Army's commander-in-chief did not receive the necessary permissions from London for large-scale recruitment and training to turn India into a base for the defence of British interests in South-East Asia. Wider expansion and recruitment commenced in May 1940 to raise five infantry divisions and one armoured division. The unprepared nature of the Indian Army in the face of an increasingly aggressive Japan led to rapid falls of Hong Kong (December 1941), Singapore (February 1942), Malaya (January 1942) and Burma (May 1942). Indeed, Menezes suggests that in 1940 'the Indian Army was comparatively less ready . . . for a jungle war with Japan than it had been in 1914 for a trench war with Germany'.[33] The Indian administration had to react quickly and by the end of the war India had recruited some 2.5 million men, one of the largest volunteer armies in the world. However, as these were largely deployed in South East Asia, the Middle East and Africa, with historiographers privileging the narrative of the war in Europe and the Pacific, their pivotal role in helping Britain win the war has remained largely obscure. This explains why the 14th Army, totalling over 700,000 men and responsible for the fight-back on the Burma front, is also known as the 'forgotten army'.

32 See India League campaign posters and flyers in British Library, London, India Office Records, L/I/1/890.
33 Menezes, *Fidelity and Honour*, p. 347.

With the British Expeditionary Force in France, 1940

The arrival of a contingent of twenty-two officers and 1,800 soldiers from the Royal Indian Army Service Corps, sent to work with the British Expeditionary Force in France in November 1939, is a little-known precursor to more large-scale deployments. The presence of animal transport companies (ATC) was an invaluable addition to British forces, as they could distribute much-needed supplies over wet, muddy and impassable ground. After Germany's invasion of the Low Countries in May 1940 and rapid advances into France, it became evident that the battle for France was lost. The contingent was widely dispersed and received orders to move to the coast. Some units transferred to St Nazaire on 17 June, from where they were evacuated under several waves of German aerial attacks. They reached Plymouth on 19 June on the penultimate ship to leave France for Britain. ATC No. 22, stationed near the Maginot line and attached to the 51st British Highland Division, was taken prisoner on 23 June, the first South Asian troops to be captured by the German army in the Second World War. ATC No. 25 and 32 experienced the carnage of Dunkirk first-hand, including relentless dive-bombing and machine-gun fire. Both were evacuated by the small flotilla of ships organized during operation Dynamo [Source 8]. Thus, South Asian soldiers were part of what is now commemorated as 'the miracle of Dunkirk'; however their stories do not feature in contemporary memorialization and the presence of Indian troops at Dunkirk remains unacknowledged. This is surprising, considering that they were the first South Asian soldiers to see action during the war and became integral to Britain's propaganda campaigns in support of the war effort, as is evidenced by much archival material. In the UK, the ATCs' Force HQ was established at Shirley Common, Derbyshire, with some companies stationed in Doncaster and Glasgow, where they received infantry training in anticipation of a German invasion. The Indian troops also offered valuable training in mountain warfare to British troops. In October 1940 the contingent moved to Southern Command where two companies were re-equipped to help with sea defences. In June 1941, the contingent moved to Brecon, South Wales. The contingent remained in Britain until December 1943.

The troops had a high-profile role on the Home Front. Seen as representative of the empire's support for the war effort, they participated in numerous ceremonial parades. Arguably, in the contexts of Britain's historical evaluation of South Asians' role in the Second World War and the myth that it 'stood alone', the South Asian active participation and lack of commemoration merit further scrutiny in present-day contexts of memorializations of Dunkirk, the Battle of Britain and the Blitz.

South Asians on the Home Front

On the outbreak of war, the South Asian community in Britain showed itself mostly supportive of the war effort, despite the precarious political situation in India and the stalemate on any negotiations for Indian self-government.[34] Even members of Krishna Menon's India League joined the war effort. In September 1939, the London *Times* praised the eagerness with which Indian students were volunteering for Air Raid Precaution (ARP) and those with medical degrees for hospital service.[35] Many South Asians, such as Finsbury Park Mayor and India League member C.L. Katial, Krishna Menon or author Sudhindranath Ghose offered to work in civil defence or as ambulance workers. Ghose, a Bengali novelist who had previously worked in Geneva for the League of Nations, describes his experiences as an ARP warden in Ealing and as a lecturer for the Ministry of Information as part of mass observation diaries [Source 9]. South Asians also responded creatively to the conflict. The editor and critic M.J. Tambimuttu recorded his reactions to the Blitz in a poetry collection titled *Out of this War* [Source 8]. These accounts offer invaluable insights into their activities and thoughts on the Home Front in Britain at this moment of crisis.

The Indian Comforts Fund, inaugurated in December 1939 and based at India House, Aldwych, is a further little-known nodal point

34 For a discussion of the contested nature of national loyalties of South Asians, particularly during the Second World War, see Chapter 3. See also R. Visram, *Asians in Britain: 400 Years of History* (London: Pluto, 2002), pp. 333–8.

35 'Indian Students: Eager Volunteers in London', *The Times* (13 September 1939), p. 3.

that highlights manifold South Asian interactions and contributions and marks an interesting example of Indian-British cooperation [Source 10]. Run by British and Indian women, the organization provided comforts and humanitarian relief work. It looked after the welfare of South Asian soldiers on the Home Front and organized leave parties to London. The Fund also fulfilled the crucial role of next-of-kin for all South Asian POW's in Europe, packing some 1.7 million food parcels by 1945. Furthermore, it supplied wool and organized knitting parties for warm clothing. At its peak, it provided wool for some 100,000 knitters across the country, involving a large number of women in the war effort. It also played an important role in providing relief, including warm clothes and funding for better facilities in lodging houses, for the large number of South Asian lascar seamen in the Merchant and Indian navies.[36]

The immense contributions of lascars to Britain's war effort have also remained largely unacknowledged.[37] Thousands of lascars were stranded in Britain for long periods of time during the Second World War, mainly in port cities Glasgow, Liverpool, Cardiff, Newport, Hull and London. They worked for the Merchant Navy and transported much-needed supplies, foodstuffs, ammunition and troops under constant threat from mines and German U-boats. Their crucial participation, along with British seamen, in the troop landings in Africa, Sicily and D-Day in Normandy in 1944 remains largely unknown to date.[38] The pressures of the war, strike action and intense lobbying by lascar unions saw a moderate amelioration to their remuneration, although they continued to be exploited by the ship owners, and were paid significantly less than their British counterparts for the same work. Lascars were vital in keeping the supply lines to Britain open, making many perilous journeys under constant threat of submarine attacks or aerial bombardment. The absence of sufficiently reliable data has led to their crucial role remaining largely unacknowledged, as ship owners were not obliged to keep proper records. The few available statistics suggest that over 6,600 lascars

36 Indian Comforts Fund, *War Record of the Indian Comforts Fund: A Record and Review, 1939–1945* (London: Indian High Commission, 1946).
37 See Visram, *Asians*, pp. 346–7.
38 Ibid., p. 346.

were killed, 1,022 wounded and 1,217 captured.[39] Very few South Asian names are on the Tower Hill Memorial to the merchant mariners killed in both world wars.[40] There are no memorials commemorating lascars' contributions.

Twenty-four South Asian pilots arrived in Britain in September 1940 to train as fighter and bomber pilots with the Royal Air Force (RAF). Overlooked until recently, they were a significant addition to Britain's flying corps in the aftermath of the Battle of Britain that had led to a shortage of trained pilots. Eighteen successfully passed their examinations. In recent years, the late Mahinder Singh Pujji spoke about the South Asian pilots' contributions [Source 12].[41] Trained at RAF Cranwell, these pilots would fly bombers over Germany or fighter planes over the English Channel and Northern France. Responding to an advertisement in Indian newspapers, Pujji joined the group chosen for an intensive training course in the UK. Pujji also flew missions in Northern Africa and was later stationed in Burma. Squadron Leader Pujji recorded in an interview that initially he was unconcerned by the lack of official recognition of the Indian pilots. For him, having won the Distinguished Flying Cross for his daring mission to save a group of American soldiers lost in the Burmese jungle was the official recognition for his work. However, during the commemorations for the fiftieth anniversary of the end of the Second World War where the sacrifices of South Asian pilots barely featured, he wrote a letter to the Ministry of Defence, asking them why as a veteran RAF pilot of Squadrons 43 and 258 he had not been invited to the commemorations for Victory in Europe Day. While Mr Pujji has laid wreaths for fallen comrades in France and Belgium, he had not received invitations to the annual commemorations at the cenotaph. However, he was invited to the 2010 memorial service for the Battle of Britain at Westminster Abbey, but passed away two days before. It is telling that hardly any history of the RAF or the Battle of Britain and its aftermath mentions South Asian

39 Government of India, *Our Merchant Seamen* (New Delhi: Government of India, 1947), p. 8.
40 The memorial records 12,000 names for the First World War and 24,000 for the Second World War. The few South Asian names were residents in Britain sailing on British articles. See Visram, *Asians*, p. 347.
41 Graham Russell, *For King & Another Country* (Ilfracombe: Stockwell, 2010).

pilots, while the stories of Czech, Polish, Caribbean and French pilots are much more widely recorded.

Other theatres of war: From the Middle East to the Burma front

India was of vital strategic significance to Britain's war effort.[42] From the mid-1940s onward, the Government of India was busy implementing the Defence of India plan. From March 1941, Britain feared that with advancing German forces through the Soviet Union, the border along the North-West Frontier Province could become the front for a future encounter with Nazi Germany.

Indian forces had to be deployed quickly abroad, even before the 1940 expansion programme was completed, with troops in 1941 dispatched to Malaya and Iraq. Continual expansion for further infantry divisions was planned for 1942, with many forces sent to North Africa and the Middle East, and in 1943 for the defence of the Arakan. Japan's entry into the war in December 1941 turned India into a beleaguered country on the front line. The ill-prepared Indian troops often received disparaging treatment by British and American commanders. Considering the inadequate equipment and lack of training they received, they did their best under very difficult circumstances. By the time the Indian Army faced the Japanese, vast resources had been diverted to other theatres, partly reasons for the falls of Singapore and Malaya in 1942 and Burma soon after. Thus, the defence of India's eastern border became the main priority. This led to a reorganization of the command structure to manage the large-scale fight-back by land, sea and air envisaged by Churchill and Roosevelt. Responsibilities for operations against the Japanese were transferred from India Command to South-East Asia Command. General Wavell was appointed viceroy and Auchinleck reappointed commander-in-chief. Both reassessed India's defence needs and overhauled Indian Army training provisions by the end of 1943. This strengthened the fighting quality of the Indian Army, making it an invaluable part of the successful fight-back by the 14th Army,

---

42 Ceylon (now Sri Lanka), which also supplied raw materials such as rubber, became strategically important to the Allies' war effort, with important naval and RAF bases for British and other empire troops, making the island a target for Japanese air attacks.

commanded by General Slim. Known as 'the forgotten army', the 14th Army constituted the world's largest land army comprising 750,000 men and divisions from across the empire, including East and West Africa. Indian Army divisions provided two-thirds of the 14th Army. The journalist D.F. Karaka covered their operations in Burma for the *Bombay Chronicle*. Educated in Britain and the first President of Indian origin of the Oxford Union, these columns formed the basis for his account *With the 14th Army* [Source 11]. Effectively an embedded journalist, Karaka recounted the daily lives of Indian and British soldiers, fighting side-by-side. Writing as an Indian nationalist and with knowledge of Britain, his accounts are a fascinating analysis of the rationale for Indian soldiers to fight with the British, offering a more nuanced account than his British counterparts. Karaka accompanied the troops in March/April 1944 during the build-up to the battles of Imphal and Kohima, which marked the turn of the war in South-East Asia in favour of the Allied Forces. He later joined British and American troops as they advanced into Germany.[43]

The Indian Army was widely dispersed in the eastern and western theatres of the war with divisions in the Middle East and North Africa. By 1942 India was the pivot of the British eastern area of defence. Its troops formed part of the Overseas Expeditionary Forces with garrisons in countries ranging from China to Libya and the Western Desert; the large Indian Expeditionary Force in Malaya was similar in size to the British, Australian and Malayan armies in the Far East; Indian troops served in Burma, Persia, Iraq, Palestine, Egypt, East Africa and Abyssinia, Syria, Aden and the Seychelles. They played crucial roles in the battles of Tobruk and El Alamein in 1942, as well as in the liberation of Greece and Italy, fighting alongside American, British and Canadian forces in the battles of Monte Cassino in 1944, the liberation of Rome and the push on the Gothic line from August to December 1944, winning numerous awards for their brave conduct.[44]

---

43 D.F. Karaka, *Then came Hazrat Ali: Autobiography 1972* (Bombay: D.F. Karaka, 1973).
44 Visram, *Asians*, p. 344.

The position of the Indian Army in the Second World War differed from that in the previous conflict. The failure of the Cripps Mission, internal disturbances and the Indian National Army all challenged British rule in India, yet the Indian Army remained largely unaffected by this. As F.H. Perry argues, 'without the Indian Army Britain would have been quite unable to meet her many commitments in the Middle East and Far East'.[45] During the Second World War, Indian Army personnel received over 4,000 awards for gallantry, including 31 Victoria Crosses. According to the India Office's Information Department, by the end of hostilities in August 1945, there had been 24,338 killed, 64,354 wounded, 11,754 missing and 79,489 Prisoners of War.[46] The impact of both wars was most keenly felt in Punjab's rural areas, where a large majority of the Indian Army was recruited. Punjabi Muslims constituted 15 per cent of troops. Yet in many ways the contributions of South Asian soldiers have not received the recognition they deserve and they are arguably both conflicts' forgotten volunteers. Commander-in-chief Claude Auchinleck explains the lack of commemoration in terms of British politicians' utilitarian approach to the Indian Army: 'I think the English never cared, ... the politicians especially, I don't think they never took any interest in India at all. I think they used it. I mean, they ... wouldn't have come through both wars if they hadn't had the Indian Army ... and I think they never really understood it.'[47]

Processes of commemoration, memorialization and historiography

Archives in Britain, Europe and India offer rich materials and manifold evidence of South Asian soldiers' dedicated service in Britain's war effort in both conflicts. Yet they feature only marginally in wider historical discourses. How do we need to interpret these

---

45 F.W. Perry, *The Commonwealth Armies: Manpower and Organisation in two World Wars* (Manchester: Manchester University Press, 1988), p. 120.

46 *India and the War 1939–1945, The Facts* (London: Information Department, India Office, 1946), p. 12.

47 British Library, Oral Archives, MSS Eur T3, 'Field Marshall Sir Claude Auchinleck'.

elisions and their impact on commemoration and memorialization in the present, and the slippages we encounter when working with archival evidence? The historian Michel-Rolph Trouillot offers some useful observations. He explains that 'history as social process, involves people in three distinct capacities: 1) as *agents*, or occupants of structural positions; 2) as *actors* in constant interface with a context; and 3) as *subjects*, that is, as voices aware of their vocality'.[48] Trouillot is especially concerned with the silences in historical discourses and the inherent manifestations of power in the process by which history is produced. This may help us understand how dominant narratives emerge through which a national consciousness is shaped. This in turn affects contemporary memorialization in the present and the silencing of other historical narratives, despite their physical presence in the archives. Trouillot argues that 'silences enter the process of historical production at four crucial moments: the moment of fact creation (the making of *sources*); the moment of assembly (the making of *archives*); the moment of fact retrieval (the making of *narratives*); and the moment of retrospective significance (the making of *history* in the final instance)'.[49] This leads Trouillot to argue that 'any historical narrative is a particular bundle of silences, the result of a unique process, and the operation required to decon-struct these silences will vary accordingly'.[50] Yet in the case of the examples mentioned it is significant to note that South Asian presences are recorded at the moment of fact creation and assembly. Although importantly these archives, too, are incomplete and partial. Records can after all be weeded, destroyed or closed for long periods of time. Nevertheless, these stories have not featured significantly at the moment of fact retrieval and retrospective significance. The sources presented here attest that South Asian involvement in both conflicts is well documented in the archives. In this respect it is perhaps more accurate to speak about lapses in memory and repre-sentation, not of silences. One might argue that these narratives are waiting only to be heard. Making audible these marginalized voices challenges the narrative of the war articulated through a narrow

48 M.-R. Trouillot, *Silencing the Past: Power and the Production of History* (Boston: Beacon Press, 1995), p. 23.
49 Ibid., p. 26.
50 Ibid., p. 27.

grouping of mainly white, middle-class men in battle histories and broadens the Eurocentric nature of the historiography of the world wars and contemporary memorialization. A new wave of critical engagement with both world wars has generated interest in different narratives, for example focusing on the working classes, women and other minority groups. As Santanu Das has pointed out, this is led by comparative, interdisciplinary scholarship.[51]

However, despite some shifts in perception, there remains a lack of awareness of South Asian contributions to the world wars, erasing them from the official radar in both Britain and India. For instance, the 2009 debates surrounding the Gurkhas' battle for citizenship rights in Britain exemplify how elisions in the historical narrative of the wars influence how the social 'value', 'impact' and contribution of ethnic minority communities in relation to a common shared British history is perceived. However, the ninetieth anniversary of the end of the First World War and the sixtieth anniversary of the start of the Second World War continue a representational shift in Britain, with an increased focus on narratives from soldiers with minority backgrounds, such as the 2008/09 'War to Windrush' exhibition at the Imperial War Museum. This is partly due to the fact that publicly funded organizations have to fulfil an outreach remit that addresses Britain's communities in all their diversity.

Britain's contemporary diversified cultural and ethnic make-up necessitates an increasingly inclusive approach to narratives of both world wars, which is slowly filtering into public acts of commemoration in Britain today, for example at the Patcham Chattri on the South Downs in memory of fallen South Asian soldiers. Considering that South Asian soldiers' vital contributions are so well documented, historiographers need to draw on this testimony to help re-focus the narrative of the world wars. This approach, then, can make a valuable contribution to overcoming the marginalization of South Asian narratives in present-day memorialization of both world wars and help provide a fuller picture of Britain's 'Finest Hour'.

---

51 S. Das, 'Sepoys, Sahibs and Babus: India, the Great War and Two Colonial Journals', in M. Hammond and S. Towheed (eds), *Publishing in the First World War: Essays in Book History* (Basingstoke: Palgrave Macmillan, 2007), pp. 61–77.

Source material for Chapter 2

First World War

1 *Open Letter by M.K. Gandhi to India Office, 14 August 1914.*
[British Library, Charles Henry Roberts Collection, MSS Eur F 170/8]

60, Talbot Road,
Bayswater, S.W.
14 August, 1914
The Under Secretary ~~of State for India~~
India Office,
Whitehall, London.

Sir,

It was thought desirable by many of us that during the crisis that has overtaken the Empire and whilst many Englishmen, leaving their ordinary vocation in life, are responding to the Imperial call, those Indians who are resident in the United Kingdom and who can at all do so, should place themselves unconditionally at the disposal of the authorities.

With a view to ascertaining the feeling of the resident Indian population, the undersigned[52] sent out a circular letter to as many

---

52 The letter has fifty-three signatories, including poet and activist Sarojini Naidu. Others represent a cross-section of London's South Asian community, mainly students (26), but also medical practitioners (8), traders and merchants (6), barristers (3), engineers (2), journalists (1), teachers (1) and secretaries (1).

Indians in the United Kingdom as could be approached during the 36 hours that the organisers gave themselves. The response has been generous and prompt, and in the opinion of the undersigned, representative of His Majesty's subjects in the Indian Empire at present residing in different parts of the United Kingdom.

On behalf of ourselves and those whose names appear on the list appended hereto, we beg to offer our services to the Authorities. We venture to trust that the Right Honble [*sic*] Marquess of Crewe[53] will approve of our offer and secure its acceptance by the proper authorities. We would respectfully emphasise the fact that the one dominant idea guiding us is that of rendering such humble assistance as we may be considered capable of performing as an earnest of our desire to share the responsibilities of membership of this great Empire, if we would share its privileges.

It may be added that some of those whose names are sent herewith, are already doing work with some of the organisations that are already rendering assistance, and we have no doubt that if our humble offer is accepted, as the news permeates the Indian community, many more volunteers will come forward.

We have the honour to be,

Sir,

Your obedient servants,

M.K. Gandhi

---

53 Robert Offley Ashburton Crewe-Milnes (1858–1945), Secretary of State for India, 1911–15.

2 Letter from Walter Lawrence to Lord Kitchener, 28 November 1914.
[British Library, Walter Roper Lawrence Collection, MSS Eur F 143/65, pp. 6–9]

94 Eaton Square, S.W.
28 November 1914

Dear Lord Kitchener,
I have again visited Brockenhurst, and have also seen the Convalescent Home at Barton-on-Sea, and the excellent Hospital arrangements which have been made for the Indians at Netley.

As regards Brockenhurst, I see a great improvement since I visited the two Hotels on the 20th. The patients are comfortable, contented, and well tended, and the dressings are done by the medical officers. This is unusual, but is greatly appreciated, and the large establishment of medical officers is some compensation for the unsuitable nature of the buildings. I can assure you that the patients are quite satisfied. The atmosphere is Indian, and rough and ready, but it is warm and congenial, and I advise that while our pressure for Hospital space continues the two Hotels at Brockenhurst be run on existing lines. They can accommodate safely 280 patients. There are now no patients in tents. When pressure for Hospitals decreases, Brockenhurst Hotels should be used as Convalescent Homes. No one should be allowed to visit Brockenhurst Hotels without a pass from the War Office.[54]

The arrangements at Netley are admirable. There the atmosphere is English. There are 880 patients in the Royal Victoria Hospital, and 223 in the Red Cross huts. I had long talks with patients and I heard no complaints. The English nurses all said that they liked the work and that the Indians were fine gentlemen. The Indians salaamed the nurses and told me that it was an honour to them to be supervised by

54 The India Office took precautions to limit interactions between South Asian wounded and the British public. This led to perceptions that they were treated like prisoners.

Englishwomen.[55] It is only supervision. At Brockenhurst the medical officers asked for English nurses, but I would not, but it is well to have two systems and to watch results. But for Brighton I advocate the Netley system – English nurses to supervise, English orderlies and Indian interpreters. There is no choice. There is no Indian personnel available, and that most essential person, the sweeper, is not forthcoming. Even if the India Office had had their Hospitals at Marseilles and Alexandria, they would have wanted sweepers, and it is remarkable that no sweepers have arrived. We do not want bhishtis[56], barbers, tailors, &c. We only want sweepers and cooks. We shall have to get the cooks from the convalescents, but here again the India Office might have foreseen the necessity for Brahmin and Mussulman cooks.[57]

Considering everything, the weather, the haste, and the lack of prevision, I think it is a matter for congratulation that the Indians are so comfortable, so healthy, and so satisfied. I tried to find a grumbler. I was often unaccompanied and talked freely to the men, and they all said they were well fed, warm, and most skilfully treated. I will not trouble you with little details. Every officer knows that he has only to ask and he will get what is wanted. So far the spirit of the personnel is excellent. The officers are devoted, and all are doing their best. I was rather doubtful as to the Indian students[58], but on the whole they have worked well. And if they can only last they will be of great assistance. I have told them that in after years of good work in the Hospitals will be a great certificate with the English in India. I wish that some hope could be given to these students that persistent work in the Hospitals would be rewarded with a medal.

55 The question of female nurses was widely debated. The Lady Hardinge Hospital was an exception to the ban on English nurses, as the Indian Soldiers Fund managed the hospital. However they were only employed in a supervisory capacity.

56 North-Indian Muslim community traditionally employed at the time as water carriers.

57 Great care was taken to cater to soldiers' religious and caste sensibilities.

58 Students from the Indian Field Ambulance Training Corps, recruited by Gandhi.

3 *Extract from War Diary, Ferozepore Brigade, 12 March 1915.*[59]
[National Archives, Kew, War Office: First World War and Army of
Occupation War Diaries, WO 95/3922]

During the night orders were received to be ready to move at 4.30
a.m. No orders having been received by that time from the Division,
at 5 a.m. the brigade moved off. At the road junction, where the units
were drawn up in close order, on either side of it the enemy
commenced a fierce Artillery bombardment using shrapnel and high
explosive shells of large calibre – the intensity and duration of this
bombardment far exceeded anything the regiment had hitherto
undergone and besides we were caught in the open which resulted in
several casualties before the men could scatter – we lost a most
promising man by the death of Sepoy[60] Zarif Khan who had already
been awarded the I.O.M.[61]

During the night SIRHIND BDE.[62] had relieved the DEHRA DUN
BDE.[63] and the JULLUNDER BDE.[64] had orders to make an attack on
the BOIS DE BIEZ[65] with them. During the violent bombardment in
the dark, regiments got hopelessly mixed up and scattered all over the
place and it was not until 9 a.m. before an advance was possible
although we were originally expected to be in position by 7 a.m. The
enemy kept up his violent bombardment to which we replied at 7.30
a.m. with even increased intensity and maintained it until dusk. Our

59 12 March, end of the Battle of Neuve Chapelle where Indian brigades from
the Meerut Division were engaged in heavy fighting.
60 Name given to a soldier serving in the infantry of the Indian Army.
61 Indian Order of Merit; military and civilian decoration. Before the Indian
Distinguished Service Medal (1907) and the Victoria Cross (1911) was
opened to native troops, it was the only award available to soldiers of the
Indian Army.
62 Sirhind Brigade; part of the Lahore Division; initially stationed in Egypt,
the brigade arrived in Marseilles on 30 November 1914.
63 Dehra Dun Brigade; part of the Meerut Division; arrived on the Western
Front in October 1914.
64 Jullunder Brigade; part of the Lahore Division; arrived on the Western
Front in October 1914.
65 Woodlands near Neuve Chapelle.

regiment, probably owing to the paucity of British Officers – we had now but 5 I.O.s[66] & 5 B.O.s[67] – seems to have been difficult to collect & only some 150 men went up into the firing line eventually and these went up to support the SIRHIND BDE: and towards 2 p.m. arrived up in the front line between the 4th and 9th Gurkhas.

66 Indian Officers.
67 British Officers.

4 *Letter from 19 Ludder Singh, 41ˢᵗ Dogras,*[68] *Barton Hospital, to Raghubir Singh, Kangra, Punjab (Hindi, 1st July 1915) [Dogra].*
[British Library, Walter Roper Lawrence Collection, Mss Eur F 143/84, p. 67]

My brother, Salig Ram was wounded on the 13th June, but he was not badly hurt. You should not be at all anxious on his account, because it is very fortunate for a man to be wounded here. For whoever is wounded escapes, but at first they used to act with great injustice and want of faith. After a man had been three times wounded, and had gone to Hospital and recovered, he was passed as fit for duty by a medical board, and having joined was sent back to the trenches. Now I hear that the men who are wounded and sent back to Hospital will not be sent again to the trenches, and that the wounded are brought before a Board and sent to Marseilles. Afterwards I heard – and this order has been promulgated – that the wounded would not be sent back during the war.[69] My brother, my heart was day and night fixed on my home, when your card arrived, and I was like a man who, once burnt, is afraid of a glowworm. My brother, on the 9th of May, there was an attack by the whole of the English and the French, and the whole line of the Indians, but as you may not understand what the 'whole line' or the 'attack' means, you should ask someone who belongs to the Army. So my friend, when my regiment went up to the trenches for the attack, it had a strength of 850 men.[70] When the attack began in the course of one hour 411 men were wounded, and 80 were killed, and 341 (sic) remained unhurt. On the 13th again

68 Part of the Bareilly Brigade, with the 2ⁿᵈ Battalion of the Black Watch, 58ᵗʰ Vaughan Rifles and 2ⁿᵈ Battalion of the 8ᵗʰ Gurkha Rifles.

69 One of the biggest grievances of South Asian soldiers was the several tours of duty on the front, after recovery from injury. Due to the shortage of men, this common practice for British soldiers was also applied to Indian servicemen, despite their having received assurances that after being wounded they would not be returned to the trenches. See soldiers' letters in Omissi, *Indian Voices of the Great War*, pp. 38–3, 61–2, 93.

70 Prelude to the Battle of Festubert. During the fighting, the 41ˢᵗ Dogras relieved the 1/4 Seaforths. In the fighting on 9 May, the 41ˢᵗ Dogras suffered heavy losses, with 401 out of 605 killed; see Merewether and Smith *The Indian Corps in France*, p. 353–4.

there was a small attack, and severe losses, and these losses that I have written of were in my own regiment alone, and the destruction that occurred in the other Brigades, God alone knows.[71] I cannot write it, for over the whole earth and the ground between the trenches bodies were lying on bodies like stones in heaps, which no words can be found to describe or relate. This is nothing but the anger of the Almighty and it is His will. When a man dies in the world, I and you think it a great event. But here in this war, corpses are piled one upon another so that they cannot be counted.

---

71 Attacks in this period were hampered by heavy rainfall.

5 Extract from article: 'The King and Queen at Brighton. Visit to the Indian Hospitals. Mohammedan Service at the Royal Pavilion. Victoria Cross Presented', *Sussex Daily News*, 23 August 1915.
[British Newspaper Library shelfmark 1915 EW 1501–1503 [1915] NPL]

Captain Godfrey-Faussett placed the Victoria Cross, the Military Cross, and the medals upon the table, and Sir Walter Lawrence[72] explained the achievements of the brave men who were to receive these coveted honours. Sir Walter also made a brief speech in Hindustani, which obviously aroused the most intense interest among the Indians.

A VICTORIA CROSS HERO
The men were then called up one by one, and it was noticed how sympathetically the Queen and Princess Mary smiled upon them. Jemadar Mir Dast, the Victoria Cross hero, was the first to approach the Sovereign's presence. He had to be brought up in an invalid chair, for he is still suffering from poisoned gas.[73] But the gallant fellow, with a little assistance, got out of the invalid chair, and stood up like the intrepid soldier he is, to receive this honour of honours from the King. The Indians know, as all know, what it means to win the V.C. in a war like this. It was not the first distinction to be won by Jemadar[74] Mir Dast. As Havildar[75] of Coke's Rifles, Frontier Force, he was awarded the Order of Merit for splendid bravery in the Mohmand campaign[76] of 1908. When the present war broke out he volunteered his service at the front. He said that his Commanding

---

72 Walter Roper Lawrence (1857–1940), Kitchener's Commissioner for the Indian sick and wounded in France and England.
73 Mir Dast (1874–1950), wounded in the 2nd battle of Ypres, during a German chlorine gas attack. The First World War marked the first large-scale use of chemical weapons.
74 Indian Army rank, lowest rank for Viceroy Commissioned Officers (VCO), commanding platoons, troops and assisting their British commanding officers.
75 Indian Army rank, equivalent to sergeant in the British Army.
76 Indian Army operations against the Pashtun Mohmand tribe in the North-West Frontier Province.

Officer had laughingly remarked, 'You have won the Order of Merit, and I shall be greatly disappointed if you don't bring back the V.C.' The greater honour was awarded to him for magnificent bravery at Ypres on 26th April of this year, when he led his platoon with great gallantry during an attack, and afterwards collected various parties of the regiment (when no British officers were left) and kept them under his command until the retirement was ordered. He subsequently, on the same day, displayed remarkable courage in helping to carry eight British and Indian officers to safety while exposed to very heavy fire.

THE KING'S SPEECH
The King, before decorating Jemadar Mir Dast with the Victoria Cross, explained that this decoration had been created by Queen Victoria for conspicuous valour by British soldiers in the field. His Majesty recalled the fact that when he attended the Durbar[77] he directed that in future this honour should also be available to Indian soldiers, and he congratulated Jemadar Mir Dast on being the first to whom it had been awarded. 'It gives me,' the King added, advancing to the hero, 'great pleasure to confer it upon you.' He then fastened it to the proud warrior's breast and shook hands with him. The Indian was deeply touched, and was again assisted into his chair and wheeled to one side to make room for other recipients of honours.

77 1911 Delhi Durbar, when George V was crowned Emperor of India.

6 *General Sir James Willcocks, 'Hurnam Singh', Blackwood Magazine*[78] *(December 1917), reprinted in General Sir James Willcocks, With the Indians in France (London: Constable, 1920), pp. vii–xi.* [British Library shelfmark V 8601]

'Hurnām Singh'

I
Beneath an ancient pipal-tree,[79] fast by the Jhelum's[80] tide,
In silent thought sat Hurnām-Singh,
A Khalsa[81] soldier of the King:
He mused on things now done and past,
For he had reached his home at last,
His empty sleeve his pride.

II
Five years before a village lout, beneath the self-same tree,
He met the Havildar,[82] who'd come
With honeyed words and beat of drum,
Cajoling all who glory sought,
And telling how the regiment fought
The Zakha[83] and the Mohmand[84] clans,
With shouts of victory.

78 *Blackwood Magazine* was first published in 1817 in Edinburgh. Conservative in outlook, it published works by writers such as Walter Scott, George Eliot, Anthony Trollope and Joseph Conrad, and critical essays and reviews.

79 Also known as the Bodhi tree, considered holy in Buddhism, Hinduism and Jainism.

80 One of the most western rivers, running for 550 miles through India and Pakistan, it is a major waterway in the Punjab.

81 Collective body of all baptized Sikhs.

82 Indian Army rank, equivalent to the rank of sergeant.

83 Tribe of the North-West Frontier Province.

84 Pashtun tribe living in the North-West Frontier Province against whom the Indian Army fought several campaigns.

III

Wah Guru Ji! rang in his ears, the famous battle cry,
And since those days Hurnām had seen,
On Flanders plains, from fierce Messines,[85]
To Festubert and Neuve Chapelle,
'Mid festering bogs and scenes of hell,
How Khalsa soldiers die.

IV

The village yokels round him flocked to hearken to his tales,
How he had crossed the Kala[86] sea,
From India's strand past Araby,
Thro' Egypt's sands to Europe's shores,
Where the wild stormy mistral roars,
And anchor'd in Marseilles.

V

'Is it the truth,' said one more bold than village yokels be,
'That men with wings ascend on high
And fight with Gods in yonder sky?
That iron monsters belching wrath,
Beneath their wheel of Juggernaut,
Claim victims for Kali[87]?'

VI

'Now list all ye,' said Hurnām-Singh, 'the aged and the youth,
The tales they told in bygone days,
Of Gods and Ghouls in ancient lays,
Are true, not false; mine eyes descried,
Mine ears have heard as heroes died,
The Mahabharut's[88] truth.

85 The Ferozepore Brigade attacked German positions there on 16–18 December 1914. It was a failure causing heavy casualties and wounded.
86 The black waters.
87 Goddess of time and change, consort of Shiva; sometimes represented as a figure of annihilation.
88 One of two major Sanskrit epics and one of the major scriptures in Hinduism.

VII

'The land of France is wide and fair, the people brave and free,
I fain would tell, but orders came,
"Push on, the foe awaits the game" –
The game of death, the Khalsa cry,
The warriors' slogan, rent the sky,
Fateh Wah Guru Ji!

VIII

'The Sahibs' faces told their tale; no craven thought or sloth
In those brave hearts, as we had learned
When Gujerat[89] the tide had turned,
And left the names of Aliwal[90]
And Chillianwala[91] as a pall
Of glory to us both.

IX

'And thus the sons of Hindustan, from Himalaya to Scinde[92],
From Hindu Kush to Deccan plains,
Rent in a day the ancient chains
Which isolate class from clan,
And joined in battle as one man,
To die for MataHind[93].

X

'Hur Mahadeo! Guru Ji! and Allah's sacred name,
Shri Gunga Jai![94] from brave Nepal,
Re-echoed loud through wild Garhwal;[95]
From Dogra vale, Afridi clan,
To the proud homes of Rajistan,
Was lit the martial flame.

89 State in Western India.
90 Town in Indian Punjab.
91 Town in Pakistani Punjab.
92 Now Sindh Province in Pakistan.
93 Mother India.
94 War cries of Gurkha, Sikh, Muslim and Hindu soldiers.
95 Princely state in North India, from where the 39th Garhwal Rifles were recruited.

XI

'As pitiless the bullets rained 'mid angry storm and flood,
Khudadad Khan![96] immortal name,
Stood by his gun, for India's fame
Was in his hands; the Huns advance,
Recoil; Retire; the soil of France
Is richer with his blood.'

XII

And Hurnām paused as he recalled, one dark November morn,
When twice three thousand foes had rushed
Our trenches, powdered into dust,
And bayonet point and Kukry blade[97]
Avenging retribution made,
Before the break of dawn.

XIII

'Garhwal will tell,' he said, 'with pride her children oft recite,
How Durwan Negi,[98] lion-heart!
Was first and foremost from the start;
He led the charge which won the day, –
Oh, brothers, 'twas a glorious fray,
For victory came with light.'

XIV

Shābāsh! Shābāsh![99] from every tongue, and mothers' hearts stood still,
As sons stepped forth and made demand
They too should join the glorious band,
They too should hear the battle's din,
Or purge the soul of every sin,
If such were Ishwar's[100] will.

---

96 First Indian recipient of the Victoria Cross, October 1914.
97 Curved knife used by Gurkhas as a tool or combat weapon.
98 39th Garhwal Rifles, second recipient of the Victoria Cross.
99 Well done.
100 God.

XV
Hurnām went on: 'At Neuve Chapelle, at Festubert, we bled,
On Wipers field, at Moulin Piètre,
We heard the German hymn of hate;
Above our lines the war-ships soared,
Our trenches rocked while cannon roared
The requiem of the dead.'

XVI
The Jehlum's banks had witnessed oft her waters stained with gore,
Had heard the tramp of countless feet,
Had known both triumph and defeat,
But never had her waters swirled
A prouder message to the world
Than Hurnām's story bore.

XVII
For India's sons had sealed their oath, according to their laws;
Sealed it with blood across the sea,
From Flanders to Gallipoli,
On Tigris' banks, on Egypt's sands,
'Mid Afric's swamps and hinterlands,
And died in England's cause.

XVIII
For ages long the Mullah's cry, the temple bells shall wile,
And call to prayer for those who died,
The father, mother, son, and bride,
Descendants of the loyal brave
Who rest in warriors' simple graves,
And need no marble pile.

Second World War
7 *Tambimuttu, M.J.,*[101] *Out of this War: A Poem* (London: The Fortune Press, 1941).
[British Library shelfmark 11657.bb.47]

> The Hero
> Where shall the innocent, curly head shelter from the blast,
> The bombs and tombs are falling on Leicester Square.[102]
> Hour-glass sand aflame on the roof-tops; the mouth
> Of fear eating air we breathe.
>
> When the halo is doffed, the bed-sown limbs regarded,
> A hero's emotions are real in the dart of a wasp.
> He will adopt the accustomed style of his fathers
> And dive into the thunder with a mask.
>
> The Teutonic Rilke[103] will cover the Hero with laurel;
> Genghiz Khan[104] allows him a hundred oyster brides.
> But remember, the hero is a fool with a theory
> That wouldn't work – the fire in his head was sand.
>
> Strike the hero on the one, receive the other cheek
> Stronger than the first with the steel of wisdom
> – The weapon of the strong and heroic, no other.
> Force does not breed in the vegetable kingdom.
>
> No better than vegetable, we have need of root and plot;
> Denied, a crimson crime will branch from the crime.
> Who fights, not the hero, but the oppressor,
> Denied the love of reason, to make him different.

101 M.J. Tambimuttu (1915–83) Ceylonese (Sri Lankan) critic, poet and editor of the magazine *Poetry London* (see Chapter 3).
102 Central London Square in the heart of the West End's entertainment district, heavily bombed during the Blitz in 1940.
103 Rainer Maria Rilke (1875–1926), Austrian poet.
104 Founder of the Mongol Empire which extended into China, Central Asia, Russia, and modern-day Eastern Europe.

The Hero will sit him down with Bible and book
Learn the stories of Indian, German and Pole.
War as the evil branching on the outraged body
Will steal from the stalking grave and wash it whole.

In a temple of weakness, war reveals its head
The disordered blood the pillar, stone and crop.
Solemn with Injustice, Vanities, Ambitions;
Both these last are deadly and Primary Evils.

A Primary Evil to rim the earth with war.
This evil resides not in itself, but causes
– The mutilated page in the book, the suffered slight,
The gnawing hunger and our accusing losses.

To rise up on the martyred blood and shriek vengeance,
And plunge the angry bayonet in the scabbard of blood,
Is the Secondary Evil, without recompense
That times the bomb of another war.

The two Evils are collateral and pledged:
The one unformulated without the other.
The resentful hand not met with force
Use violence again will not bother.

O for the clean wind that will split the fruit
And pluck the golden heart for the common earth,
Singing of the frosted time when Evil will rise
Not one-accusing, but laid across its causes.

It probes into the infinite reaches of space
And graded life below, the Buddha said.
Evil is the all-flavouring element
Blowing equally on the new-born and the dead.

O to hold this terrifying vision in the mind,
Roll the hills and grooves, like a well-known bead!
Half this battle and the murder over;
The hero stirring in the common weed and seed.

This his fond task, to ride the sky
Between his knees the iron time gripped and curled.
The chart of cause and effect unfurled before him,
This his creation he swings on the shoulder of the world.

8 *Extract from 'Report of Operations in France', 19 July 1940.*
[British Library, India Office Records, War Staff Papers, L/WS/1/355]

32 Animal Transport Company[105]
This unit was originally located at ORCHIES, LANNAY and
BOURGHELLES and allotted to 1 & 2 Divs., 1 Corps. When these
Divisions advanced into BELGIUM, the Company less one sub-
division moved from ORCHIES and LANNAY to
VILLERS-au-TERTRE, a distance of twenty-five kms., which was
carried out by night. The sub-division at BOURGHELLES moved to
FAUMONT, about 20 kms., during the early hours of the day, night
movement having been forbidden by the local Commander. These
moves took place during the night 11/12 May and on 12 May.

On 18 May orders were issued by the local Commander for the
unit to concentrate at OSTRICOURT and THUMERIES. Owing to
the non receipt of a message despatched by D.R. to the sub-division
which had been detached from the Coy.[106], the unit did not concentrate as a whole until its arrival at the outskirts of DUNKIRK[107],
which it reached on 23 and 24 May, staging near NEUVE
CHAPELLE, VIEUX BERQUIN and SOCX.

The Unit embarked complete at DUNKIRK in the early hours of
25 May; on that date arrived at DOVER and were despatched to
ALDERSHOT. The O.C.[108] unit, Major K. JERMYN, handled his unit
with determination and skill and in spite of enemy activity, the unit
had only two casualties, one of which occurred at VILLERS-au-
TERTRE. Unfortunately it was not found possible to provide
shipping for animals, equipment or supplies, and orders were
received to abandon them.

. . .

---

105 The extract covers the retreat of one of the four Animal Transport
    Companies of the Royal Indian Army Service Corps stationed in France
    with the British Expeditionary Force in 1939–40.
106 Company.
107 Dunkirk evacuation, code-named operation Dynamo. 330,000 soldiers
    were evacuated from the beaches of Dunkirk in late May to early June 1940.
108 Officer Commanding.

Policy:

In view of the fact that this Contingent is the only military formation from parts of the Empire other than the British Isles, which has had personnel in the front line, and that other Empire troops are remaining in this country, I suggest that to return the Contingent to India would have an enormous and adverse political repercussion in that country, and be a golden opportunity for anti-British propaganda by the enemy, although I am well aware that it needs only one personnel to misbehave for adverse criticism to be directed at the Contingent; I am of the opinion, however, that this factor must be ignored.

The Contingent wishes to remain in ENGLAND, which will, I suggest, remain either the main theatre of operations or will be the country from which another expeditionary force will be despatched. Personnel have much sympathy for the French people, and are only too anxious to assist in every way they can in the liberation of that unfortunate nation.

9 *Extract from Indian Comforts Fund Progress Report October 1941 to March 1942.*
[British Library, India Office Records, Military Department Library, L/Mil/17/5/2327]

PRISONERS OF WAR

As far as is known, the maximum number of Indian prisoners of war in Europe[109] is some 2,300, made up of approximately 1,750 military and 550 seamen. The Fund continues to pack and despatch the weekly food parcels and the quarterly next-of-kin clothing and comforts parcels as allowed by the International Convention. The cost of the weekly food parcel for each man, including cigarettes, is 10/-,[110] and is paid by the Indian Red Cross. With effect from 1st January 1942, the salaries of the Food Packing Centre will also be paid by the Indian Red Cross.

At the present time, 2,600 food parcels are being packed at India House[111] each week. This number will be gradually increased until the maximum output of 3,000 per week is obtained by the end of April, thus creating a reserve against loss in transit or other unforeseen emergency.

Similarly, approximately 240 quarterly clothing parcels are packed each week, making a total of just over 3,000 for a quarter of 13 weeks.

On leaving India House, food and clothing parcels are taken over in bulk by the G.P.O.[112] and the War Organization of the Red Cross and St. John[113] respectively, who arrange for their transport to Geneva. It then becomes the responsibility of the International Red Cross to distribute them in sufficient quantities to all camps where Indians are known to be. To facilitate this distribution, Indian food

---

109 By 1942, the Axis powers, including Germany and Italy, had taken a number of South Asian soldiers prisoner during operations in France and North Africa, as well as lascar seamen working in the Merchant Navy. The Indian Comforts Fund acted as their next-of-kin.

110 About £17.49 in 2010.

111 Indian High Commissioner Firoz Khan Noon made rooms available for the Indian Comforts Fund at India House, Aldwych.

112 General Post Office.

113 St John's Ambulance Service.

parcels[114] are packed in distinctive carton and the bales of clothing parcels bear special stencilled markings.

Tobacco and cigarettes are sent in bulk from stocks at Geneva under arrangements made between the British and Indian Red Cross Societies. Bulk distribution of special items acceptable to Sikhs has also been arranged.

...

WORKING PARTIES
There are now 1,683 working parties registered in England, Wales and Scotland, varying from a minimum of six persons to whole schools. It is estimated that some 60,000 people receive our wool to knit up into an equivalent weight of garments. During the last six months, 29,316 lb. of wool has been bought and distributed. And the number of knotted garments received has been 78,915. In addition, 4,767 knitted garments have been received as gifts, made up from wool other than our own, chiefly from America, Canada and India – the latter including excellent sea-boat stockings from Kalimpong.

...

INDIAN CONTINGENT
Many men of the Indian Contingent were called upon to face the rigours of an English winter for the first time. A full scale issue of woollen garments was made to all ranks and 'windcheaters' sent to those who had not previously received them. At Christmas, every man received a special present of handkerchiefs and razor blades. Other despatches included boot polish, brass polish, shaving sticks, sports equipment and books. The Fund also made a grant of £20 towards a magic lantern, kindly provided by the Y.M.C.A.

The Mosque at Woking[115], which is the home of the weekly leave parties, was presented with a wireless set by the Welfare Department of the War Office. The Fund made a grant of £25 for the purchase and installation of four loud-speaker extensions to the men's living

114 Based on calorific tables for British food parcels, the Indian Comforts Fund would pack parcels with Indian foodstuffs such as rice, dhal, atta, and curry powder.
115 The Woking Mosque's association with South Asian soldiers in Britain continued in the Second World War, providing accommodation for leave parties visiting London. Soldiers also worshipped at the Mosque and joined in the annual Eid celebrations.

huts. The Fund also pays the bus fares of these leave parties when they visit London three days each week.

INDIAN SEAMEN

In addition to the distribution of clothing and comforts, the welfare of the Indian Seamen on shore remains very much the concern of the Fund. During the previous six months, the following grants have been made from the gracious gift of Her Majesty The Queen, allocated for this purpose:

£60   to the Indian Hostel, Missions to Seamen, Salford, for bathing cubicles.

£75   to the Indian Seamen's Hostel, Missions to Seamen, Glasgow, for more shower baths.

£150   for furnishing the recreation rooms of a new Indian Seamen's Club (Mersey Mission to Seamen) to be opened at Liverpool on 10th April 1942.

£40   for the purchase of a radiogram, which has been loaned to Mr. S.T. Alley's[116] boarding house at Coatbridge, Glasgow.

At Christmas a grant of £30 was made to the Indian Institute, Mersey Mission to Seamen, Birkenhead.

---

116 Surat Alley (1905–?) South Asian activist and trade union leader, particularly active among the lascar community. In 1942 he was the London representative of the All-India Seamen's Federation. In 1943 he formed the All-India Seamen's Centre with branches in London, Liverpool and Glasgow.

10 *Sudhindra Nath Ghose,*[117] *Excerpts from 'War Diary' June/July* 1942.

[British Library, Sudhindra Nath Ghose Collection, MSS EUR F 153/19]

Back to London, find a note from 'George Orwell'[118] asking me to prepare a script for the B.B.C. 'Indian Programme'. Bokhari[119], his boss, is bound to turn down any script prepared by me. Just for the fun of preparing an original script undertaken the job – 'Hinduism in 2000 A.D.' Circulate my script informally among a few most intimate friends, Dr. J.C.G., Dr. A.D., Miss Ch. (of St. Andrews), and others – including the 'old war horse' Sir Francis[120]. All find it extremely interesting – only criticism the Sanskrit texts should accompany translations ... The text is rejected and the B.B.C. wishes to buy up the script so that it might not be published anywhere! Had a talk with Sir Frank Brown who said that Bokhari ... In other words you can't touch him, he is protected by Lady Gigg. See Dr. M ... (whom I christened Gama Muck!..S.N.G.) According to Gama Muck, Bokhari's Programme is generally irritating to the listeners in India and this is probably part of a deliberate policy to 'blackmail' the B.B.C. My comment: Mysterious are the ways of the Mighty!
... A.R.P. Wardens meeting.[121] The Home Securities Dept. has decided to cut down A.R.P. post in North Ealing and elsewhere; we are to be disbanded. A few days later, Berlin wireless in Russian announced: 'Berlin and London have come to a mutual agreement to disband A.R.P. services. Russians! Where is the second front promised in the Anglo-Soviet Treaty[122]?' We of the A.R.P. lodge a

117 Sudhindra Nath Ghose (1899–1965), Bengali novelist and art history lecturer for the India and Burma Association and Imperial Institute.
118 George Orwell (1903–50) worked as Talks Assistant for the Indian Section of the BBC's Eastern Service from 1941 to 1943.
119 Z. A. Bokhari (1904–75), director of the Indian Section of the BBC's Eastern Service.
120 Sir Francis Younghusband (1863–1942), former Indian Army officer; became known for his spiritual writings. He was also a member of the India Society and befriended many South Asians living in Britain at the time.
121 Air Raid Precaution.
122 1942 treaty establishing military and political cooperation between the British Empire and the Soviet Union during the Second World War and for twenty years after.

strongly-worded protest and are informed that in future we might run our centre, provided we do not cost the Government or the Local authorities a penny; we accept the offer. It means my refusing all engagements in the evenings.

... While checking up my typewriting bills, find that Ministry of Information has not paid for my articles sent to Mallet Street two months ago! Get in touch with Grafton Greene and am told that I ought not be impatient, and the articles have been accepted, and if I would care to write another one, and all the rest of it.

... Find that the British Council has – at long last – accepted my suggestion made more than a year ago and the pamphlet 'British Scholarship and Arabic Studies' and 'British Scholarship and Persian Studies' have come out; these are all right, but, Good God! These are so very different from what I proposed and they will not serve the purpose I had in mind.

... Had a long talk with the new High Commissioner[123]. According to him, I need not worry – because if the British authorities are satisfied with their stupid methods of publicity, it is not my job to point out their shortcomings. You will, he says, get no thanks but kicks for your troubles; they knew that the collapse of France was to a large measure due to their methods of diplomacy and publicity and they know today what they are doing ... As far as India is concerned, they are apparently following the devilish policy of insulting the Hindus, the majority community; if your article on 'Hinduism in 2000 A.D.' has been rejected it is simply because it did not sufficiently insult the Hindus; tackle diplomatic representation; preference is given deliberately to the Moslems; the Government of India's ministers in Great Britain, China, South Africa, etc are all Moslems – the only exception is Sir Girja Sanker Bajpai[124] and you know why ... Do not find any consolation in these remarks. Even if Sir Azil. H. happens to be right, my aim would be to strive to bring about a change in the existing state of affairs ...

Foreign Office needs a Press Attaché, one knowing French – with travelling experience and some knowledge of publicity work; apply for the job ... Sir Francis – without my asking for it – called on a few

---

123 M. Azizul Huque (1892–1947), Indian High Commissioner 1942/43.
124 Girja Shankar Bajpai (1891–1954), Indian Civil Servant.

of the mighty and reports ... I know all about the 'Colour Bar'[125] and the rest of it ...

They seem to be suspicious of those Indians who want the Axis Powers to be defeated. For the Bengali broadcasts the B.B.C. has finally hit upon A. Sen Gupta who a few weeks ago supported the policy of Gandhi, namely let Britain be defeated in this war! I find Bokhari giving preference to Mulk Raj Anand[126], Selvankar[127], and others of their school.

125 Term refers to racial discrimination, barring people from employment or lodgings.
126 Mulk Raj Anand (1905–2004), novelist and regular contributor to programmes for the Indian section of the BBC's Eastern Service.
127 Krishnarao Shelvankar (1906–96), Indian journalist and author, regular contributor to programmes for the Indian section of the BBC's Eastern Service. He was also a member of the India League.

11 *Extract from D.F. Karaka,*[128] *With the 14ᵗʰ Army (London: Dorothy Crisp and Co., August 1945), pp. 28–30.*
[British Library shelfmark T 2743]

The ordinary day-to-day news of the Burma and Arakan fronts[129] is not exciting enough to be reproduced here. Unlike the Battle for Stalingrad[130] or the *Blitz* over London, where every moment was exciting, there is not enough sustained dramatic action to report. In Arakan the war is slow-moving, long-drawn. It is the story of the taking of one hill-feature and the bombing of another. All this can become monotonous after a while.

But there is another story – a human story of the lives of men standing the test of endurance under the most difficult circumstances. It is a story of character and this to my mind will prove to be one of the important factors in the winning of the Burma war[131].

Wendell Willkie[132], that Great American, once said in a moment of

128 D. F. Karaka (1911–74), journalist. The book was first published in India in September 1944 by Thacker and Co Ltd (Bombay). The Indian edition features the following note, which is not included in the British edition: 'This is not meant to be a war book, nor an authoritative treatise in the 14th Army. It is nothing more than a personal diary. Every line of it has been adequately censored, though censorship has, I must admit, been particularly tolerant on this occasion. For this I am grateful.' The book contains despatches Karaka sent to *The Bombay Chronicle* while with the Indian Army in Burma during the first half of 1944.

129 The Arakan and Burma fronts became an increasingly important theatre of war with the threat of a Japanese invasion of India with its push towards Imphal and Kohima in March/April 1944. The Allies had first successes recapturing part of the Arakan in January 1944.

130 17 July 1942 to 2 February 1943; the Soviet Army defeated the Wehrmacht decisively, marking a significant turning point on the Eastern Front in the Second World War.

131 The Burma campaign of the Second World War was fought between 1942 and 1945. By 1944, the Allies were embattled along India's eastern border. Japanese attempts to invade India failed after Allied victories at Imphal and Kohima. The Allies successfully re-conquered Burma in 1944/45.

132 Wendell Willkie (1892–1944), American politician and activist. Trained as a corporate lawyer, he later became a diplomat, author and political activist. He is the author of *One World* (1943), which includes early ideas about international peace-keeping. The book became an international bestseller.

inspiration: 'Men need something more than arms with which to fight and win this kind of war.' Therefore, it is relevant to find out the thoughts and feelings of these men who are fighting on the Eastern front. What is it that keeps them there in the jungle – waiting, waiting, waiting?

It is not an easy thing to live month after month torn away from one's home and one's people. It is not pleasant to go for weeks without a bath in the dustiest of terrain. It is not very enjoyable to have to eat bully beef for most days of the week and to live life without wine, women and song. And at nights after a hard and tiring day it is not exactly restful to have to battle with flies and mosquitoes and to sleep for days together on the ground. The men in Burma and Arakan have been living like this for many months on end.

What is it that sustains them through all these hardships? It is true that in wartime British soldiers are conscripted. It is equally true that the Indian soldier often joins because the Army offers him a job. But there is something more in it than that.

In the minds of those British and Indian Servicemen who can think and feel, there are, generally speaking, two ideas that have taken root. To most men they have become essential to ordinary, decent living. The first is the idea that a soldier must fight for his *izzat*.[133] *Izzat* does not necessarily imply loyalty and patriotism. Its peculiar shade of meaning is difficult to bring out in a single English word. A man fighting for *izzat* fights as he thinks a man of his country is expected to fight. *Izzat* implies both self-respect and one's respect in the eye of his fellow men.

The other idea is that with all its faults the democratic idea of living is the only one worth while and that, properly developed, it is the only way of life that will bring peace and greatness and dignity to the civilized world.

I do not suggest that the ordinary soldier thinks in these terms all the time, but there is a vague idea of righteousness which he feels but cannot properly express.

There are many thinking men who feel that after the war there must follow re-orientation of ideas and an overhauling of the social systems in all the countries of the world. A revolution of the mind

133 Urdu term: honour and reputation of a person.

and thought of the common people there must come. It has been described as a Silent Revolution. Various conflicting ideologies must adjust themselves to find some common meeting ground on which the people of the world can live without strife. Already the Communists of Soviet Russia have dissolved their Comintern[134] and the Conservatives of Britain have overhauled their educational system. Tolerance and equal opportunity seem to be the keywords of the age that is to come – the age of the common man of the world. So that in the minds of many fighting men there is a certain feeling that this war is being fought for the preservation of ordinary, decent living, and it is something which these men believe is worth fighting for.

134 International Communist organization, founded in 1919 to fight by all means possible, including armed conflict, for the overthrow of the international bourgeoisie with a view to establish an international Soviet republic; dissolved in May 1943.

12 *Interview with Squadron Leader Mahinder Singh Pujji.*[135]
The interview took place in Gravesend on 18 February 2009. Present
were M.S. Pujji (D.F.C., B.A., L.L.B.), Dr Rozina Visram, Dr Florian
Stadtler.

FS: What was it like to arrive in Britain in 1940 at such a difficult
time, when the country was very much embattled and Indian soldiers
were called upon to help Britain out?

MSP: My answer will startle you. It's not conventional and nobody
expects that. I loved to join, because I loved flying and I saw an ad in
the newspapers inviting pilots for the Royal Air Force. What else did
I want? Because in India whenever I wanted to fly there were
problems; it's expensive. So I volunteered and twenty four of us from
all over India were selected for the Royal Air Force and we were all
excited. To answer your question, we were excited, looking forward to
it. I wrote to my Dad. He said, 'I don't understand what's gone wrong
with you. You have a good job, good wages, a good salary and here
you are going abroad to kill yourself. I think it's very stupid.' But I was
determined so I wrote a couple of more letters to him and I finally
put to him that I will go. So when we departed from Delhi they all
came to see me at the railway station. They were all crying and
feeling so bad, but it didn't affect me. We came to Bombay, then
from Bombay by ship to England. You have to remember that at that
time all services were suspended. Now, because we were King's
Commissioned Officers[136] we got the VIP treatment. We stayed in a
five star hotel, when we came to the ship we travelled first class and I
wrote back to my father after about a month and I said 'I'm having a
wonderful time. I've got my first class cabin, etc.' I mean I was well-
to-do but this was a luxurious thing, you see. So when we reached
Britain it was different. England with the black-out here, all dark. We
came to Liverpool and then to London. Here in London again we got

---

135 Mahinder Singh Pujji (1918–2010), one of twenty-four Indian pilots
   arriving in Britain to join the RAF in 1940. He flew missions in Britain,
   North Africa and Burma. For his gallant conduct in battle and his distinguished service he was awarded the DFC.
136 King's Commissioned Officers had authority over British troops.

the VIP treatment. The Secretary of State[137] was at the station to receive us and then after about a week again he said the King and Queen would like to meet you. What else did we want, it was wonderful; so we were taken to Windsor Castle, because Buckingham Palace was out of bounds at that time. There I met King George VI, the Queen and the two Princesses. They offered us refreshments. We sat down round the table with Princess Elizabeth sitting on my right and the other girl, Princess Margaret on my left ... So we got the VIP treatment and we had to undergo the RAF commercial course. It was called a crash course, but they said let's not call it 'crash'. While we were undergoing this course, we were experiencing the effects of the war. And that's where your question comes in, were we horrified, afraid. I personally, I can only speak for myself, I was enjoying every-thing. In the night when there were bombings, and every night there were bombings, and people would be asked to go to the shelters, I never went there. I've not seen a single shelter in the whole of the UK, because I didn't want to, I wanted to see. And at one time there was a warden who shouted to me 'get into the shelter' and I said it is very far. Then he said 'ok then you lie down'. Well I had to obey him. Then after that I was worried about my uniform – I was more worried about my uniform than the bombs.

What I am trying to say to you is that I wanted adventure, I got adventure and I loved it. Even when we were undergoing this course, we were bombed many times. The first time we were bombed was in Piccadilly in the Overseas League Club[138] during the weekend we were spending there along with one more colleague. And at about 2 o'clock in the night we were woken up 'come on get out, evacuate the place'. We asked what had happened. They said the building is on fire. So we didn't panic. Then I woke up the other chap. I don't drink, but he used to drink a lot. He was half-drunk and I woke him up and I said 'come on, let's go out' and he said 'oh no, let me sleep', even when the building was on fire. A few minutes after that again there were knocks on the door 'Come on get out, get out! You must leave the building.' We had to go out. What did we see? Fire engines all over

137 Leo Amery (1873–1955), Secretary of State for India, 1940–45.
138 During the Second World War, the Overseas League Club, St James's Street, London, offered accommodation for Empire troops on leave.

London. There were fires burning in many places and it is a horrific scene but it didn't frighten me, but of course we thought 'oh God, such a lot of problems coming'. I wasn't scared but it gave me an idea what it was like …

FS: and also what you were up against …

MSP: That's right and actually that will also apply a little later, when I started flying. At that time we were the receivers, the victims, just like other civilians, you see. I marvelled at the bravery and courage of the people of London especially because when we went to the movies there would be sirens and a sign would come up and the picture would stop and it would say 'anyone wanting to go to a shelter, there is a shelter right below the picture house, they may leave quietly' and I would see nobody leave. I looked left and right and nobody was afraid. They were all middle class ladies and they were very cheerful and I asked them: 'Are you really not scared, are you not afraid?' And they said 'No, our mothers are gone our children are gone; we are quite happy.' And every day in the evening there were dances and entertainments, that sort of thing.

FS: You mentioned that you were in London with lots of other friends, other Indian RAF pilots. Did you meet other Indian soldiers?

MSP: Where were they?

FS: They were stationed in the Midlands, Scotland and some were also in North Wales, but would visit London on leave.

MSP: I was in Scotland also, but I didn't meet them. The only people I met were civilians. They were students and there were families of high commissioners and others. They were the only people that we saw.

RV: Did you meet Krishna Menon in the India League?

MSP: Yes!

RV: I've seen your name as a member of the India League on one of their membership lists.

MSP: I knew him very well. I've got photographs of his ... I was very fond of him. He was a staunch Indian very much pro-Indian[139], at the same time he was not anti-war.

FS: Your main motivation to join the RAF was your passion for flying. When did you realise that you were up against a very serious threat?

MSP: After I started operational flights, and I was in the operations, then I found the horror of war. Because every time we went out on an offensive sortie, and at some times we went three times a day, all the pilots never came back. There were always one or two missing. That's the time I realised that we were up against something very serious. And because in the morning for breakfast there would be thirty pilots, for dinner there would be less. We would miss them, you see. In the morning when the commanding officer of the station would come, he would say 'for today's job I want two squadrons and not more than 24 people. Firstly I ask for volunteers, please raise your hands.' And everybody would raise their hands. I looked left and right and also raised my hand, because I wasn't sure what I was in for, you see. But these boys they knew they may be killed. You see flying, you have to understand, as you probably do understand, a pilot's life is very different from the army life ... For a pilot every time he takes off, he is in the thick of it. Every time he goes up he may not come down. That's the situation that relates to the fighter pilot, not the bomber pilot.

FS: For the bomber pilot it's a different story again.

MSP: Yes.

FS: Regarding the twenty-three Indian pilots that came with you, did you all fly in the same squadron together or were you actually spread out?

139 A supporter of Indian independence.

MSP: Twenty-four of us came, went for that course, six were rejected; they were not up to the standard, in spite of their qualifications. So that left only eighteen of us. Out of those eighteen they wanted the most brilliant to be fighter pilots and I was lucky enough to be one of them. I was among the six fighter pilots. The other twelve became bomber pilots. At that time, fighter pilots were the elite and when we went out in the streets in London, wearing the uniform, we wanted it to be known that we are not like other pilots. We were fighter pilots. So going against convention, we unbuttoned the top button of our uniform, until some senior officer said 'come on, come on, button up, button up' and we said 'sorry sir' and buttoned up, but as soon as he was gone we unbuttoned again. We wanted people to know that we were fighter pilots, you see. And during that period, I don't know if you are interested to know how I was treated here ...

FS: I am very interested in that ...

MSP: Wherever I went – incidentally I bought a car three months after I've been here – because I wanted to look around. I had come to enjoy and I like an adventurous life. I made the best of it, you see. Now, there was a movie, *Gone with the Wind*. There was a long queue starting all the way round the building, so I thought this must be a really good movie, so I decided to see it. So I parked my car, got out with an overcoat like that and stood at the back of the queue. As soon as the man in front of me saw my turban and uniform he said 'Sir you don't have to stand in the queue.' I said 'no, no, it's ok'. But he ushered me direct in front. No one objected or grumbled. When I went to the counter and I asked how much a ticket would be, they looked at me and she just kept on looking at me, because she had never seen an officer with a turban and with the air force wings on. She said no sir you come in for free. So why wouldn't I like a place like this? I enjoyed every minute of my stay in this country. I liked adventure, I loved flying, I liked the people I was with and I was treated far better than they were treated ...

FS: And did you get similar treatment within the RAF, within the Armed Forces?

MSP: Yes. There were six Muslims, five or six Sikhs and the rest Hindus; I mean we didn't even know what religion they were. My roommate was a Muslim. He never did any prayers and I didn't know how to do prayers. There was no such thing. Nobody ever said who they were. They never knew what their religion was and even if they did, it was a personal thing, we never discussed it. In the RAF they treated us with respect, but respect means curiosity. They would normally ask us where do you come from, what is it like in India, but they treated us as equals and they treated us as well as they possibly could. We had good manners because we had all come from very good families and we knew the British way of living, so that helped us, you see. That helped us to merge with these people. An American Volunteer Group came along also to the same station as we were. They were in the New Forest. They were unmannered. They would always keep on chatting and talking and the other RAF staff would say 'look at these people'. And then on the breakfast table we would have special garlic tablets and fish oil with a notice there 'for pilots only' and the sugar, with a notice 'one lump each please'. But the Americans each one of them would take three or four and we were looking at them and once I told them 'Look, only take one', but they said 'never you mind'. But we Indians were meticulously disciplined. We did exactly how we were expected to behave, whether it was off duty or on duty.

FS: You mentioned that despite the fact that you were all trained pilots already, you had to go through the intensive RAF training course. What kind of training did you actually have to go through? Was it frustrating for you having to have to wait, because obviously you wanted to get up in the air as soon as possible?

MSP: It was very frustrating, because we wanted to fly. And the course we went through fortunately did not include marking and rifle drill. Oh we were so lucky, thank God. I do not know how to hold a rifle even till today. That portion was eliminated from our course, but other courses – we had six or seven subjects – I remember only the majority: armament, all related to aviation, navigation, and they were extensive courses and we had to pass them all. We had to get 80% and above before we qualified, you see. So that was the part of the training including the flying training, which was no problem at all; and at the end of it there was a test and 18 of us qualified and we got our Royal Air Force Wings. There was a big parade and I think some big military – I forget who it was – came and presented us with these wings.

FS: I also see from photographs, you always wore your turban when you were flying. I gather you were the only Sikh pilot who asked to continue wearing his turban.

MSP: I'm the only Sikh pilot in the world who was able to fly with a turban on, because there were other Sikh pilots. They would readily take off their turbans and fly with a helmet and I thought it was terrible to fly without a turban, so I asked permission and they went out of their way to prepare a helmet for me with the earphones here like this which came on top of my turban. I was very grateful.

FS: And were you able to use the oxygen mask?

MSP: I could use it but not as efficiently as I should have. That I discovered when I fell ill six years later with TB. I got Tuberculosis and no one in our family or our neighbourhood had this. So they said the only reason was that I wasn't careful with my oxygen mask. Because I did fly at that time in the dogfights because I was so excited, so keen to find the other fighter and shoot it that I forgot about my mask and put it on later on, but it did affect my lungs. If I had had a helmet it would have been permanently on.

FS When you got your permission to wear your turban. How did the other Sikh pilots react?

MSP: They were furious. They used to tell me in the evening 'Pujji why have you done this thing now? This looks bad.' ... 'I'm telling you, put on the helmet'. We did discuss this. But I was adamant, you see. I was not willing to take off my turban.

Princess Sophia Dhuleep Singh selling "The Suffragette" outside Hampton Court Palace, where she has a suite of apartments.

1.1 Sophia Duleep Singh selling *The Suffragette* newspaper outside Hampton Court Palace, 1913.

We the Jamiat-Ul-Muslimin of whome the undersigned represent
but a small proportion to hereby strongly wehemently and and angerly
protest against the false, cowardly and maliciously slanderous statement made by H.G.Wells in his short History of the World against our
revered, respected and honoured prophet Mohammad (peace be upone Him)
and our holy Quran.

We cannot understand the reason which could have prompted Mr.
H.G.Wells to make his unfounted and nauseating, calumnious statement
without any justification knowing as he must have done that, he was
offending a nation of true believers, we cannot imagine by the greatest
stretch of imagination that Mr.H.G.Wells intended to insult such a
large number of Mohammadans and we throw out a challenge to him to
prove his assertions, we demand that Mr.H.G.Wells immediately with-
draw the allegation and offer us an immediate public apology.

We demand and crave your excellency kind intercession to bring
about a speedy and satisfactory ending to our very strenuous and
urgent complaint for which we shall for ever be indebted to your
most gracious excellency.

Petition to His Most Excellent the High Commissioner
for India presented by the executive Committee of The Jamiat-
UL-Muslimin on this 18th day of August 1938.

Mohamad Bukhari
Ghulam mohammad
a.h. ......
S.A. Shah
T.M. Shaukt
Allah Dad Khan
Syed Fazal Shah
Akhtar egul
G. Din
Budhu
F. mohammed
Z. Kim
N. Khan
Boato
MUKHTAR AHMED
...
Khudu

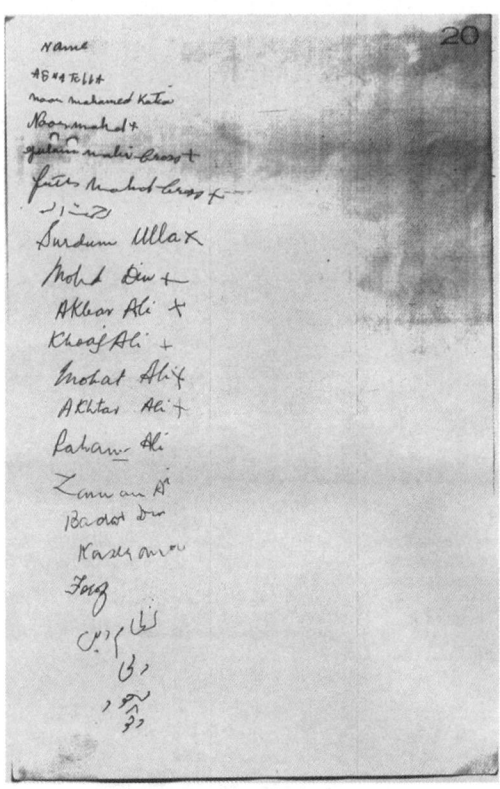

1.2 Petition of Jamiat-ul-Muslimin, August 1938.

1.3 Jamiat's protest march, 1938.

Son of Ind wins Britain's most Coveted Honour

The second Indian soldier to gain the V.C. was Naik Darwan Sing Negi, of the First Battalion 39th Garhwalis. Part of the British trenches had been taken by the enemy, and violent attacks to recover it were made. The final assault was delivered by the First 39th Garhwalis. A murderous fire was poured on the Indians by the Germans, but Darwan Sing, bayonet in hand, led the attack again and again. Half-a-dozen trench sections were soon cleared of the enemy, and there remained but three traverses to take when the heroic Indian was wounded by a bomb. He continued fighting until the last position fell.

2.1 Artist's impression of Naik Darwan, VC, on a bayonet charge with other Sikh soldiers, *War Illustrated*, 13 February 1915.

2.2 Highlander and Dogra soldiers in a trench with dugouts near Fauquissart, France, July 1915.

2.3 Indian RAF pilots meeting an English policeman on arrival in London, October 1940.

Sarojini Naidu

3.1 Sarojini Naidu from the frontispiece of the first edition of her collection of poems *The Golden Threshold* (William Heinemann, 1905).

PELICAN
BOOKS

W

PUBLISHED BY PENGUIN BOOKS

THE INTELLIGENT WOMAN'S GUIDE TO SOCIALISM, CAPITALISM SOVIETISM & FASCISM

IN TWO VOLUMES
(I)

BERNARD SHAW

WITH ADDITIONAL CHAPTERS SPECIALLY WRITTEN FOR THIS EDITION

6ᵈ

6ᵈ

COMPLETE

UNABRIDGED

3.2 Cover of Bernard Shaw's *The Intelligent Woman's Guide to Socialism, Capitalism, Sovietism & Fascism*, 1937. V.K. Krishna Menon was editor of the Pelican series.

3.3 M.J. Tambimuttu at work at the Manchester Square office of *Poetry London*, date unknown.

4.1 The Opening of the Imperial Institute, *Graphic*, 13 May 1893.

4.2 The renowned Indian dancer and choreographer Uday Shankar in a variety of poses influenced by the dance-drama form Kathakali, which originated in Kerala. *Illustrated London News*, 20 March 1937, p. 480.

4.3 Rafiq Anwar's company of Indian dancers at the Ambassadors Theatre in London, May 1943.

3

Textual culture and reception (1870–1950)

Ruvani Ranasinha

This chapter shows the varied and complex ways in which a dispro-portionately influential minority of South Asian writers, intellectuals and editors not only mediated representations of the subcontinent to British readers, but also infiltrated and shaped British literary, cultural and intellectual life more broadly. During the period under scrutiny (1870–1950) at least 80 different South Asian authors published over 180 books at the most conservative estimate.[1] While poet and artist Rabindranath Tagore (in Britain during 1878–80, 1890, 1912, 1913, 1920, 1921, 1926 and 1930) produced over 20 publications between 1912 and 1941, others produced a single volume. South Asian writers include poets Toru Dutt (in Britain during 1870–73) and Manmohan Ghose (1879–93), reformers and memoirists B.M. Malabari (1880s) and Cornelia Sorabji (1889–94, 1900–04, 1938–54), poet and politician Sarojini Naidu (1895–98, 1912–14, 1919–21 and 1931/32), novelist and activist Mulk Raj Anand (1930s and 1940s) and novelist, broadcaster and actress Attia Hosain (1947–98). As even this sample suggests, many of these figures straddled several roles. Thus their influence was often not purely literary. In fact, the majority of books by South Asians published in Britain during this period were non-fictional texts on imperialism, South Asian history, religion, art, anthropology or philosophy.

1 I refer only to books authored by South Asians published in Britain by British publishers.

The primary consumers of these South Asian books, often aimed at deepening the British public's understanding of 'the peoples of India', were English readers with some exposure to the subcontinent, or those 'anxious to understand Indian life',[2] alongside colonial subjects[3] within Britain. However, certain subcontinental figures penetrated wider British readerships, notably the journalist, lawyer and activist V.K. Krishna Menon mentioned in Chapter 1.[4] In his role as editor at Penguin he made economics, history and political theories accessible to a broader range of British readers through his founding of the innovative and affordable Pelican non-fiction paperback list (Figure 3.2). Similarly, the journalist, translator and editor Clemens Palme Dutt (who like his elder brother Ranjani Palme Dutt was an active member of the Communist Party of Great Britain) disseminated politics to left-wing readerships in his book *Labour and the Empire* (London: Communist Party of Great Britain, 1929), and as the editor of over nine volumes of Marx, Engels and Lenin published by Martin Lawrence. The Sri Lankan poet and critic

2 S.S. Townsend, 'Review of *The Coolie*', *Times Literary Supplement* (20 June 1936), p. 520.

3 South Asian readerships were not exclusively middle class, but complex and multilayered as the 1922 Muslim protest against H.G. Wells explored in Chapter 1 has shown.

4 V.K. Krishna Menon (1896–1974): activist, lawyer, labour Councillor for St Pancras and editor. He arrived in Britain in 1924. He studied law and then politics at LSE. In 1928 he joined and swiftly radicalized the India League campaigning for Indian Independence alongside key British and South Asian figures for the next two decades. Menon was editor at Bodley Head (1932–1935) where he launched the Twentieth Century Library Series and commissioned the publication of Nehru's autobiography, before becoming the founding editor of Pelican books the non-fiction, educational imprint of Penguin books in 1935. Krishna Menon's key role has been written out of official accounts of history of the Pelican Books, which began when Shaw gave Menon permission to produce a paperbound Penguin edition of *The Intelligent Woman's Guide to Socialism*. Menon played an important role within a broader context of British writers wishing to popularize their works. Other Pelican titles include H.G. Wells's *A Short History of the World* (Pelican, 1937) and Sigmund Freud's *Psychopathology of Everyday Life* (Pelican, 1938).

Tambimuttu engaged with 'English' poets, the liberal aesthetes of London's Soho and Fitzrovia he gravitated towards and published in his poetry magazine *Poetry London* (1939–50) [Source 6 and Figure 3.3]. Less well-known, but no less significantly, writer Sirdar Ikbal Ali Shah provided a scathing critique of 'refined, soulless ... English novels through Eastern eyes' in *The Bookman* in 1931,[5] while the writer and critic Ranjee Shahani wrote *Shakespeare Through Eastern Eyes* (Herbert Joseph, 1932).[6] The academic Narayana Menon's (b. 1911) fearless critique of Yeats in his book *The Development of William Butler Yeats* (Oliver and Boyd, 1942) was reviewed by Mulk Raj Anand and George Orwell. The writer and critic Balachandran Rajan (1920–99) wrote not on South Asian poets but on *Milton* (Chatto & Windus, 1947) and *Modern American Poetry* (Dennis Dobson, 1950).

This discussion, then, testifies to the enormous range of South Asian writers, and their different responses to the discursive pressures facing South Asian authors as colonial subjects. As noted in the Introduction, in the aftermath of Queen Victoria's 1858 proclamation granting colonial subjects 'citizenship' (in theory at least) when India was transferred to the British crown, and the opening of the Suez Canal, an increasing number of English-educated, Anglophone or bilingual travellers, reformists, memoirists, activists, novelists and poets visited the 'mother country'. At the same time, the 'Mutiny' of 1857 in India reified distinctions between the colonizers and the colonized. Such competing discourses of identification and demarcation of difference (sometimes within individual writers) mark the cultural output of the South Asian writers who visited or came to study in Britain. Certain writers, notably Alice (Sorabji) Pennell, saw their role as negotiating 'a voice for those of us who are loyal to Britain'. Pennell wrote, as John Murray describes, 'a loyal

5 Sirdar Ikbal Ali Shah, *The Bookman* (October 1931): 7–8, p. 8.
6 See also Shahani's review of Anand [Source 10]. Significantly H.G. Wells quotes at length from Shahani's *Shakespeare Through Eastern Eyes* to suggest that Indian minds are unable to comprehend the cynicism and criticism of religion by Englishmen in H.G. Wells, *Crux Ansata: An Indictment of the Roman Catholic Church* (2nd edn; Book Tree, 2000) pp. 68–71.

book with good effects as propaganda'.[7] Conflicting discourses of colonial discourse also influenced the British reception of these authors. In tracing the differing degrees of complicity and resistance of South Asian writers and their metropolitan interpreters to the dominant cultural values of each decade, this chapter offers a vivid portrait of the diverse, ideological viewpoints among South Asian Anglophone writers based in Britain, *alongside* their varied reception from different sections of British society and the literary establishment.

This discussion juxtaposes a selection of annotated sources from literary texts, reviews and correspondence in chronological order from 1870 to 1950. Locating each within its moment of cultural production and consumption enables me to chart the shifting historical and cultural conditions, and political, academic and commercial agendas that have influenced the selection, content and presentation of South Asian Anglophone cultural texts at different historical moments during the spread and decline of empire. Within an overarching imperialist political framework, we will see how the more liberal white British publishers, authors and reviewers supported the cultural inroads made by their South Asian counterparts in Britain, and identify the fissures within the not so homogenous imperial capital. Revealing a history of vigorous interaction between South Asian individuals and groups and their white British allies, this chapter places these South Asian figures not as part of an isolated 'South Asian tradition', but within the developing context of the historically local movements and milieus in which they found themselves. These include the Left Book Club (1936–48), a nexus between left-wing anti-imperialist white British (Harold Laski, Sidney and Beatrice Webb, Leonard Woolf, George Orwell) and South Asian and black intellectuals (Ranjani Palme Dutt, Ayana Angadi, Santha Rama Rao, Bhabani Bhattacharya, Paul Robeson) and the BBC which, operating similarly as a contact zone, facilitated and sustained the interaction between British and South Asian writers resident in

---

7 Cited in Shane Malhotra, 'Writing the Raj: The Search for Anglo-Indian Understanding in the Novels of Alice Sorabji Pennell', unpublished paper, *Making Britain* conference, 13 September, 2010.

Britain.[8] The reception and interpretation of these South Asian writers is explored in terms of intellectual and cultural exchange under the shifting conditions of colonial modernity and the move towards Independence.

Contrary perhaps to expectations, it was not only small publishers like Michael Joseph, but also a significant number of prestigious, influential publishing houses (notably Macmillan, Routledge, Oxford University Press, John Murray and Allen & Unwin) who provided a platform for these founding authors of South Asian Anglophone writing, sometimes taking on a financial risk.[9] Many of these publishers had prior interests in South Asian markets or in publishing British authors on South Asian topics.[10]

In addition to specialist journals (*The Asiatic Review*, 1885–1952,

8 For a fuller discussion of the role of South Asians in the BBC, see Ruvani Ranasinha, 'South Asian Writers and the BBC', *Journal of South Asian Diaspora* (March, 2010): 57–71.

9 Longmans (Dutt Family Album, 1870; Bhawani Singh, 1904; Maharani of Baroda, 1911), Routledge (Toru Dutt, 1880 and 1882; Prince Kapurthala, 1895), John Murray (Alice Pennell Sorabji, 1926, 1928, 1931; Ranjee Shahani, 1934), Oxford University Press (Cornelia Sorabji, 1924, 1932; Feroz Khan Noon, 1939), Macmillan (Rabindranath Tagore [13 books between 1913 and 1936]; Lal Behari Day 1883; R.K. Narayan, 1935), Edwin Arnold (J. Vijayatunge, 1935), Allen & Unwin (Tagore 1931, 1932; Gandhi 1930; Bhabani Bhattacharya 1930; S. Radhakrishnan, 1932 and 1939; Nehru, 1936; Raja Rao, 1938; R.P. Masani, 1939, Basanta Kumar Mallik, 1939 and 1940; Atul Chandra Chatterjee, 1948), Bodley Head (Nehru, 1936), Lawrence & Wishart (Mulk Raj Anand, 1935, 1936, 1937, 1940; C.P. Dutt, 1934, 1936, 1938, 1940 and 1942), The Hogarth Press (G.S. Dutt, 1929; R.P. Dutt, 1938, C.L.R James, 1933; Ahmed Ali, 1940), Chatto & Windus (Aubrey Menen, 1947; Balachandran Rajan, 1947), Cape (Anand, 1939, 1940, 1942; J. Chinna Durai, 1941), T. Fisher Unwin (Mallik 1907, T. Ramakrishan, 1915), Secker & Warburg (Cedric Dover, 1930, 1937, 1943), Michael Joseph (D.F. Karaka, 1938; Shahani, 1939; Sudhin Ghose, 1949).

10 John Murray published British authors, E. Yule's *Hobson Jobson*, F. Younghusband's books on India and Tibet, and E. Havell's books on Indian art. Edwin Arnold published Leonard Woolf's *Village in the Jungle* (1913) and E.M. Forster's *Passage to India* (1921).

Indian Art and Letters, 1925–64, *India and England,* 1937–39, *India Bulletin,* 1932–39, *Asian Horizon,* 1948–51), national newspapers and high-profile literary magazines published and reviewed some of these writers, sometimes to great acclaim. These magazines include *The New Age* (particularly after Orage became sole editor in 1909), *The Spectator* (especially when edited by Francis Yeats-Brown, author of the best-selling *Lives of a Bengal Lancer*), the *Times Literary Supplement, Life and Letters, Left Review, New Statesman* (particularly after Kingsley Martin became editor in 1931) and *The Bookman* (under the editorship of Hugh Ross-Williamson reviewed a number of books on India and Indian politics before being incorporated into the *London Mercury* in 1935, and then *Life and Letters* in 1939). *Life and Letters* also commissioned special issues on India including articles on 'Indian Folk Art' (by Ajit Mookherjee) and on the 'Music of India' (by Narayana Menon) in 1948.

Of course this is not to underplay the obstacles South Asians faced in penetrating British literary establishments, and the pressure to conform to Eurocentric standards. The nineteen publishers that turned down as well-connected a writer as Anand have become a proverbial marker of parochial white British literary hostility to South Asian writing. Several publishers, including Grant Richards, rejected the reformist Bengali poet-politician Sarojini Naidu's first collection. The 'cosmopolitan' publisher Heinemann took it on, but Naidu had to bear the cost – fourteen pounds plus binding charges – of the publication. Other writers had to self-publish (Balachandran Rajan privately printed 200 copies of his volume of verse *Monsoon* (1945) while at Cambridge), or publish with small, obscure presses: Sri Lankan writer Lucien de Zylwa published his novel *The Dice of the Gods* with Heath Cranston in 1917. As I have shown in my book *South Asian Writers in Twentieth-century Britain: Culture in Translation* (OUP, 2007), it was much harder for South Asians to be taken seriously as fiction writers than as social historians in the British context. Furthermore, while some publishers and reviewers were ahead of their time in giving South Asian writers a platform, this was not always offered to them on their own terms. Thus some of the sources trace the difficulties some South Asian writers faced in gaining acceptance by the more conservative members of the literary establishment. For example, the positive reviews of Anand's fiction in

Life and Letters (by Arthur Calder-Marshall, cited below, p. 170) and *The New Statesmen* contrast with those that dismiss his work in the *Times Literary Supplement* [Source 8].

Influential British metropolitan writers (Yeats, Pound, Gosse, Forster, Spender, Woolf) mediated between these South Asian writers and a hostile reading public often not prepared to engage with cultural difference, or only on specific terms, by writing reviews or prefaces to their work. Yeats's foreword to Tagore's *Gitanjali* (Macmillan 1913), Eric Gill's to Ananda K. Coomaraswamy's *Handicraft: One Hundred Examples of Indian Sculpture* (Luzac, 1914) and to Anand's *A Hindu View of Art* (Allen & Unwin, 1933), E.M. Forster's to Anand's *Untouchable* (Lawrence & Wishart, 1935) or Leonard Woolf's to Anand's *Letters on India* (Labour Book Service, 1942) are all fascinating documents raising questions about the relationships both supportive and patronizing, productive and restrictive between metropolitan 'mentor' and colonial 'ingénue'. Championing these writers, these introductions often seek to dictate the terms within which these authors are perceived, sometimes with pervasive influence, and provide insights into the ways in which their works were framed or co-opted into prevailing discourses of the moment.

Certain tropes reoccurred in the ways in which South Asian writers in Britain were conceived and represented. Notably, within and across the decades we see a simultaneous desire to both savour and domesticate the cultural specificity of these writers' South Asian contexts. The perceived Eastern mysticism of exoticized figures – Indian Theosophist Mohini Chatterji, Tagore, and subsequently of Tambimuttu – at distinct junctures reflect versions of primitivism, a valorizing of authentic differences to provide a critique of the host society's limitations, with their various white British interpreters seeking renewal through a romantic engagement with otherness. Simultaneously, other white British reviewers feared Tagore's poems would seem too 'fantastic and alien' to white British readers,[11] just as decades later, the subcontinental backdrop of Indo-Anglian novels by Anand, Raja Rao, Ahmed Ali and other writers were seen as too different and of marginal interest to the metropolis, therefore

11 A.C. Brock, 'Mr Tagore's Poems', *Times Literary Supplement* (7 November 1912), p. 492.

requiring special pleading. Hence these early South Asian writers' negotiations with mainstream literary culture are important, not only because they are not widely appreciated, but also because they have an impact on later literary formations.

While noting recurrent tropes, this chapter is also sensitive to cultural shifts, and identifies several strands of cultural representation within which subcontinental writers shaped British literary and cultural life at specific historical moments. Books were crucial to the representation of India particularly within Britain; India was endlessly 'translated' to the West especially in the late nineteenth and early twentieth centuries by a range of British individuals (Edwin Arnold, Max Müller), but also South Asian writers in Britain and organizations including Home Rulers, theosophists and British feminists. A dominant motif within these translations was the figure of spiritual India. But literary culture in Britain was crucially shaped not only by the figure of India or Asia, but also by the South Asian writers themselves, notably diverse Indo-Anglian poetic voices [Sources 1 and 3], travellers' tales in the form of an outsider's views of Britain [Sources 2 and 4], and reports on the colonial territories. Some of these accounts particularly emphasized Britain's economic exploitation of India, such as D. Naoroji, *Poverty and Un-British Rule in India* (Swan and Sonneschein, 1901) and R.C. Dutt's influential *The Economic History of India* (Gollancz, 1904) that inspired the work of J.A. Hobson and was considered so inflammatory that Gollancz agreed not to publish it in India. Others notably (Malabari and Sorabji) focused on the trials of subcontinental women. Supported by English and Irish feminist friends of India, such texts were also sometimes deployed as a way of justifying imperialism [Source 5b]. Subsequently, in the 1930s, a period that saw increasing political tensions between Indian nationalists and the British, the shift away from a reformist agenda towards bids for independence and the Round Table Conferences 1930–32, there was an emergence of heightened political writing, notably Gandhi and Nehru's politicized autobiographies when – as Sarojini Naidu describes in 1931 – the 'Gandhi craze' was at its height in London.[12] The late

12 Sarojini Naidu, Letter to Padmaja and Leilamani Naidu, 23 September 1931. Cited in M. Paranjape (ed.) *Sarojini Naidu: Selected Letters, 1890s–1940s* (New Delhi: Kali for Women, 1996), p. 248.

1930s and 1940s saw increasingly forceful critiques of imperialism in South Asian journals like *Indian Writing* [Source 7] published in Britain, and in narratives of nationalism in the novel form published by writers like Ahmed Ali and Anand in Britain [Sources 9 and 10], and articulations of transnational traditions of cosmopolitanism in the work of other early diasporic writers Sudhin Ghose, Aubrey Menen, and Raja Rao that foreshadow the post-1980s Indian writers' subsequent engagement with cosmopolitanism.

Early poetic voices: imitation or influence? Toru Dutt and Manmohan Ghose

Everyone knows the usual style of books written by the Bengali Baboo. He delights in long words and complicated sentences ... He puts the adjectives in the wrong places, and applies the most inappropriate expressions to every emotion ... He deals with words much like a child before it can read, plays with a box of letters.[13]

The Bengali poet Toru Dutt (1856–77) is noted as an exception to this 'usual style' in this review: 'In Miss Dutt we find none of these faults.' This review displays the prejudices Anglophone writers faced at this historical moment, and underscores the role Dutt played in dispelling them. Educated in Nice and Cambridge, Dutt published a collection of translations and commentary on French poets, *A Sheaf Gleaned in French Fields* (Bhowanipore: B.M. Bose, 1876; republished by Kegan Paul in 1880), that caught Edmund Gosse's attention as a reviewer for the *Examiner*. A couple of reviews dismissed Dutt's collection as 'a literary curiosity, as being a product of a Bengali lady'.[14] But the majority (over 12 reviews) praised 'the absolute and unaffected exactness' of her translations into French, excusing occasional lapses by reflecting that 'it was the work of a Hindoo girl of less then mature age'.[15] After Dutt's untimely death the reviews become noticeably more emphatic in praise.

Dutt, 'arguably the first modern Indian poet in English', was also one of the earliest of the many individuals who 'translated' India

13 Anon. 'Review', *The Examiner* (4 January 1879), p. 25.
14 Anon. 'Various Versifiers', *The Graphic* (4 November 1876), n.p.
15 Anon. 'Review of Toru Dutt', *The Examiner* (26 August 1876), p. 967.

to the West in this period.[16] Her Western poetic manner is seen
to override the subcontinental content of her poetry: 'As to the
ballads, we say, Miss Dutt's manner is better than her matter. The
legends of Hindostan are less interesting to Europeans than those
of almost any other people'.[17] The combination of Dutt's talent
and extreme youth contributes to the fascination with her poems.
Dutt is prized in raced and gendered terms as 'the most remarkable literary example of the precociousness and the strange
imitative power which is noticeable in many Oriental races, and
perhaps even more so in the women of these races than the men'.[18]
While labels such as 'imitative' or 'derivative' get frequently
employed in a colonial context rather than influence, Oscar Wilde's
review of the young poet Manmohan Ghose (1869–1924),
schooled in Britain, is striking in terms of its emphasis on the
influence (of Keats and Arnold) rather than imitation [Source 1].

Spiritual India?

Towards the end of the nineteenth century, key translations of Hindu
and Buddhist texts by Max Müller, Annie Besant (*The Bhagavad Gita*,
1895), Edwin Arnold (*The Light of Asia or the Great Renunciation*,
1879) alongside R.C. Dutt (the *Ramayana* and the *Mahabharata*) –
the first Indian to translate the epics of ancient India into English
verse – contributed to the widespread identification of India with the
spiritual within Britain. This identification developed along multiple
strands that include the Theosophical Society, the impact of the
Bengali reformer Keshab Chandra Sen and the National India

16 R. Chaudhuri, 'The Dutt Family Album', in A. Mehotra (ed.), *A History
   of Indian Literature in English* (London: Hurst, 2003), p. 65. See also
   Inderpal Grewal's scholarship on Toru Dutt in *Home and Harem:
   Nation, Gender, Empire and Cultures of Travel* (Leicester: Leicester
   University Press, 1996).
17 Anon. 'A Hindoo Poetess', *Pall Mall Gazette* (21 April 1882), n.p.
18 Anon. 'Review of Toru Dutt', *Guardian* (17 August 1881), p. 7, emphasis
   mine.
19 Keshab Chandra Sen visited Britain in 1870. His Brahmo-religious
   ideals had developed through an interaction with Christian particularly
   Unitarian beliefs. With his assistance, Mary Carpenter founded The

Association.[19] It emerged as a key discourse within books published in Britain on South Asia by Europeans, and by South Asians themselves.[20]

The Theosophical Society's London publishing house produced Besant's *Bhagavad Gita* and later F.L. Woodward's *Dhammapada* (1921). However, it is also significant as an early publisher of books by South Asian writers: Mohini Mohara-Dhara's *Krishna* (1917), Jinarajadasa Curupumullage's *Life, Death and What Then?* (1918), *Art and the Emotions* (1920), *The meeting of the East and the West* (1921), *Offering* (1928); J. Krishnamurti, *Christ the Logos* (1920), *At the Feet of the Master* (1927) and *The Divine Vision* (1928). In parallel, a subcommittee of the National India Association, the Northbrooke Indian Society, became a separate society in 1881, and its secretary Dr. S.A. Kapadia alongside L. Cranmer-Byng became the driving force behind John Murray's successful *Wisdom of the East* series (1905–58) of 122 English translations of classic Eastern works including ancient Hindu, Buddhist, Islamic and Parsi texts, translated by South Asian and British writers.

Müller's *Upanishads* (1879) is reviewed as 'aptly the first volume of the Sacred Books of the East, for India naturally occupies, or rather should occupy the first place in the East'.[21] On the other hand, *The Saturday Review* condemns the work of such European scholars as revealing 'their hatred of the faith in which they have been nurtured'. It argues that these 'translations will bring a conviction of the futility of such hopes and the vanity of expecting any spiritual illumination in "the light of the East"'.[22] Such negative responses identify the very target audience of these texts 'designed as ambassadors of peace and goodwill between East and West': 'all who imagine that there is no knowledge worth having outside Europe and America'.[23]

National India Association in aid of social progress in India in Bristol in 1870.

20 Dent published a number of comparative studies of great world religions by South Asians.

21 A. Burnell, 'The Sacred books of the East', *The Academy* (9 August 1879), p. 95.

22 Anon., 'Review of Müller's *Upanishads*', *The Saturday Review*, 48(1) (13 September 1879), p. 335.

23 Puff, citing *Bristol Mercury* review of *Wisdom of the East*.

In contrast, *The Examiner's* review of Arnold's *The Light of Asia* conveys the high esteem in which certain informed Westerners regarded Buddhism. It notes that 'higher ethic doctrines are scarcely to be found anywhere'. However, the same review reinforces Orientalist tropes of a feminized, ethereal Orient defined in contrast to the masculine, active West: 'If the sweetness of language sometimes cloys our Northern taste, which requires more of the rugged and heroic as a foil to the ethereal, the fault must not be charged upon the singer, but upon the subject with which he deals.'[24] The translations by British writers received more coverage than those by their South Asian counterparts, but the few reviews were respectful to the 'distinguished' subcontinental contributors across all religions.[25]

The first 4,000 copies of Dr S.A. Kapadia's *The Teachings of Zoroaster and the Philosophy of the Parsi Religion* (John Murray, 1905) were sold out, resulting in a further printing of 4,000 copies in a second edition in 1913. This kind of circulation suggests the extent to which spiritual versions of the Indian subcontinent preoccupied British readers, and conditioned and determined the reception of many South Asian writers within Britain. This emphasis resurfaced during both the First[26] and Second World Wars particularly by those who sought refuge from the perceived crises in the 'already deadened' West.[27]

---

24 Anon., 'Review of Arnold's *Light of Asia*', *The Examiner* (30 August 1879), pp. 1127–8.

25 Burnell, 'The Sacred books of the East', p. 95.

26 See Bahman Wadia, *Will the Soul of Europe return?* (LTP, 1921).

27 Kathleen Raine, letter to Tambimuttu, November 22 no year, Ms. Coll. Poetry London-New York Records, 1943–1968, Columbia University Rare Book and Manuscript Library. On the eve of the Second World War, Tambimuttu's assimilation into literary society was similarly mediated by essentially spiritual representations of the subcontinent, set up in opposition to Western rationality. Echoing Yeats's preface to Tagore, Kathleen Raine wrote 'Tambimuttu discerned in my work some quality India looks for and recognizes whereas England, since the war … does not. All is cerebral and political and mundane whereas Tambi heard in my verses some music of the soul; the music of the goddess Sarasvati who was the form in which he himself worshipped the

Of course it was Rabindranath Tagore (1861–1941) and his poetry that became for many British readers the ultimate embodiment of 'essential Oriental mysticism'.[28] Like Keshab Chandra Sen, Tagore was seen to regenerate religion in Britain, and provide a valuable spiritual counterbalance to the advance of scientific thought, alongside an antidote to Western modernity. Tagore's *Gitanjali* 'has a serenity which is one of the lessons most needed by the restless peoples of the West'.[29] This kind of response served to figure the East in mystical, philosophic and contemplative terms and as ultimately ineffectual in contrast to the West, defined as an arena of action and power: 'in spite of spiritual accomplishment, [Tagore's] work exercises, upon a Western mind at any rate, a somewhat numbing effect'.[30] Mary Sturgeon's priviliging of Naidu's poems above Tagore's reinforces this ideological construction. She affiliates Naidu's '*sensuous, human* and *passionate*' poems to 'the energy of the active, strenuous West' unlike the 'mystical, philosophic, and contemplative' Tagore who remains 'oriental to that degree'.[31]

Yeats's famous preface to *Gitanjali* similarly invoked a static 'supreme culture': 'Mr Tagore, like the ... unbroken ... Indian civilisation itself has been content to discover the soul and surrender himself to its spontaneity.'[32] Yet as Elleke Boehmer has shown, Tagore's impact on his Western interpreters is much more complex: Tagore suggested to Yeats a model for a national poet: 'how to give form to a national culture emerging out of a [shared] history of

Goddess'. Kathleen Raine, *India Seen Afar* (Devon: Green Books, 1990), p. 12. See also J. Curupumullage, *The War and after: a Theosophist's Viewpoint* (LTP 1940).

28 Anon., 'Review of *Gitanjali*', *The Athenaeum*, No. 4438 (16 November 16 1912), n.p.

29 Anon., 'Review of *Gitanjali*', *The Athenaeum*, No. 4458 (5 April 1913), p. 382.

30 Anon., 'Review of *Gitanjali*', 1912.

31 M. Sturgeon, *Studies in Contemporary Poets* (London: George C. Harrap, 1916), 235–46, at 236, emphasis mine.

32 W.B. Yeats, Introduction, Rabindranath Tagore, *Gitanjali* (London: Macmillan, 1916), p. xiv.

dispossession'.[33] Yeats insists 'and yet we are not moved because of its strangeness, but because we have met our own image ... heard perhaps for the first time in literature, our voice as in a dream'.[34] Another review similarly urges British readers to see Tagore's *Gitanjali* as more than 'the curiosities of an alien mind'. Furthermore, it praises Tagore, not for his acculturation to Western poetic norms (as in the reception of Toru Dutt), but again as a *model for English poets*, as 'prophetic of the poetry that might be written in England if our poets could attain to the same harmony of emotion and idea. That divorce of religion and philosophy which prevails among us is a sign of our failure of both'.[35]

While these responses do not escape the taint of Orientalism, it is important to remember that not everyone saw Eastern ideas as a force for the expansion and enrichment of traditional Western outlooks. In a letter to Lady Ottoline Morrell (dated 24 May 1916), the novelist D.H. Lawrence scorned the veneration of Tagore, revealing how the denigration of 'Eastern' civilizations enabled an inflated sense of European self-worth among certain constitutiencies:

> I become more and more surprised to see how far higher, in reality, our European civilizations stands than the East, India or Persia ever dreamed of. *And one is glad to realize how these Hindus are horribly decadent* and reverting to all forms of barbarism in all sorts of ugly ways. *We feel surer on our feet*, then. But this fraud of looking up to them – this wretched worship-of-Tagore attitude – is disgusting. 'Better fifty years of Europe' even as she is.[36]

Tagore's diverse, variegated reception by his English and Indian interpreters in Britain (a subject that warrants a chapter in itself) complicates any easy identification of Tagore with a spiritual

33 Elleke Boehmer, '"Immeasurable strangeness" in Imperial Times: Leonard Woolf and W.B. Yeats', in N. Rigby and H.J Booth (eds), *Modernism and Empire* (Manchester: Manchester University Press, 2000), pp. 93–111, at pp. 101–2.
34 Yeats, *Gitanjali*, p. xviii.
35 Brock, 'Mr Tagore's Poems', p. 492.
36 D.H. Lawrence, *The Collected Letters* (London: Heinemann, 1970), p. 451, emphasis mine.

India.[37] Moving beyond the broad strokes of this familiar paradigm, my reading of the reception of Tagore and other early South Asian writers shows how they became focal points for broader debates comparing British and South Asian societies, and underscoring the intellectual connections between East and West, which had political implications with regards to reconfiguring relations between the colonizers and the colonized.

'Oh, East is East and West is West, and never the twain shall meet ...'

Just as Rudyard Kipling's (1865–1936) literary output perpetuated racial stereotypes in the popular imagination, this much quoted idea ascribed to his poem *The Ballad of East and West* (originally published in 1889) casts a shadow over South Asian writers and their reception in Britain in the early twentieth century. As is still the case, the closing lines that modify the apparent racial hierarchies ascribed to Kipling are omitted:

> Till Earth and Sky stand presently at God's great Judgment Seat;
> But there is neither East nor West, Border, nor Breed, nor Birth,
> When two strong men stand face to face, though they come from
> the ends of the earth!

Consequently, the aphorism is usually taken to refer to the complete incommensurability between (superior) European and (inferior) Asian cultures. This idea of cultural incompatibility with a stress on irreconcilable, absolute difference had a powerful hold on the public imagination.

37 S. Radhakrishnan contests certain British representation of Tagore's outlook as the result of his absorption of Christianity, but also argues Tagore is neither the anarchist nor the unpractical being he is supposed to be. See S. Radhakrishnan, *The Philosophy of Tagore* (Basingstoke: Macmillan, 1918). For a similar refutation of perceptions of Tagore as a mystic poet, see E.J. Thompson, *Rabindranath Tagore* (Oxford: Oxford University Press, 1926). While British reviews fête Tagore's self-translated poem, Sukumar Ray writes on the impossibility of doing justice to Tagore's original Bengali in 'The Spirit of Tagore', *The Quest* (October 1913): 40–57.

In response, South Asian writers in Britain in the first few decades of the twentieth century published several books concerning the juxtaposition and comparison of both cultures and peoples: notably art-historian Ananda Coomaraswamy's *The Deeper Meaning of the Struggle between Englishmen and Indians* (Essex House Press, 1907), Manmath Mallick's *Orient and Occident, A Comparative Study* (Fisher Unwin, 1913), Jinarajadasa Curupumullage's *The Meeting of the East and the West* (London Thesophical Publishing House, 1921) and A. Yusuf Ali's *India and Europe* (London: Drane's, 1927). Tagore reconfigures Kipling's lines, maintaining that differences enable a more productive cross-cultural union:

> East is East and West is West – God forbid that it should be otherwise – but the twain must meet in amity, peace and understanding; their meeting will be all the more fruitful because of their differences.[38]

Such an emphasis reflects these authors' own preoccupations, stimulated by the cultural contact of which they were products as a consequence of their hybridized colonial upbringing in South Asia, now enhanced by their experiences within Britain. Syed Ameer Ali attended the Universal Races Congress held in London in 1911 in order to debate this question of relations between East and West.

Equally, these authors may have been encouraged to explore these questions at the instigation of publishers, as part of a broader agenda and recognition that sympathetic international relations are fostered through cultural contact between 'civilizations' as reflected in certain British journals of the period. Positive reviews of Tagore and Naidu's poems contest Kipling's 'over-quoted aphorism' presenting these authors 'as a cultural link between India and England'.[39] However, Naidu's role is privileged over Tagore's because she is writing in *English*: 'without the ... distortions of translation'.[40] *The Bookman* notes while Naidu retains her

---

38 Cited in Anon., 'Dinner for Mr Tagore', *The Times* (13 July 1912), p. 5.
39 F. Bickley, 'Review of Naidu's *The Broken Wing*', *Bookman*, 52(308) (May 1917): 51.
40 Mrs Westbrook, address, *The Indian Magazine and Review*, No.686 (November–December 1931): 130. Naidu's brother Harindranath

'Indian nationalism and ... soul ... East and West blend in her Anglophone poetry in a way which they do not ... in Tagore's.'[41] Sturgeon's question how 'two children of what we are pleased to call the changeless East, under conditions nearly identical, should have produced results, which are so different?' articulates the burden of representation on these early writers .[42] This burden includes remaining 'truly native to [one's] motherland' as the *Bookman* reviewer was careful to stress.

In the wake of the formation of the The India Society (established in 1910) to promote South Asian arts and culture in Europe through the exhibitions and lectures of Tagore and Coomaraswamy, *The Asiatic Review* began a regular section in 1915 entitled 'Where East and West meet' delineating events in Britain relating to 'Asiatic questions'. The *Africa and Orient Review* had a similar aim of educating the British public, and facilitating a dialogue with her colonies. This dialogue appears particularly crucial during strained Indo-British relations, as the publisher's preface to Sarath Kumar Ghose's romantic novel *The Prince of Destiny, the New Krishna* (1909) indicates. Ghose's tale of the princely state of Barathpore functions as an allegory of India's relationship with Britain. The publisher's foreword highlights the importance of this 'Indian view' of the 'present unrest' referring to Indian protests against the limited Morely-Minto reforms noted in the introduction to the present volume. It warns British readers of the 'unseen peril in India': 'if Britain loses India it will be by the neglect of such a warning.'[43] Writing a preface to his own novel *My Brother's Face* (1924) as 'an Indian anxious for the future of India' in the aftermath of 'the Amritsar shootings' in 1919, Dhan Gopal-Mukherji alludes to how this event marked a fissuring of shared Indo-British

---

Chattopadhyaya's plays are praised in similar terms: 'India speaking with careful mastery, not in an unknown, but in an English voice'. S. Fowler Wright, introduction, Harindranath Chattopadhyaya, *Five Plays* (High Holborn: Fowler Wright), p. iii.

41 Bickley, 'Review of *The Broken Wing*', p. 51.
42 Sturgeon, *Studies in Contemporary Poets*, p. 235.
43 Foreword, S.K. Ghose, *The Prince of Destiny, the New Krishna* (London: Rebman 1909), p. iv.

viewpoints.[44] Immediately after Amritsar, in a private letter to Gandhi, Naidu observes, 'I see a woeful and even wilful ignorance and indifference about India in England – it is so precious to us, so rotten, a valueless thing to them, except as enriching their coffers.'[45] Later the House of Commons' debate on the excessive use of martial law in the Punjab in the wake of Amritsar shatters 'the last remnants of [Naidu's] hope and faith in British justice and goodwill towards the new vision of India. It is in vain to expect justice from a race so blind and drunk with the arrogance of power'.[46] These documents reveal the cracks behind the public rhetoric of accommodation and mutual understanding exemplified in the tellingly short-lived *Britain and India* (January–December 1920) set up as a monthly journal to promote understanding and unity between the two countries.

The trials of Indian women

> The Simon Commission [1930] came to the conclusion that the women's movement in India holds the key of progress, and the results it may achieve are incalculably great.[47]

From the late 1800s debates on India's fitness for independence circled around the status of Indian women. This emphasis is both reflected in and shaped by books by South Asian writers in Britain and their reception. The Age of Consent Act of 1892 is attributed in no small measure to Bombay social reformer and journalist B.M. Malabari's tireless campaigns in Britain and India, and the impact of his and R.C. Dutt's publications, alongside Syed Ameer Ali's writings on status of Muslim women.

Malabari's visits to Britain coincided with those of the affluent, anglophile Parsi-Christian supporter of British rule in India, Cornelia Sorabji. Her conservative opposition to women's franchise

---

44 D. Gopal-Mukherji, *My Brother's Face* (New York: Dutton, 1924), p. iv.
45 Naidu, letter to Gandhi, 17 July 1919. Cited in M. Paranjape (ed.) *Sarojini Naidu*, p. 142.
46 Naidu, letter to Gandhi, 15 July 1920. Cited in M. Paranjape (ed.), *Sarojini Naidu*, p. 147.
47 Cited in F.H. Brown, 'Review of Cornelia Sorabji's *India Calling*', *The Observer* (27 January 1935), p. 7.

on the grounds that the majority of Indian women were uneducated, illiterate and not ready for the vote contrasted with Malabari and Naidu's positions. Scrutiny of the reception of Malabari and Sorabji's works reveal an appetite for stories of the suppression of subcontinental women: Malabari's 'missionary zeal, [which] a year or two ago, did much to familiarise the more thoughtful classes in this country of the miseries inflicted by child-marriage, the cruel servitude of the Hindu widow, the oppressive seclusion of the Mahommedan wife'.[48] A reviewer of Cornelia Sorabji's seminal work, *Between the Twilights: Being Studies of Indian Women by One of Themselves* (London: Harper, 1908) writes in the same vein:

> The social aspects of Hinduism are so sinister to the ordinary English eye ... that no excuse is needed for a book which enables us to look with comprehension if not sympathy ... [at] the injustices fostered by the Hindu ... that blight Hindu women which our author has helped alleviate.[49]

In contrast, Naidu's insistent demands for an independent Indian nation centred around women's equality and participation in public life was in part a response to the reliance of British feminists on this kind of trope of the helpless, backward Indian woman. Drawing on R.C. Dutt's translations Naidu's poems [Source 3], like her numerous political speeches, constantly refer to the self-determination, self-reliance and self-sacrifice of the heroines Damayante, Savitri, Sita, and Draupadi of the ancient *Ramayana* and *Mahabharata* epics. Her insistence on the precolonial emancipated position of women in ancient India contests the received idea that the British were responsible for emancipation of Indian women. Instead Naidu was motivated by an international feminism of equals: 'Mrs Naidu spoke of the delight it gave her ... to realise the indivisible kinship of women the world over'.[50] In *The Awakening of Asian Womanhood* (1922) Irish suffragette, theosophist and campaigner for Indian home rule Margaret Cousins delineates Naidu's impact on like-

---

48 Anon., 'Review of *The Indian Eye of English Life*', *The Saturday Review*, 76:1 (11 November 1893), p. 548.

49 Anon., 'Review of *The Indian Eye of English Life*', *Athenaeum*, No. 4220 (30 January 1909), p. 129.

50 Our London Correspondent, *Guardian* (12 November 1913), p. 8.

minded women. Nevertheless, the focus on the suffering of Indian women remained a persistent trope among metropolitan reviewers. Stanley Rice's praises Sita and Santa Chatterjee's *Tales of Bengal* (OUP, 1922) as 'delicate six short stories of Bengali women' that 'speak of the suffering which is the lot of women, especially Indian women'.[51]

Travellers' tales[52]

Reports of the colonial territories from 'migrant' writers such as Malabari's *Gujarat and the Gujaratis* (London: W.H. Allen & Co., 1882), Rev. T.B. Pandian's *Indian Village Folk, Their Works and Ways* (London: Elliot Stock, 1898), Cornelia Sorabji's *Sunbabies*, and J. Vijayatunge's later vignettes of Ceylonese village life, *Grass for My Feet* (1935) remained popular among metropolitan readers, although later South Asian fictional narratives would be seen through such an anthropological lens.

Some of these writers also wrote memoirs offering converse views of Britain: Malabari appraises English culture in his *The Indian Eye on English Life* (Constable: 1893 Source 2), as does Rev. T.B. Pandian in *England to an Indian Eye* (Elliott Stock, 1897). Notwithstanding their 'outsider' status, both implicitly distinguish themselves from Jewish Londoners whom they depict as aliens and as oppressed. This kind of book flourished at the turn of the century with T.N. Mukharji's *A Visit to Europe* (Newman, 1889), Manmath Mallick, *Impressions of a Wanderer* (T. Fisher Unwin, 1907), and T.

51 S. Rice, 'Indian writers of English verse and prose', *Indian Art and Letters*, xiv(2) (1940): 94–104, at 102.
52 For developing scholarship on colonial South Asian travel to Britain and the West, see M. Fisher, S. Lahiri and S. Thandi, *A South Asian History of Britain* (Oxford: Greenwood World, 2007), pp. 110–18; A. Burton, 'Making a Spectacle of Empire: Indian Travellers in Fin-de-Siècle London', *History Workshop Journey*, 42 (1996): 127–46; Simonti Sen, *Travels in Europe: Self and Other in Bengali Travel Narratives, 1870–1910* (New Delhi: Orient Longman, 2005); J. Majeed, *Autobiography, Travel and Postnational Identity* (Basingstoke: Palgrave, 2007); and S. Lahiri, *Indian Mobilities in the West, 1900–1947: Gender, Performance, Embodiment* (Basingstoke: Palgrave, 2010).

Ramakrishnan's *My Visit to the West* (T. Fisher Unwin, 1915).

This trope of a stranger's fresh perspectives on aspects of everyday British life recurs across the decades. Bhawani Singh's *Travel Pictures* (Longmans, 1912) is similarly praised for having 'found matter for observation in customs ... over which an European would pass in silence'.[53] It resurfaces thirty years later in strikingly similar terms in George Orwell's description of British-based South Asian contributors' role in the BBC Indian Service's cultural broadcasts to India (1941–43) designed to maintain India's conditional allegiance in Britain's war effort, in the fraught context of the Quit India movement of the early 1940s, as noted in the introduction to this volume:

> The general idea is to interpret the West, and in particular Great Britain, to India, through the eyes of people who are more or less strangers. An Indian, or a Chinese perhaps, comes to this country, and because everything is more or less new to him he notices a great deal which an Englishman or even an American would take for granted.[54]

Across the decades the role expected of the 'Asiatic' stranger is a complex one: the writer should not be too fawning, but neither too critical. One review while appearing to welcome 'the contemplation of ourselves as others see us' is unable to actually accept Malabari's criticism of English peoples' 'unbelief', 'mania for novelty', and propensity for 'drunkenness' that 'debases, brutalises and maddens', on the grounds that Malabari has neither 'long residence in the country' nor 'natural kinship'. The reviewer criticizes the very criteria that supposedly enable Malabari to provide a fresh, exterior perspective. Malabari is accorded authority *only* when he criticizes Indian customs, such as the position of women in India: 'In Asia woman is a vague entity, a nebulous birth absorbed in the shadow of artificial sexuality. This seems a hard saying, but Mr. Malabari should know.'[55]

Decades later in the 1930s, Indian journalist D.F. Karaka's criti-

53 R. Gorrell-Barnes, 'An Indian Prince in Europe', *Times Literary Supplement* (5 December 1912), p. 561.

54 G. Orwell, Memo, 1 Feb. 1942, in P. Davison (ed.), *The Complete Works of George Orwell: All Propaganda is Lies* (London: Secker & Warburg, 2001), p. 163.

55 Anon. 'Review of *The Indian Eye on English Life*', *Calcutta Review*, 105(209) (July 1897): 107–20, at 107 and 110.

cisms of racism in British society were similarly dismissed as jaundiced and unreliable, at a time of heightened Indo-British tensions.[56] This suggests how texts that challenge hegemonic notions of Englishness and offer transforming reflections were often dismissed. Similarly, the limits of expertise of the South Asian fiction-writer were clearly demarcated. A review of Anand's novel *The Coolie* claims:

> The author would have done better to leave out the English characters, for all of them are caricatured, from the baronet – who apparently wore a frock coat when visiting his mill in Bombay – downwards in the social scale ... He is at his best when he is concerned with the simplest phases or incidents of life.[57]

Another reviewer of Anand's novel *The Village* (1941) writes 'There is some ... penetrating perception of Indians – he wisely avoids that stumbling block the 'European'.[58]

In contrast to Malabari's critical Indian eye, the more appreciative memoirs (discussed in Chapter 4) of the conservative patrician Prince Raja Jagatjit Singh of Kapurthala made more palatable reading. Kapurthala praises Queen Victoria's 'real affection for her Indian subjects [which] has done much to encourage them in feelings of loyalty for the throne'.[59] Similarly entranced by 'our wonderful empress' the Dowager Maharani of Cooch Behar, Sunity Devee's *Autobiography of an Indian Princess* (1921) describes meeting

56 'There is too much bitterness, too little thought in this book', cited in Anon., 'Review of Karaka's *Oh you English!*', *Times Literary Supplement* (18 July 1935), p. 468. The prolific Parsi journalist D.F. Karaka studied law at Oxford (1930–33) and published an article on the Colour Bar in 1934 in the *Daily Herald*, one of the most widely read newspapers in the 1930s. He also dealt with the position of Indians in the British Empire and Britain in his books *The Pulse of Oxford* (Dent, 1933) and *I Go West* (M. Joseph 1938). See Chapter 2, p. 97 for a discussion of his role as war correspondent.

57 Townsend, 'Review of *The Coolie*'.

58 H. Brown, 'Review of *The Village*', *Times Literary Supplement* (15 April 1941), p. 215.

59 Raja Jagatjit Singh of Kapurthala, *My Travels in Europe and America 1893* (London: Routledge and Sons, 1895), p. 62.

'the ideal ruler ... linked to our hearts across "the black water" by *silken chains* of love and loyalty' in a telling textual slippage.[60]

Malabari, Pandian and other writers' collective critique of British slums and social inequality provide a reversal of British perceptions of India's poverty and lack of 'civilization', and challenge linear narratives of imperial progress. Yet Prince Kapurthala's diary converges with other memoirs across the social spectrum when he notes the recurrent 'striking dissimilarity of thought and action between the Englishman in his own country and the same individual when he is abroad'.[61] This kind of contrast alerts British readerships to the broader discrepancy between notions of 'Englishness', of justice and fair play, and how these are distorted in praxis in the rule of the colonies: a contradiction that fuelled a dominant strand of the anticolonial movement.

Narratives of nationalism (1930–1950)

As noted in the introduction to this volume, during this period London was a hotbed of radical nationalist activity, and a cosmopolitan, dynamic site for contact between a wide variety of students, intellectuals and anticolonial activists from a range of colonial backgrounds. The synergy and intersection between Indian and Irish cultural nationalism [Source 11], and Left politics and literature (the Left Book Club, Progressive Writers' Association) continued to characterize many of the literary endeavours of South Asian writers and their interactions with British writers, especially during the Roundtable discussions, the lead-up to the Second World War, and the subsequent failure of the Cripps' Mission discussed in the introduction. Collectively, Krishna Menon's *Condition of India* (India League, 1932 with a foreword by Bertrand Russell), R. Palme Dutt's *India Today* (1940), and Nehru among others' numerous India League pamphlets, alongside E.J. Thompson's *The Reconstruction of*

---

60 S. Devee, *Autobiography of an Indian Princess* (London: John Murray 1921), p. 108.
61 Kapurthala, *My Travels in Europe*, p. 161. See also N.L. Dodd, *Reminiscences, English and Australian* (Calcutta: M.C. Bhownick, 1893), p. 40.

India (1930) formed a distinct strand of Leftist political writing on India distinguished by rational analysis, logical argument and accessible prose.[62]

Simultaneously, sources [6, 7, 9, 10] reveal not only the diverse, ideological viewpoints among South Asian writers in Britain, but also how different diasporic individuals in Britain dealt with these tensions in diverse ways, and expressed these differences in a range of literary texts at this historical juncture; how different newspapers and critics received these texts, and how ideological ties override racial ones. In contrast to the dismissive review [Source 8] reproduced from the *Times Literary Supplement*, British novelist Arthur Calder-Marshall (1908–92) provides a much more sympathetic view of Anand's novel *Across the Black Waters* and 'his extraordinary technique'. Anticipating the response 'that a war book devoted to the experiences of Indian privates would have too narrow an outlook to appeal to English readers', Calder-Marshall cites men in his barrack room who 'have picked it up and gone on reading it in every minute of their spare time. Though Anand's characters are always Indians, they are always soldiers; his quiet realism, his assessment of fear and homesickness and loyalty and groping intelligence enable the white conscript to identify himself with the Indians'.[63]

Gandhi and Nehru dominated the 1930s not only politically but also publishing more than eight books in London between 1930 and 1941. *The Spectator* noted *Mahatma Gandhi's Ideas* 'should be studied by all who would try to understand the subtle beauty of the Hindu mind', while *The New Statesman* observed 'it throws valuable light on the career of a remarkable personality'.[64] Both reviews reflect the distinct ideological views of each magazine's constituent readerships.

The reviews of Nehru's *Autobiography: With Musings on Recent*

62 See S. Khilnani, 'Gandhi and Nehru', in Mehrotra (ed.), *A History of Indian Literature in English* (London: Hurst, 2003), p. 148.

63 A. Calder-Marshall, 'Review of Anand's *Across the Black Waters*', *Life and Letters Today*, 28(4) (1941): 83–8, at 85–6.

64 Cited on cover *Mahatma Gandhi's Ideas*, ed. C.F. Andrews (London: Allen & Unwin, 1930).

Events in India (Allen Lane, 1936)[65] and *India and the World* (Allen & Unwin, 1936) were mostly appreciative but not all were as 'ecstatic' as Sunil Khilnani suggests.[66] *The Times* attempts a fair appraisal: 'a sincere book written in an easy, almost conversational style, a book to read, however much one may disagree with the outlook of the author'. Anticipating scepticism from British readers, it emphasizes that the book written during Nehru's incarceration by British authorities (1934–35) is 'on the whole ... without bitterness'.[67] Another review of Jawaharlal Nehru's *India and the World* (Allen & Unwin, 1936) conveys the impact of Nehru's de-familiarizing 'unflattering portrait' on more responsive white British readers, encouraging them to re-imagine themselves differently: 'It is however well, that we should see ourselves through the eyes of an Indian nationalist leader, unflattering though the portrait may be to our self-esteem'.[68]

However, five years later the reviews of Nehru's writings become more critical as the tensions between Indian nationalists and the British establishment come to a head, and the future of empire is hotly debated in London as well as Delhi. A review of *Unity in India* (Lindsey Drummond, 1941) describes Nehru as occupying an 'extremist position that India will be satisfied with nothing less than complete severance of the British Connexion'. Under the heading 'Discordant Voices', it compares Nehru's book with more moderate books by Indians (J. Chinna Durai, *The Choice before India*, Cape, 1941; N. Awab Zada, *Indian India*, Quality Press, 1941; and Feroz Khan Noon, *India*, Collins, 1941) that 'counter Nehru's extremist position'.[69] Another *Times Literary Supplement* review adopts a

---

65 The subsequent edition in 1941 was reprinted as *Towards Freedom: The autobiography of Nehru*. This reflects the changes in the political context and in Nehru's status. It was reprinted in 1947, 1949 and 1962 suggesting its popularity.

66 S. Khilnani, 'Gandhi and Nehru', in Mehrotra (ed.), *A History of Indian Literature in English*, 135–56, at 150.

67 Anon., 'Review: Nehru's Autobiography,' *The Times* (28 April, 1936), p. 10.

68 Anon., 'Review of Nehru's *India and the World*,' *The Times* (14 July 1936), p. 11.

69 P. Tomlinson, 'Review of Nehru's *Unity of India*', *Times Literary Supplement* (6 September 1941), p. 446.

similar strategy: Zada's *Indian India* is more 'objective' than Nehru's 'one-sided' book because Zada is critical of customs such as *purdah* and comments on the 'benefits' of British rule.[70] At this juncture, Allen Lane and Allen & Unwin's role in publishing Nehru and Gandhi, contrasts with the more conservative reviewing culture that mirrors political attempts to disunite Indian nationalists and marginalize Nehru as an extremist.

The Second World War (1939–1945)

As Chapter 2 explores, the outbreak of the Second World War had a decisive impact on the diverse range of South Asians resident in Britain at this time, producing conflicting responses. For some of the writers the war represented a crisis within Western civilization. In 1940, contributing editors to *Indian Writing* [Source 7] Iqbal Singh and Ahmed Ali forcefully voiced their objection to the use of Indian soldiers as 'cannon fodder' and to 'the spectacle of innocent nations and peoples being dragged into the homicidal delirium of rival imperialist powers'.[71] Others like Shahani saw such critiques as undermining support for a global war effort against a greater evil, fascism, at a critical juncture [Source 10]. As Source 6 indicates, Tambimuttu distanced himself from radical anticolonial politics and evaded any discussion on the debates on the role of South Asians in the war – although see his own war poems discussed in Chapter 2. A fervent supporter of Indian Independence, Eurasian writer Cedric Dover served in the Royal Army Ordnance corps during the war [Source 12].

As a comparison of contemporary magazines *Poetry London* [Source 6] and *Indian Writing* [Source 7] makes clear, Tambimuttu's privileging of aesthetic and formal considerations contrast sharply with *Indian Writing*'s radical critique of Indo-British relations and politicized conceptions of 'culture', and more broadly with the nationalist, anticolonial agendas of his more politically motivated activists in London. Some of these writers like Anand were engaged

---

70 E. Blunt, 'Discordant Voices', *Times Literary Supplement* (10 May 1941), p. 220.

71 Ali et al., Editorial, *Indian Writing*, 1(2) (1940): 68.

with cultural fronts against fascism in Europe, while developing a critique of colonialism that often put them in difficult positions. Anand's interaction with the BBC Indian Service is a particularly illuminating case study of the tensions between anti-fascism and anti-imperialism during the 1940s, and underscores the role of metropole, and its institutions and intellectual milieu in fostering diasporic nationalism.[72]

The Second World War meant that not only were promises of independence shelved, but that mainstream British readerships were more sensitive to 'anti-English' propaganda. Correspondence in the Hogarth Press Archive reveals the extent to which fiction – notably Ahmed Ali's *Twilight in Delhi* (1940), a depiction of a well-off Muslim family in Delhi during the 1920s in the context of a vehement Indian nationalism that retaliates against 'the foreign yoke' – was censored by 'national policy'. The printers refused to print Ahmed Ali's novel *Twilight in Delhi* (1940) unless 'subversive' passages were deleted and passed by the Censor. John Lehmann finally called on Harold Nicholson and E.M. Forster to support the publication.[73] Nevertheless the late 1930s and 1940s saw a peak of writing and coverage of these South Asian writers, particularly because of the rise of left politics as a counter to rise of fascism, as evinced by the Left Book Club and the Progressive Writers Association discussed earlier. The *Left Review* (1934–38) and the *New Statesman* (under David Garnett's editorship) reviewed all the key South Asian novels of the 1930s and 1940s and featured South Asian reviewers. While journals like *Indian Writing* were short-lived with small circulations, D.P. Chaudhuri set up the New India Publishing Company in 1946: the first publishing venture run by Indians to supplement the more ephemeral pamphlets, leaflets and news bulletins produced by Indian organizations in Great Britain, to meet the need for 'Indians themselves' to evaluate Western as well as Indian social issues.

72 See Ranasinha, 'South Asian Writers and the BBC', 2010.
73 Reading Special Collection MS2750, Ahmed Ali, *Twilight in Delhi*, 1940–54.

Nationalism/Transnational cosmopolitanism

In their early foundational fictions published in Britain, Anand, R.K. Narayan and Raja Rao projected homogenizing visions of an 'Indian' language, space, narrative forms, through their representation of Gandhian heroes, Indianized English, their concern for the Nehruvian ideal of socialism and their projections of such idealized spaces like Malgudi and Kanthapura. After independence, Indo-Irish author Aubrey Menen alongside Sudhin Ghose and Nirad C. Chaudhuri, also domiciled in England, and Raja Rao (in his later work written from self-exile in France) began to negotiate with the consciousness of the greater world and the international communities. This shift away from nationalist politics appears in work of the new poets Nissim Ezekiel, Francis Newton Souza and Maria Souza who emerged at independence, visiting Britain at this time. Through their collective internationalism these writers questioned the boundaries of national self and space and can be located within an existing tradition of cosmopolitanism that prefigures contemporary cosmopolitan writers such as Salman Rushdie and Amitav Ghosh. This tradition of cosmopolitanism within Indo-Anglian writing dates back to the nineteenth and early twentieth centuries, and had run parallel or even counter to the contemporary nationalistic fervour with intellectuals like Rabindranath Tagore and Mabendranath Roy providing trenchant criticism of nationalism, and spiritual philosophers like Sri Aurobindo (Ghose) providing visions of cosmopolitanism in works like *The Ideals of Human Unity*. These ideas of 'world-citizenship' stem in no small way to these writers' encounters with Britain and their South Asian visions of 'home' and 'abroad'.

Source material for Chapter 3

1 Extract from Oscar Wilde's[74] review of *Primavera: Poems, by Four Authors* (Stephen Phillips, Laurence Binyon, Manmohan Ghose, Arthur S. Cripps) (*Oxford: B.H. Blackwell, 1890*)[75] in the *Pall Mall Gazette* (24 May 1890), p. 3.
[British Library shelfmark: LON LD28 NPL]

'*PRIMAVERA*'
In the summer term Oxford teaches the exquisite art of idleness, one of the most important things that any University can teach, and possibly as the first fruits of the dreaming in grey cloister and silent

74 The Anglo-Irish poet and playwright Oscar Wilde (1854–1900) met Ghose in London.
75 The inclusion of Manmohan Ghose and the non-mention of his Indianness in the *Primavera* collection itself can be read as an example of late nineteenth-century homogenization of Indian literary expression with British literary expression, but this can also be seen as an inclusive gesture. In her review of *Primavera* in *The India Magazine*, the journal of the National India Association, Mary Hobhouse suggests that Ghose's 'familiarity with English habits and feelings have enabled him to express sentiments common to both English and Indian youths, in fluent English verse'. She observes that Ghose's 'English ideas and modes of expression makes it more natural to use the expression "fellow-countryman" rather than Indian fellow subject'. This denotes how markers and ideas of citizenship resonate in these literary critical discussions. M. Hobhouse, 'Review of *Primavera*', *The India Magazine*, No. 238 (October 1890): 512. See also Leela Gandhi's discussion of Manmohan Ghose in *Affective Communities: Anti Colonial Thought, Fin-de-Siècle Radicalism, and the Politics of Friendship* (Durham, NC: Duke University Press 2006), Chapter 6.

garden, which either makes or mars a man, there has just appeared in that lovely city a dainty and delightful volume of poems by four friends. These new young singers are Mr. Lawrence Binyon, who has just gained the Newdigate; Mr. Manmohan Ghose, a young Indian of brilliant scholarship and high literary attainments who gives some culture to Christ Church; Mr. Stephen Phillips, whose recent performance of the Ghost in 'Hamlet' at the Globe Theatre was so admirable in its dignity and elocution, and Mr. Arthur Cripps, of Trinity. Particular interest attaches naturally to Mr. Ghose's work.[76] Born in India, of purely Indian parentage, he has been brought up entirely in England, and was educated at St. Paul's School,[77] and his verses show us how quick and subtle are the intellectual sympathies of the Oriental mind, and suggest how close is the bond of union that may some day bind India to us by other methods than those of

76 Manmohan Ghose (1869–1924): poet and academic. His younger brother was the politician and spiritual leader Sri Aurobindo (Aravinda Ghose). Ghose's anglophile Bengali parents Dr Dhan Ghose and Swarnalata Basu sent him to be educated in Britain at the age of seven. He attended Manchester grammar school (1881–84) and then St Paul's School in London (1884–87) where he became close friends with fellow poets Lawrence Binyon and Matthew Arnold. Binyon credited Ghose for introducing him to Indian literature, art and philosophy. Ghose won an open scholarship to Christ Church, Oxford which he took up in 1887, where he was regarded as an outstanding scholar and became fluent in Greek. Binyon joined Oxford a year later and they collaborated on the poetry publication *Primavera* published in 1890. Ghose returned to India at the age of 25 after his father's death and held various academic posts. He went on to publish *Songs of Love and Death* (Blackwell 1926).

77 Wilde's distinction between Ghose's 'purely Indian parentage' and upbringing in England is a remarkably early counter to received ideas of origins as a determining factor.

78 Wilde's review is significant in its anticipation and wish for different 'bond of union' between India and Britain other than 'those of commerce and military strength'. Wilde makes this point at a time when roughly 85 per cent of India's imports in the 1880s and 1890s came from Britain, which amounted to almost 20 per cent of all foreign exports during the period. See T. Parsons, *British Imperial Century, 1815–1914* (Oxford: Rowman & Littlefield, 1999), p. 50.

commerce and military strength.[78] There is something charming in finding a young Indian using our language with such care for music and words as Mr. Ghose does.[79] Here is one of his songs:-

> Over thy head, in joyful wanderings
> Through heaven's wide spaces, free,
> Birds fly with music in their wings;
> *And from the blue, rough sea*
> *The fishes flash and leap;*
> There is a life of loveliest things
> O'er thee, so fast asleep.
>
> In the deep West the heavens grow heavenlier,
> Eve after Eve; *and still*
> *The glorious stars remember to appear;*
> The roses on the hill
> Are fragrant as before:
> Only thy face, of all that's dear,
> I shall see nevermore!

It has its faults. It has a great many faults. But the lines we have set in italics are lovely. The temper of Keats, the moods of Matthew Arnold have influenced Mr. Ghose, and what better influences could a beginner have? Here are some stanzas from another of Mr. Ghose's poems:-

> Deep-shaded will I lie, and deeper yet
> In night, where not a leaf its neighbour knows;
> Forget the shining of the stars, forget
> The vernal visitation of the rose;
> And, far from all delights, prepare my heart's repose.

79 There is some fetishizing of Ghose, 'something charming in finding a young Indian using our language with such care' in Wilde's review. Yet the Oxford aesthete sees Ghose as part of a group of like-minded writers sharing 1890s aesthetics, styles and tropes. Ghose was known to 'The Rhymers' Club' set of young London poets that included Yeats, Arthur Symons and Ernest Rhys. Ghose was particularly close to members Lionel Johnson and Ernest Dowson. Dowson wanted to include Ghose's work in *The Book of the Rhymer's Club* (1892) but Ghose could not afford to share the cost of the expenses.

O crave not silence thou! too soon, too sure,
Shall Autumn come, and through these branches weep;
Soon birds shall cease, and flowers no more endure;
And thou beneath the mould unwilling creep,
And silent soon shall be in that eternal sleep.

Green still it is, where that fair goddess strays,
Then follow, till around thee all be sere.
Lose not a vision of her passing face;
Nor miss the sound of her soft robes, that here
Sweep o'er the wet leaves of the fast-falling year.

The second line is very beautiful, and the whole shows culture and taste and feeling. Mr. Ghose ought some day to make a name in our literature.

... On the whole 'Primavera' is a pleasant little book, and we are glad to welcome it. It is charmingly 'got up', and undergraduates might read it with advantage during lecture-hours.

2 Preface, Behramji Merwanji Malabari,[80] *The Indian Eye on English Life or Rambles of a Pilgrim Reformer* (London: Archibald Constable & Co., 1893).
[British Library shelfmark ORW.1986.a.2101][81]

PREFACE TO FIRST AND SECOND EDITIONS
These notes were jotted down during a brief holiday, mainly with the object of diverting thought. They are now offered to the British Public by a stranger in blood, in creed, and in language; by a student too early withdrawn from the advantages of systematic study.

In contrasting the New Civilisation with the Old, the writer cannot pretend always to maturity of experience or soundness of conclusion. All that he claims is a friendly conversation, in open council, with

80 Behramji M. Malabari (1853–1912): Parsi poet, journalist and reformer. He made several visits to London from Bombay to win support for a reform of Hindu marriage customs from British reformers. His publications include Behramji Malabari, *Gujarat and the Gujaratis* (London: W.H. Allen & Co., 1882); *Infant Marriage and Enforced Widowhood in India: Being a collection of opinions for and against received by B.M. Malabari from representative Hindu gentlemen and officials and other authorities* (Bombay: Voice of India Printing Press, 1887); *An Appeal from the Daughters of India* (London: Farmer and Sons, 1890); *India in 1897* (London: A.J. Combridge, 1897) and *Bombay in the Making: being mainly a history of the origin and growth of judicial institutions in the western Presidency, 1661–1726*, with an introduction by George Sydenham Clarke (London: T. Fisher Unwin, 1910).

81 This preface provides an insight into the way Behramji M. Malabari offers his book in a somewhat tongue-in-cheek manner 'to the British public by a stranger in blood and creed and language'. *The Calcutta Review* discussed in this chapter emphasizes this perspective. The book itself functions as an early reversal of the dominant metropolitan gaze with an Indian writer's ambivalent commentary on English social mores, alongside a social and topographical mapping of London. For scholarship on Malabari, see Inderpal Grewal, *Home and Harem: Nation, Gender, Empire and Cultures of Travel* (Leicester: Leicester University Press, 1996) and A. Burton, *At the Heart of Empire: Indians and the Colonial Encounter in Late-Victorian Britain* (Berkeley: University of California Press, 1998).

Englishmen on the one hand and Indians on the other. That granted, he hopes these rambles in the field of Humanity may not prove altogether to be the ramblings of a vacant mind.

Bombay, Xmas 1891.

3 Sarojini Naidu,[82] 'Damayante to Nala in the Hour of Exile' from *The Golden Threshold* (London: Heinemann, 1905), pp. 75–6.
[British Library Shelfmark T39389]

'Damayante to Nala[83] in the Hour of Exile'
(A fragment)

> Shalt thou be conquered of a human fate
> My liege, my lover, whose imperial head
> Hath never bent in sorrow of defeat?
> Shalt thou be vanquished, whose imperial feet

82 Sarojini Naidu (nee Chattopadhyaya 1879–1949): poet and politician. Naidu was born in Hyderabad to Aghorenath Chattopadhyay and Varada Sundari, who were both involved with the Brahmo Samaj, a Bengali movement founded in 1828 by Rammohun Roy and committed to educational, religious and social reform. Naidu won a scholarship from the Nizam of Hyderabad to study in England. She chose King's College London and arrived in London with Annie Besant for the first time in April 1895, and stayed until 1898. She returned in 1912–14 and after meeting Gandhi in London in 1914, she worked with him on all the *satyagraha* campaigns from 1919 onward. She visited London and Ireland in the period 1919–21, arriving with a delegation giving evidence to the Joint Committee on Indian Reforms on the question of female suffrage. She joined Gandhi (and 75,000 followers) on the coast at Dandi to harvest salt and contravene British salt laws, and led a raid on Dharasana Salt Works, and on release from Yeravda prison she returned to London in 1931/32. Naidu authored four volumes of poetry: *The Golden Threshold* (1905), *The Bird of Time: Songs of Life, Death and the Spring* (1912) and *The Broken Wing: Songs of Love, Death and Destiny* (1917), as well as *The Feather of the Dawn* which appeared posthumously in 1961. Anna Snaith shows how contrary to conventional interpretations of Naidu, her poetry (emerging from a fin-de-siècle, late Romantic, aesthetic) and feminist nationalism were interlinked. See A. Snaith, 'Sarojini Naidu in London', Postcolonial Seminar, King's College, 19 March 2010 and *Colonial London: Gender, Nation and Modernity 1890–1945*, Cambridge University Press, forthcoming.

83 The poem is an example of the feminist revivalism discussed in this chapter. Damayante, a mythological princess from the *Mahabharata*, overcomes the trickery of demi-gods by recognizing her husband, King

Have shattered armies and stamped empires dead?
Who shall unking thee, husband of a queen?
Wear thou thy majesty inviolate.
Earth's glories flee of human eyes unseen,
Earth's kingdoms fade to a remembered dream,
But thine henceforth shall be a power supreme,
Dazzling command and rich dominion,
The winds thy heralds and thy vassals all
The silver-belted planets and the sun.
Where'er the radiance of thy coming fall,
Shall dawn for thee her saffron footcloths spread,
Sunset her purple canopies and red,
In serried splendour, and the night unfold
Her velvet darkness wrought with starry gold
For kingly raiment, soft as cygnet-down.
My hair shall braid thy temples like a crown
Of sapphires, and my kiss upon thy brows
Like cithar-music lull thee to repose,
Till the sun yield thee homage of his light.

O king, thy kingdom who from thee can wrest?
What fate shall dare uncrown thee from this breast,
O god-born lover, whom my love doth gird
And armour with impregnable delight
Of Hope's triumphant keen flame-carven sword?

Nala, in several guises. Damayante is celebrated for her loyalty and her
strength in exile. Naidu went on to write many more poems of this kind,
notably 'Nasturtiums'.

4 Maharani of Baroda and S.M. Mitra, *The Position Of Women in Indian Life*[85] (*Longmans Green and Co*, 1911), pp. 13–15.
[British Library shelfmark 2356.b.7.T4302]

Though not permitted to play an immediate part in English politics, women here, even without the vote, are, as they can be if they chose in all countries of the world, a great indirect power. Particularly in English society do we find ladies taking up the causes of their husbands, fathers and brothers, helping them to win election-fights, charming the hearts of constituents by their enthusiastic championship, and promoting the welfare of the poor and suffering by their appearance on public platforms. In England they have peculiarly ample opportunities for such influence, since there for many centuries social and political functions have been harmoniously interwoven. Those who would form an idea of the wide influence exercised by ladies of the highest rank in England, will find a very thoughtful and interesting account of this phase of political life in some of Mrs Humphrey Ward's novels, and, in a lighter vein, in Lady Randolph Churchill's witty and amusing 'Reminiscences'.

But how has it fared with the woman of India through the long centuries since civilization dawned upon her land? We have seen that

84 The Maharani of Baroda co-authored (with S.M Mitra) the first book published in Britain by the wife of a ruling Indian chief. Titled, Chimnabai II, she was the second wife of Sayaji Rao III (1863–1939), a descendant of the Marathi family which had created the state of Baroda in Gujarat during the eighteenth century. (He was installed on the gadi or throne of Baroda in May 1875 and invested with governing powers in December 1881). She went on to become the first president of the All-India Women's Conference in 1927.Their daughter married Maharajah of Cooch Behar and became the daughter-in-law of Sunitee Devy (discussed in this chapter, pp. 168–9).

85 Although entitled *The Position Of Women in Indian Life*, as reviews note, the Maharani of Baroda's book aims to show 'her untravelled Indian sisters the wide avenues of employment and interest open to their sex in Europe or America'. Reviews negate the 'bookworm diligence of her collaborator' S.M. Mitra in contrast to the Maharani's 'talented personality'. F.H. Brown, 'The Women of India and the West', *Times Literary Supplement* (12 October 1911), p. 384.

in the early ages of the world while Northern Europe was yet steeped in barbarism, she enjoyed the highest public honour, and was a participant in all the wisdom and activities of her day. Neither should we omit to recall the fact that in ancient India the laws of Manu and of other Hindu lawgivers touching women's property rights, known as the Stridhana, though introduced about 2,000 years ago, have hardly yet been excelled by any laws in any country in the West. Mahomedan women also have long enjoyed their share in the property of their male relations, which is granted to them by their laws.[86] But succeeding years in India checked women's glory. Our land became prey to external invasion and internal strife, and in the ceaseless struggle that was waged, the cause of learning, and with it that of woman, was forced to the wall. The arts of peace had no room to expand, and with the constant warfare that devastated India in the seventeenth and eighteenth centuries, women's interests and education fell into a depth of miserable neglect and suppression, from which they are only now recovering.

Fortunately there is no longer need to ask by what means woman may rise to a higher and nobler position. The woman of the East, like the woman of the West, may depend on this, that in the proper use of education lies the salvation of her sex. As long as she is ignorant, so long will she remain dejected, oppressed, incapable of sharing man's pursuits and ideals. But educate her, help her to organize her efforts, and she will respond to the changed environment. It is

---

86 The Maharani draws attention to the relative empowerment of women in 'the early ages of India ... while Northern Europe was yet steeped in barbarism'. This alongside her emphasis in her preface on the selective importation of Western feminist ideas rather than 'too slavish imitation of Western notions' (Preface, p. xv) suggests the articulation of alternative sub-continental feminisms within Britain, that distinguishes between 'intelligent observations of other lands' and the wholesale, uncritical adoption of its customs: 'My countrywomen should bear in mind the need to guard against too slavish imitation of Western notions. Every country by intelligent observation can learn something from other lands, but at the same time each should try to preserve its own racial characteristics, just as each sex should endeavour ... to make the most of its own peculiar distinctions of character' (Preface, p. xv).

education and useful organizations that alone can give true freedom and enlightenment. By means of women's Associations woman has gained in Europe and America, and should acquire in the East, a broader outlook, wider interests, a brighter, more generally useful attitude to life than she has had in the past. High and low, rich and poor, all are shaking themselves free of the lethargy and indifference which seemed in past ages to envelop them.[87] The movement is confined to no one rank or creed, country or continent; its professed aim is the uplifting of the feminine mental and public status throughout the world. In this matter there can be no separation of the interests of the sexes. The good of woman is the good of man. Many famous men have recognized the importance to the race of the well-being of its women-kind, and have agreed that it is by the character of its women that the standard of a nation's civilization is judged.

87 At times, in alluding to Indian women's cooperation in their own subordination, the Maharani reinforces Orientalist tropes of Indian women as inherently passive that also surface in Cornelia Sorabji's prose and reception. See also her preface where she writes 'I wanted to awaken my Indian sisters from their lethargy of ages, to enable them to take their proper place in Indian life' (Preface, p. x).

5a Extract from Cornelia Sorabji[88] introduction to *India Calling: The Memories of Cornelia Sorabji* (London: Nisbet, 1934), pp. 5–7.
[British Library W48/2930 DSC]

At one of the many delightful visits, which I paid in my youth to the Grant Duffs at York House, Twickenham – Sir Mountstuart said of me, making a necessary introduction, 'A Friend who has warmed her hands at two fires, without being scorched.' ... Yes – it is true that I have been privileged to know two hearthstones, to be homed in two countries. England and India. But though it is difficult to say which 'home' I love best, there has never, at any time, been the remotest doubt as to which called to me with most insistence ... Always, early or late, throughout the years, it has been 'India Calling' ...

And it has been such a happy life that, before I begin to try to tell what can be told in words, I want to glance back over my shoulder and savour it ... patches of dappled sunshine lying all along the road from the very beginning – sunlight scented with rosemary and lavender. I inhale the Past in great whiffs. The eyes of my Mother, whatever her mood: my Father's laugh: the clearings in the woods near our home and the many games we played as children ...

Sunsets – flaming gold and red-gold: or bruised and blue: or pale mauve and primrose: the deep shadows on the hills, folds in the broidered mantle of God: gold mohur trees trailing bloom: the green paroquets at Budh Gaya: the blue wood-smoke in an Indian village. A thrush in an English garden, his throat swelling with song: the dark wood of trees in early spring bursting with swollen buds, or powdered with blossom: chestnuts alight: sheets of bluebells set in woods of grey beeches. Somerset, and the view from my window – old trees and flower-beds and sloping fields where the quiet cattle grazed: a dinghy on the Cher: Bagley Woods and fritillaries: tramps in Oxfordshire or over Welsh hills, or in the Riviera: and always and always the Earth springing flowers.

88 Sorabji (1866–1954): lawyer, author and reformer. She studied in Oxford and London (1889–94) and settled permanently in Britain from 1938. This introduction provides us with a tantalizing glimpse of what Sorabji might have written about her experiences in England had she chosen to.

Burnham Beeches aflame at Autumn's ending: beeches again in the New Forest; the lovely brown leaves on the browner earth and the feel of crushing them as you walked. Scotland and the feel of heather when you lay upon it: and the little streams in Scotland and in Cumberland, with the stones showing through, held so safe and cool among the peat of their green – and – brownness.

London, and the way it caught one's heart, first seen ... the feeling of standing at the core of the traffic, one morning at the Exchange, and knowing one's self utterly insignificant and alone, yet alive and perfectly companioned. My first robin, my first fall of snow: the ache when snow melted and got dirty: the Irish crossing-sweeper with her bonnet awry, who smiled at me – 'One must keep up one's speerits, *and* one's appearance!': the exhilaration of London fogs: dream cities: the Towers of Westminster in a white mist: the lion in Trafalgar Square with whom I shared all my jokes and my anxieties – the one nearest the Strand: tiredness after work done: many an apt phrase heard or read: special loves in Books and Music and Pictures. Venice and Assisi: things seen, loved, felt, admired: and best of all, Friendships everywhere, and the faces of little children.

No! the goodness and happiness of it all can never really be gathered up to be bound into a book; it spills too much elusive golden grain, which only the heart remembers and recognizes.

But the Giver will know, and will take this for my inarticulate *Te Deum.*

Cornelia Sorabji

56 Review of Cornelia Sorabji,[89] India Calling: *The Memories of Cornelia Sorabji, Times Literary Supplement*, No. 1713, Thursday 29 November 1934, p. 851.
[*Times Literary Supplement* Centenary Archive, British Library[90]]

India Calling: The Memories of Cornelia Sorabji (Nisbet. 12s. 6d. net) The book will be a protection to the future biographer of Miss Sorabji – a protection against the charges of flattery and exaggeration. It reveals, with no trace of consciousness on the author's part, such devotion, selflessness, power of intellect and will, courage, charity and (by no means least) fun that acquiescence will be easy when it is claimed for her that she was – as some might put it, a saint, others, a great woman.

Ten to one, when the reader has finished the book his immediate reflection will be what a lot of good yarns[91] there are in it. There is the yarn of how Miss Sorabji once had an elephant for a client and won his case through a bull-dog. There is the yarn of the man who came climbing over a wall to murder her, but dropped his naked sword and 'retrieved his limbs in hast' when she looked up from her book and said to him: 'There is no foothold; be careful.' There is the yarn of the 'dearest old priest in the world,' who was sent to sit at her gate and curse her till she dwindled and died; was invited to come in, was lodged with the gardener, was encouraged to curse in the greatest comfort – and gave it up in despair after a fortnight. 'I do not believe in curses: I believe in blessings,' said his intended victim; but her clients – her wards, her children, would be better words – did believe in curses; and she took her risk on the day when she cried: 'Bring out

89 Sorabji (1866–1954): lawyer, author and reformer.
90 At the time of publication, *Times Literary Supplement* reviewers were anonymous. This reviewer has still not been identified. This review gives a sense of the recuperation of Cornelia Sorabji for the imperialist project by the more right-wing elements of the British press in the 1930s. As is more widely known, she was befriended and supported by influential sympathizers in Oxford and London, and so these reviews are evidence of the variegated nature of her reception.
91 'Yarn' seems to diminish the scope of this narrative. *The Times* review (4 December 1934), p. 20 deploys the same term, which suggests it could be the same reviewer.

the bone!' The bone was under the bed of the head of the house; and the head of the house, being aged five, was the only person present small enough to get at it. If it had been a human thigh-bone, he would have been irrevocably cursed. It was 'a darling little leg-of-mutton bone,' put there, not by his grandmother but by a dog.

Yarns for their own sake are good; but the most memorable of all the stories in this book are those which show Miss Sorabji doing a sort of intellectual ju-jitsu, and, out of her reverence for all things Indian, using the force of error to confound itself. When a mere child, herself in childbed, was just going to be put to some horrible ritual torture with a hot tin plate, Miss Sorabji suggested that Ganga Ma (the Ganges) might like to share the honour with the God of Fire – and a couple of rubber hot-water bottles ministered both to holiness and to health. In a small-pox epidemic, when Kali wanted blood, she was given it – with the vaccination needle. In protecting the rights, managing the affairs, and composing the quarrels of a people so subtle and so crafty Miss Sorabji had need of all her own subtlety and craft; and such a reflection as, 'when you have forced two quarrelling women to make friends, separate them immediately,' proves her worldly wisdom. But, though we have been tempted to linger on the lighter side of her book, none who knows anything of her career will doubt the existence of its serious side and of a higher than worldly wisdom.

'Brought up English,' and Christian, this Parsee lady[92] was self-

92 Note the emphasis on Sorabji as 'Brought up English' and in 'Christian household', and how this is presented as inextricably entwined with her 'self-dedication' and 'high ideals of intellect and service'. This ostensibly favourable review of Sorabji's memoirs, then, is in fact a validation of a European Christian value system. In this way, Sorabji is represented as a remarkable Westernized exception to, and separate from her fellow-countrymen and women who are 'so subtle and so crafty' and, as the review suggests with some relish, ever-ready to inflict 'some horrible ritual torture' on their women. Similarly, F.H. Brown's review notes 'Sorabji is 'free from the narrowness and fanaticism which sometimes accompany dedication to a great cause, and which have not been absent from the more aggressive side of the Indian feminist movement. Her balance and sanity of judgement is largely due to an early nurture in which the best conceptions of the East and West were mingled'. Brown, ' Review', *Observer*, p. 7.

dedicated from childhood to the service of the women of India, and especially of the Hindu purdah-women[93] who were denied contact with the men that might have helped and protected them.[94] It was mainly for their sake that she came to England, studied law at Oxford, fought a long and only partially victorious battle[95] against official and other obstacles, and at last induced the Government to create and to give her the post of Legal Advisor to the Court of Wards.[96] Her work for India by no means ended when she retired, some years after the War, from the post that died with her; but it is from her account of her journeyings, her perils, her watchings, and her joys as she worked among the purdah-women that the reader will draw the best proof of her quality and the fullest light on the horror and the beauty, the wickedness and the holiness of the India to which her life has been devoted.[97]

93 See also Sorabji's *Love and Life behind the Purdah* (London: Freemantle and Co. 1902), *The Purdahnashin* (Calcutta: Thacker, Spink and Co., 1917).

94 Note the point that 'the Hindu purdah-women who were denied contact with the men that might have helped and protected them' overlooks the roots of purdah in patriarchal systems underpinning Indian society and religion.

95 The reviewer omits that Cornelia Sorabji's anti-nationalist and pro-empire attitudes (dating from the late 1920s) hampered her achievement, costing her the support she needed for her social reforms among Indians.

96 Her efforts to petition the India Office for a legal advisor date from 1902.

97 Note the reviewer's recurrent reference to an India of 'extremes', alongside the emphasis on Sorabji's devotion to and 'reverence for all things India', asserted perhaps to authenticate the privileged status of this native informant, and counter her criticisms of Indian nationalism and aspirations for Indian self-rule.

6 Tambimuttu,[98] First Letter,[99] *Poetry London,* **February 1939.**
[British Library Shelfmark PP5126 bbbi]

Extract, FIRST LETTER
I wish to take my stand and I start by restating a few fundamentals,
well-known enough maybe, but which seem to have been lost in the
ramifications of modern thought and to need restatement for the
purpose of this magazine.

Every man has poetry within him. Poetry is the awareness of the
mind to the universe. It embraces everything in the world.

Of poetry are born religions, philosophies, the sense of good and
evil, the desire to fight diseases and ignorance and the desire to better
living conditions for humanity.

98 M.J. Tambimuttu (1915–83): Sri Lankan poet and critic. Related to
Ananda Coomaraswamy, Tambimuttu arrived in London from colonial
Ceylon in 1938. He established himself with an assortment of poets,
artists and bohemians who were to be regularly found in 'Fitzrovia' –
the name given by Tambimuttu to the area between Fitzroy Square and
Soho Square. Tambimuttu co-founded *Poetry London* with Anthony
Dickin. He went on to edit the first fourteen numbers of *Poetry London*
as well as a number of books (an anthology of poems, *Poetry in Wartime*
(1942)), commissioned by T.S. Eliot, together with *Out of this War*
(1941) and *Natarajah: a Poem for Mr. T.S. Eliot's Birthday* (1948), while
participating in the BBC Overseas Service to India during and after the
Second World War.

99 *Poetry London* was the main poetry magazine of the war. In it
Tambimuttu published the important English and international writers
of his day such as Walter de la Mare, Spender, Louis MacNeice and
Dylan Thomas. He was among the first to recognize then emerging
talents such as Keith Douglas, Lawrence Durrell, Michael Hamburger,
Elizabeth Smart and Kathleen Raine. He published some of their first
books or volumes of poetry. His imprint *Editions Poetry London* also
published the first London editions of novels by Anaïs Nin and
Vladimir Nabokov. He had a dynamic influence on the content and
format of British books, commissioning artists such as Henry Moore,
Lucian Freud, Mervyn Peake, Graham Sutherland and Barbara
Hepworth to design covers for his publishing imprint and for his illustrated texts. Tambimuttu aligned himself with the New Romanticism of

Poetry is the connection between matter and mind. Poetry is universal.

Poetry is not individual. It exists as whole in the universal mind. It is a universal force and like God it can never be *discovered*, although it will always be present directing thought.

It can never be *discovered*, because it is a large universal thing and a man would have to write a hundred paragraphs at the same instant with a hundred hands in order to represent it truly.

For the instant a man starts to write, he ceases to live. Before he began he had the universe in him, but the very moment he put pen to paper he went into a tiny coil of intellectualisation and became only partially alive.

It is this fact that surrealists wanted to teach, but they intellectualised even this simple fact and made it into a system to discover the great force Poetry that cannot be intellectually discovered. Life and the understanding of it is surrealist, but writing about it is intellectual. Therefore it is futile to practice surrealism purposively. The very nature of it defeats its end.

Surrealism is not a new thing, since it has always existed. It has

---

1940s Britain as a robust rejoinder to the poetry magazines *New Verse* and *Twentieth Century Verse*, and to the poetry of political commitment of the thirties, such as John Lehmann's left-wing *New Writing*. *Poetry London* retained its position as a leading vehicle for modern poetry. *Poetry London* survived *New Verse* (1933–39), *New Writing* (1936–46), *Twentieth Century Verse* (1937–39), *Kingdom Come* (1939–42) and *Horizon* (1940–49), a considerable achievement considering the constraints on paper and publishing during the war. In marked contrast to the literary coteries of the day, *Poetry London* was to be characterized by its catholicity. From the first number, *Poetry London* represented all schools of contemporary English poetry, the Imagists, a Stephen Spender and MacNeice group, a Dylan Thomas group. It was a proving ground for promising younger, albeit exclusively, European poets, apart from a review of N. Menon's book on Yeats (PL10), and a *bhajan* dedicated to Gandhi in 1948 after he was assassinated. The absence of material on the subcontinent and of South Asian contributors (B. Rajan is the only exception) in this and subsequent issues of *Poetry London* is striking especially in contrast to mainstream literary magazines like *Life and Letters* and the *New Statesman* which featured South Asian writers and reviewers.

always influenced creative activity, but to know it one has to give up all cruder attributes. To think surrealistically, spontaneously, and entirely – that is without sacrificing large portions of the mind, one would be forced to develop a finer sensibility and like the yogis dispense with cruder forms of expression, for instance the writing of poetry. At any rate, the results of the surrealist movement have shown us that the mental equipment of mankind is not yet perfect enough to practice surrealist thought. If we should ever achieve the perfection necessary to understand it, which is possible only as a hypothesis, it would be because we had persevered in our traditional form of thought.*

I have said that poetry is not individual and than one man could not analyse or formulate it.

Although a fine intellect may see the whole of poetry with its inner light, the effect of translating this vision into words splits it and only part of the vision is transmitted. Man can transmit only part of a whole vision at a given instant.

But by the reception of many different expressions of poets, a mind that has not already *felt* the whole truth is educated to feel it. This is one of the uses of written poetry, to educate every man into this consciousness.

No man is small enough to be neglected as a poet. Every healthy man is a full vessel, though vessels are of different sizes. In a poetry magazine we can only take account of those sizes of vessels which represent humanity as a whole.

*An analogy that lends point to this statement – a few years ago cowboy films were not considered to be unreal or ridiculous; but today people perceive these elements in them merely because they persevered to be *within* the reality of these films until they grew out of it, and are now able to see it objectively.

7 *Indian Writing*[100] Opening Editorial, 1(1) (Spring 1940): 3–4.
[British Library PP 5939 CAS]

The epoch of Wars and Revolutions is no longer a vague shadow on the horizon: it is an immediate reality. At least the Wars are here, and revolutions may follow. It is, of course, possible to take the view that in times like these any form of cultural activity is irrelevant. But so to

100 The opening editorial of the literary magazine *Indian Writing* set out the aspirations of its founding editors Iqbal N. Singh (b. 1912): Activist and writer; Ahmed Ali (1908–94): Activist and writer. Ali co-founded the League of Progressive Authors, which evolved into All-India Progressive Writers' Association in 1936. He visited England in 1939 and arrived with manuscript of his first novel in English *Twilight in Delhi* published by Hogarth Press with E.M. Forster's support. K. Shelvankar: author and activist; Alagu Subramaniam (b. 1910): Sri Lankan Tamil short-story writer. All were at the centre of anti-colonial activities with strong links to the India League, and with the Congress party and Indian Progressive Writers' Association. *Indian Writing* ran irregularly in the period 1940–45. Its office was based at Sasadha Sinha's bookshop 'The Bibliophile' in London's Little Russell Street, which opened in 1935 as a meeting place for politically minded South Asians. In his book *Two Cheers for Democracy*, E.M. Forster expresses his disappointment that in 1945 modern 'Indian "intellectuals" were more deeply preoccupied with politics than art: when I spoke about the necessity of form and individual vision in literature ... their attention wandered. Literature in their view should inspire a political creed'. E.M. Forster, *Two Cheers for Democracy* (London: Edwin Arnold, 1951), p. 324. This comment perhaps explains the frustration that these politicized writers felt towards such a notion that art and politics should be mutually exclusive, and clarifies the *Indian Writing* editors' perceived need to literally create their own space in the form of a literary magazine, to articulate their own views on politics and culture – which would have been seen as radical and extremist at the time. The sparsely produced magazine provides a radical critique of Indo-British relations from the perspective of these activists in London. *Indian Writing* charted the Cripps' mission to India, criticized Allied War Propaganda, and the BBC's staging of 'a mock debate on India, in which the BBC presented as representatives of Indian opinion, a number of abjectly illiterate non-entities, incapable of even representing themselves'. Iqbal

argue is to acquiesce in a tragic position created by the very forces which are working towards the degradation of human values. As Gorky observed: 'Culture is more necessary in storm than in peace.' It is more necessary because it is precisely in the stormy periods of transition that it becomes imperative to maintain some sense of the continuity of human thought and endeavour, and even more, to understand the processes which lead to new cultural integrations.

In launching *Indian Writing* we take Gorky's view. And for good reason. It does not seem altogether fantastic to suggest that we are witnessing today a significant shift of the bases of culture, that initiative in cultural matters is passing to those vast masses of humanity who have so far served only as pawns for the profit of Western Imperialism. In this respect the awakening of India is one of the most important facts of contemporary history. No single magazine could possibly claim to represent this great movement in all its complex aspects. We only hope to interpret its specifically cultural implications.

This condition defines our main purpose. We are interested primarily in publishing imaginative literature which is alive with the realities of to-day. Much work is being done in the major Indian languages as well as in English. It may lack the particular graces of magazine literature of the west, but it is not wanting in the genuine qualities of expression. And, within the limits of our resources, we will try to give it the recognition it deserves. We are aware than writing in English, so far as India is concerned, can never become an adequate substitute for vernacular literature. We feel, nevertheless, that at present it can supplement the latter and be instrumental in bringing the works of significant Indian writers before a larger international public.

Intellectual inbreeding is not in the interests of cultural eugenics. The bulk of the material in *Indian Writing* must necessarily be Indian. At the same time, however, we will take the opportunity peri-

---

Singh 'Indian Art at the Imperial Institute', *Indian Writing*, 1(3) (March 1941): 151–5, at 155. Although the magazine was called '*Indian*' *Writing*, the co-editor Subramaniam, as well as several regular contributors including Pieter Keuneman and J. Vijaya-tunge were in fact Sri Lankan, or Ceylonese to use the terminology of the time.

odically of publishing examples of the writings of other oppressed peoples with whom we share a common background of experience and aspiration.

The difficulties of bringing out a magazine, particularly an Indian magazine, in war-time need hardly be stressed. Moreover, a non-commercial journal like ours cannot take for granted those means of subsistence which are open to magazines run on strictly commercial lines. We therefore expect the active support of our readers and contributors. Indeed, their co-operation will be the measure of our success.

8 R.D. *Charques, Review of Ahmed Ali's Twilight in Delhi and Mulk Raj Anand's Across the Black Waters, Times Literary Supplement* (7 *December*, 1940), p. 619.
[*Times Literary Supplement* Centenary Archive, British Library]

TALES OF INDIANS
Twilight in Delhi: By Ahmed Ali, Hogarth Press. 7s. 6d.
It requires an effort to adjust one's imagination to the unfamiliar setting and strange atmosphere of 'Twilight in Delhi,' and at the end one is not at all sure how rewarding that effort has been. It may be that the failure to discover pattern or significance in this chronicle of Indian social customs springs from an insufficiently attentive or sympathetic reading. On the other hand, it seems possible that Mr. Ahmed Ali in this first novel of his is as yet too inexperienced to make satisfying use of his material. The picture he draws of Delhi and a life of a moderately well-to-do Mahommedan family a generation or so ago, is a queer confusion of heat and sand, food, washing and sleeping, street shopping and begging, marriage ceremonies and ceremonial feasts, Urdu and Persian poetry, all of it topped by a vehement Indian nationalism that discovers the source of all evil in 'the foreign yoke.'

The author may have had it in mind to elaborate in this chronicle, the sentiment of the poetry of Bahadur Shah, pausing now and again to echo a line or two of Hafiz or of some other Eastern poet. The purpose of the novel, however, seems mainly descriptive and the reader will discern what imaginative significance he can in the detail given here concerning matters of personal hygiene, for instance. Amidst the confusion stand two principal figures, the middle-aged Mir Nihal the manager of a lace shop, and an enthusiastic pigeon-flyer, and his volatile and slightly effeminate son Ashgar. The latter, who is much taken up with dancing girls and dreams and wishes to marry Bilqeece, but a sternly conservative parent forbids the marriage with a 'low born' until Ashgar is on the verge of suicide. The festivities take place shortly after the Coronation Durbar of 1911, which apparently woke violent memories of the Mutiny (history is handled in a rather glibly preposterous fashion in this connection), and the description contains much curious detail. Ashgar's passion is soon spent, but something of tenderness appears in him after his child is born: Mir Nihal has a long spell of illness and having given up pigeon-flying takes to trapping rats; Bilqeece dies in the epidemic of 1918 and Ashgar is at the last moment prevented from marrying her younger sister. The story is informative in its way, but is somewhat too remote and obscure in feeling to engage any deep interest.

ACROSS THE BLACK WATERS BY MULK RAJ ANAND[101]
Cape 8s. 6d.
Writing as usual with great attention to detail, and with plentiful quotations of trivial talk, Mulk Raj Anand tells in this tale of an Indian infantry battalion, which went to war in the early part of the four years' war. When the 69th got to the front there were some of them who felt that 'it didn't matter if they had big guns or small guns or whether they lay on the mats like beggars or slept in feather beds like the princes ... they hadn't died in crossing the black waters.' They marvelled at the ease with which they forgot their caste prejudices and they soon gained ideas of white women that were quite different from those they had formed in India. When they went into the trenches (the position is delightfully given in a letter one of them wrote to his mother as 'a village near Ypres, Tehsil Ypres, District Ypres, Subah Flanders, near Franceville') they began to form strange ideas of the Government which had sent them to fight. 'The Sarkar is like a bitch son, it barks its orders and does not explain.' And 'they did not know what they were fighting for or what anyone else was fighting for.' The wretchedness of it all, the moments of terror, the filth and the discomfort are well described. But it is all rather pointless, except as a study of men in strange surroundings and in the sort of war for which they have not been trained, and the little group of Hindu soldiers that figures in the book becomes tedious. The author makes them talk with worse iteration of bad language than is probable. These are blemishes, which spoil the general effect of a picture built up with care and skill.

---

101 Anand dedicates his novel *Across the Black Waters* to 'my Father Subedar Lall Chand Anand M.S.M. Late 2/17th Dogras'.

9 Mulk Raj Anand,[102] Review, *Indian Writing* 1(3) (March 1941): 175–7.
[British Library, PP 5939 CAS]

Twilight in Delhi: By Ahmed Ali (Hogarth Press 7s. 6d.)
Night in Bombay By Louis Bromfield (Cassell 9s.)

There is a certain appropriateness in reviewing contemporary Indian and European books together. For reviewing in England has, particularly since the intensification of this war of rival Imperialisms, become increasingly insular, self-centred and chauvinistic.[103] And the only corrective to such retrogression can be offered by the assertion of the point of view of the subject peoples, whose aspirations though nationalistic, are certainly not predatory, and tend, through their urge for emancipation, towards a more balanced and internationalist outlook.

It is only in such a way that one can understand the insanity which leads to the acclamation of *Night in Bombay* as a 'great' work, and to its choice by the Book Society and the *Daily Mail* Book Club,[104] while so sensitive a narrative as Ahmed Ali's is dismissed by most of the reviewers with perfunctory notices, not even gracious enough to offer the author helpful criticism.

Now one thing is quite certain: the intellectuals, the writers and artists of the present generation of India will never accept the *Night in Bombay* kind of spurious book, the successor in direct descent from Kipling through Yeats-Brown's *Bengal Lancer*, and through its author's own Book Society choice and Hollywood success, *The Rains*

102 Mulk Raj Anand (1905–2004): writer, editor, journalist and activist based in Britain in the period 1925–45.
103 In the context of the 'insular' reviewing culture Anand describes, his own review of Ali's novel serves as an important corrective to the *TLS* review [Source 8] and suggests that the Book Reviews section of *Indian Writing* served as a crucial space for these South Asian writers to comment on each other's work.
104 As Anand suggests, the favourable reviews of the work of English writers set in India such as Louis Bromfield, R. P. Russ and Maud Diver confirm a fascination for stories in exotic locales, yet always preferably filtered through the vehicle of the European novel.

Came. No, we will not have these P. and O. coloured cartoons of glamorous India, where rubies are stolen and New England blondes go gold-digging, where saints, wastrels and missionaries abound; no, we will not accept this India with its 'fierce romance and no less fierce vices, its strong medley of Eastern and Western desires'.

Some of the younger writers in the various vernaculars of India have, during the past few years, been practising modestly, and without sensationalism, the lyric art of the short story as a kind of extension from the feudal folk tale to a more modern idiom and purpose. Ahmed Ali is one of the pioneers of this form of narrative in Hindustani. He writes a masterly Urdu prose which is a fluent mixture of the old patrician style and the language of the gutter of Delhi. The nuances of this prose are difficult to translate, but some of his stories translated into English, have brought over enough of their original charm. The desire to get an international audience and the exigencies of Imperial censorship persuaded him to attempt a novel in English. Essentially, however, this book like most imaginative writings by Indians in English, reads like a translation from the vernacular by a bi-lingual artist who thinks mostly in his own language even though he writes in a foreign language. This accounts for some of the Americanisms and colloquialisms that put off the conservative English reviewer.

But, apart from the delicately poetic style of *Twilight in Delhi*, this study of a vanishing age, symbolised by the chief character Mir Nihal, a man whose links with the court of the last Mughal were broken by the butchery of Metcalfe, through the coming in of alien rule and the passing of old convention, is a profoundly moving and inspired narrative, giving promise of the development in Ahmed Ali's hands of a new Urdu tradition of the novel.

The germs of the new books Ahmed Ali may write are present in this book. Thematically he seems to be preoccupied with the decay of feudal culture in northern India. This preoccupation must lead him, one day or other, to write about the Mutiny of 1857, when the Mughal nobility and its satraps gave pitched battle to the more organised forces of the English conquerors. At present, his intimate knowledge, and even love, of the graces of upper class Muhammadan life, make for subjectivity and nostalgia; but there is enough anguished awareness in his book of the putrescence of this nobility to show the inevitability of their tragedy. Technically his prose will rid itself of all remnants of lubricity without losing its poetic quality. The result will be a novel which will come in translation to foreign languages, an Indian novel which, because it will not be modelled on the books of our masters, may be India's distinctive contribution to world literature.

MULK RAJ ANAND

10 Ranjee Gurdasing Shahani[105] 'Review of Anand's *The Sword and the Sickle*', *Times Literary Supplement* (2 May 1942), p. 221.
[*Times Literary Supplement* Centenary Archive, British Library]

Mr. Mulk Raj Anand is a writer who promised to take a leading place among the novelists of his generation. But something has happened to him: he becomes more and more prejudiced in his outlook. The telescope which he turns on the world has three specks: the anti-bourgeois speck, the anti-White (which in substance means anti-British) speck. These not only limit his horizon, but lead him to errors and injustices.[106]

However, being a professed champion of the humble and the downtrodden, he must be judged by his portraits of these. On the whole Mr. Anand is successful here. His peasant, coolie, outcast and soldier are not marionettes, but living and growing human beings. We watch their adventure with life with fascinated interest. But the final impression is one of disappointment. We do not feel that these unhappy beings, though plundered and profaned are, in essence, the offspring of the stars. Mr. Anand does not show the power to relate a particular destiny to the Creative Whole of existence. He is content to scratch the surface of life and reality.

This is particularly noticeable in his new novel 'The Sword and the Sickle' which recounts the doings, both private and political, of Lal

105 Ranjee Gurdasing Shahani (1904–68): author of *A New Pilgrim's Progress* (World Congress of Faiths, 1936), *A White Man in Search of God* (Lester & Welbeck, 1943), *The Amazing English* (Adam Charles Black, 1948), contributor to *The Sufi: A Journal of Mysticism*, 1933–39 and editor of the literary magazine *Panchila*.

106 George Orwell objects to Shahani's review in a Letter to the Editor. Given the nature of Shahani's critique, Orwell appears to assume the then anonymous reviewer to be an English writer: 'And if Mr. Anand makes it plain that he is anti-imperialist and he thinks India ought to be independent, is he not saying something which almost any English intellectual would echo as a matter of course? In novels written by Englishmen a "left" viewpoint is taken for granted, yet when your reviewer finds exactly the same coming from an Indian, he is annoyed.' G. Orwell, Letter to the Editor, *Times Literary Supplement* (23 May 1942), p. 259.

Singh, a Punjabi soldier who returns from capture in Germany to find everything topsy-turvy in India. His family has disappeared: his father's farm has been sold: the countryside is in the grip of a 'money famine': and, to make matters worse, the Sarkar has not only wrongfully discharged him from army, but 'without the reward of a square of land that had been promised to each soldier, without the good conduct medal.' The man turns into a rebel. He elopes with the girl whose father had ruined his people; joins the service of a generous but ineffectual Princeling who is organising the peasants, and devotes his energies to improving the lot of the peasants. We are kept interested in the ex-sepoy's struggles, hopes and dreams, but these do not enlarge our knowledge of the man or stir us profoundly: the depths are not plumbed. The writing, too, lacks original force; indeed, there are passages which an ill-natured critic might call a new form of Babuism.[107] Moreover, the frankness appears to be unrelated to a large view of life. Also, Mr. Anand's references to Europeans betray a lack of insight. What is really disagreeable, however, is the spirit of the novel; it tends to create bad blood between Indians and British, which is a bad thing at any time and a dangerous one at this hour. The reader will regret this separation of talent and wisdom in a writer with the gifts of Mr. Anand.

107 Again assuming an English reviewer, Orwell responds ' I quite agree that it is undesirable to create bad blood between Indians and British; and one way of doing that is to use words like 'Babuism'. Orwell, Letter to the Editor, 1942. See also the reviewer's criticism of Orwell's 'timid patronage' of Anand.

11 Transcript of Letter from B.B. Chaudhuri[108] to George Bernard Shaw,[109] 27 July 1944.
[British Library, Dept of Manuscripts, add 50524, f. 109]

Dear George Bernard Shaw,
Greetings on your 88th birthday. It is on this occasion, which reminds us how deeply India is indebted to you for your support and sympathy to the cause of Indian independence. The India struggle draws its inspiration from the people of Eire whose common enemy is British imperialism.[110] Eire is fortunate to have De Valera, as we were Gandhi. Indians are fortunate to be inspired by the greatest poet of the East, Tagore, just as the people of Eire drew inspiration through your immortal oeuvre.
Yours sincerely,
B.B. Chaudhuri

108 B.B. Chaudhuri, Secretary to the Tagore society and author of a book of verse *A Lover's Lute* (Stockwell, 1930).
109 George Bernard Shaw (1856–1950). Irish playwright and socialist charter member of the Fabian Society and a pioneer of feminism and racial equality. Shaw alongside fellow Fabians and Irish nationalists was sympathetic to Indian nationalist aspirations.
110 This letter underscores the ways in which Indian nationalists simultaneously forged ties with other 'subject peoples', namely Irish nationalists 'whose common enemy was British imperialists'. They formed their own cultural institutions such as the Tagore Society that emphasized an affinity between Indian and Irish nationalism at a literary and political level, and sought links with George Bernard Shaw, Harold Laski and other Irish and British sympathizers of Indian independence. See the growing body of work on cross-cultural nationalisms, in particular Irish and Indian revivals. For instance, Kate O'Malley, *Ireland, India and Empire* (Manchester: Manchester University Press, 2009).

12 *Cedric Dover's*[111] *poem 'Brown Phoenix' (London: College Press, 1950).*
[British Library, 11657.1.6]

'BUT STILL BELIEVING WE CAN CLIMB'

> BROWN PHOENIX
> I am the brown phoenix
> Fused in the flames
> Of the centuries' greed.
>
> I am tomorrow's man[112]
> Offering to share
> Love, and the difficult quest,
> In the emerging plan.
>
> Do you see a dark man
> Whose mind you shun,
> Whose heart you never know,
> Unable to understand
> That I am the golden bird
> With destiny clear?

111 Cedric Dover (1904–61): biologist and writer. His mixed Indian and European descent and scientific training influenced his thinking on race and scientific humanism. His books, published by Secker & Warburg, include *Know This of Race* (1930), *Half Caste* (1937) and *Hell in the Sunshine* (1943). He settled in Britain in 1934 on a government scholarship to Edinburgh University. An ardent supporter of Indian nationalism, he worked in civil defence and served in the Royal Army Ordinance corps during the Second World War and contributed to the BBC Indian Section of the Eastern Service. Cedric Dover's poem, like his writings, challenged 'race' theories by showing the intermingling of people and political and economic movements. Dover writes 'Prejudice has no place in rational Civilisation'. C. Dover, *Half-Caste*, London: Secker & Warburg (1937), p. 77.

112 This poem articulates a similar sense of the balance of power shifting at last towards formerly subjugated peoples that we saw in the *Indian Writing* editorial [Source 7].

Fools cannot destroy me,
With arrogant fear.

Listen brown man, black man,
Yellow man, mongrel man,
And you white friend and comrade:
I am the brown phoenix – I am you.

'There is my symbol for us all.'

For we are tomorrow's men,
But not you.
Little pinkwhite man,
Not you!

No dream this, but history in process
And already denied by prose waffles
Of Self drowned in sweet objectivity.
(The reely scientific view, you know,
Is palsy-walsy with the status quo.)

Here there is no such mixture: only
The personal responses prevail
(In poor metric if you please to say so).
Like high marks on the pulse and fever chart
Of one brown bastard malarial hot
From the swamps and the sticks and loan companies.

The one is many, and the many you.
Not now perhaps, but inescapably,
In the night's end, the many will be You.

Acknowledgements

The headings under which the poems are arranged are gratefully and obviously derived from W.H. Auden.

4

The representation and display of South Asians in Britain (1870–1950)

Sumita Mukherjee[1]

This chapter will consider the ways in which South Asian visitors were represented and put on 'display' in Britain from 1870 to 1950. It should be read as an introduction to the accompanying sources. South Asians from all social classes and regions were increasingly visible in Britain from the late nineteenth century and their presence challenged and reinforced existing 'Orientalist' stereotypes about the East. The discourse of 'Orientalism' accentuated dissimilarity and strengthened an idea of a 'Western' superiority of 'Self'. Although we know a good deal about British perceptions of the Indian subcontinent during this period, and earlier, we know less about British reactions and ideas about South Asians in their midst within Britain. Therefore, the framework of 'Orientalism' should not be the only lens through which to think about these depictions because these South Asians were bringing the 'East' to British soil and asserting their own personalities. Did the British climate (environmental and political) challenge the ways South Asians were perceived? And how did South Asians in Britain represent themselves to a wider British audience?

These sources reflect particularly on the physical representation of South Asians in Britain over an eighty-year time period, whether on

1 I would like to thank Ruvani Ranasinha, Sarah V. Turner and Rozina Visram for their comments on an earlier version of this chapter.

the stage as exhibits and performers, as objects of reportage and commentary, or more generally as subjects of the British imperial 'gaze'.[2] We will see that there were certain similarities in tropes used to describe South Asians of varied social groups from Indian artists and dancers to lascars, ayahs and craftsmen. In particular, the regional differences of South Asians were hardly appreciated as similar terms were used to label and limit different cultural traditions. However, there were developments in the representation of South Asians over time, as public discourse in Britain moved away from imperial hierarchies. These changes in representation reflect developments in the political relationship between India and Britain, in British ideas of race and in Indian nationalist ideas, but also changing social tastes and growing appreciation for 'Indian culture'.

We will see that some South Asians capitalized upon and accentuated features of difference in their manner and appearance when in Britain, using certain stereotypes as necessary tools for perceived gain. But, we will also see how essentialized descriptions of South Asian individuals and groups were used to demean and infantilize these visitors. Depictions of South Asians in this period usually emphasized differences that were used to portray South Asians as inferior. However, emphasis on difference could also be part of a positive discourse that appreciates multiple cultural traditions. Therefore, it is necessary to look beyond instances where the exotic was remarked upon in these sources, but also to seek out which particular tropes and adjectives were relied upon, if any, and to interrogate the images they depicted of South Asians in Britain to gain a deeper understanding of the public discourse about empire and the Indian subcontinent prevalent at the time.

Imperial ceremonies and exhibitions

One of the most visible social groups of South Asians in Britain, particularly following the coronation of Queen Victoria as

---

2 For more on the imperial gaze see A. Burton 'Making a Spectacle of Empire: Indian Travellers in Fin-de-Siècle London', *History Workshop Journal*, 42 (1996): 127–46, and S. Lahiri, *Indian Mobilities in the West, 1900–1947: Gender, Performance, Embodiment* (New York: Palgrave Macmillan, 2010).

Empress of India in 1877, were Indian princes. As part of the spectacle and splendour of empire, Indian princes, and soldiers, were encouraged to be present at imperial ceremonies in Britain as well as in India. Therefore, princes could be seen at the celebrations of Queen Victoria's jubilees (1887, 1897), the coronation of Edward VII (1902), and at the opening of imperial exhibitions in Britain (1886, 1895, 1911 and 1924). Indian princes were emblems of the wealth and opulence of the empire and symbols of the 'ornamentalism' of empire.[3] They were expected to appear in full ceremonial regalia and participate in formalized rituals of their subservience to the Queen.

Indian princes were representatives of the 'exotic' East, typified by bright colours, precious metals, stones, spices and wild animals. When the *Graphic* sought to illustrate the opening of the Imperial Institute in South Kensington, it is of little surprise that they should choose to symbolize the presence of Indian subjects in London through the illustrations of elephants and lions (Figure 4.1). The image includes men with a variety of turbans, men bearing weapons and bare-chested boys from the colonies. At the end of the nineteenth century, the British public's ideas of the Indian subcontinent relied heavily on a self-serving circle of stock, stereotypical descriptions of Indian presences from the press and various forms of literature.

The presence of South Asians in British public life at this time attracted a great deal of attention. As noted in Chapter 3, [pp. 168–9] Jagatjit Singh of Kapurthala published a diary of his visit to Europe in 1893. His entry for 10 May 1893 on the opening of the Imperial Institute recounts the interest the crowds expressed in his presence within the procession to the ceremony: 'They constantly cheered me, and I deeply appreciated this token of welcome on the part of the populace to a representative of their Indian brethren. The streets were lavishly decorated, and the balconies crammed with ladies and gentlemen, who waved parasols and handkerchiefs as we passed.'[4]

---

3 As opposed to 'orientalism', 'ornamentalism' emphasizes the ways in which the British bound empire through affinities of hierarchy, particularly through allegiance to the imperial monarchy. D. Cannadine, *Ornamentalism: How the British Saw Their Empire* (London: Allen Lane, 2001).

The admiration for Indian royalty was at one extreme of the spectrum of ways in which South Asians were represented, particularly at the turn of the century. As the 'jewel in the crown', India was favoured for any events or displays associated with the glorification of the empire. As India had not been colonized in the same manner as Africa, and did not have the same status as the white dominions, the representation of India and South Asians took on a different space within the colonial imagination, as we shall see.

The Imperial Institute in South Kensington was partly designed as a museum for goods from the Empire and was built after a number of temporary imperial exhibitions were organized within Britain. These exhibitions were organized by the British Government, usually under royal commissions, and with financial help from the colonies. Imperial exhibitions often put people as well as material objects on display. Indians and Africans became exhibits that were categorized and objectified. Portrayals of Africans often emphasized the 'savage', for example the 'Savage South Africa' show held in London in 1899, or Africans in nearly nude illustrations in *Boy's Own Magazine* in the mid-nineteenth century.[5] Indians were also compartmentalized, but not necessarily in the same way. In exhibitions, there was more emphasis on the 'village', but also on handicrafts. In 1885, Liberty's Department Store in London created a 'living' display of Indian village artisans in Battersea Park. The group consisted of forty-two villagers, including two female dancers, and a variety of craftsmen. The handicraft skills of Indians were lauded, but they were also used to accentuate difference from the industrialized West. It is this 'cult of the craftsmen' that Saloni Mathur refers to, illustrating the tensions within the modernizing mission of imperialism, which sought to modernize and 'civilize' on the one hand but also benefited from

4 His Highness the Raja-i-Rajgan Jagatjit Singh of Kapurthala, *My Travels in Europe and America 1893* (London: Routledge and Sons, 1895), p. 61.

5 See J. Green, *Black Edwardians: Black People in Britain, 1901–1914* (London: Frank Cass, 1998), K. Castle, 'The representation of Africa in mid-Victorian children's magazines', in G.H. Gerzina (ed.), *Black Victorians/Black Victoriana* (New Brunswick, NJ: Rutgers University Press, 2003), pp. 145–58. For an interesting comparison with regards to the representation of Egyptians in France see T. Mitchell, 'The World as Exhibition', *Comparative Studies in Society and History*, 31(2) (1989): 217–36.

keeping colonial subjects in the pre-industrial and pre-national past.[6] This is evident in other imperial exhibitions in this period. For example, the 1886 Colonial and Indian Exhibition in South Kensington, presided over by the Prince of Wales, included a display of thirty-four 'native artisans' from Agra, in fact inmates from Agra Jail, demonstrating various crafts and professions, from sweetmeat maker to potter to carpet weaver. The account of the 1888 Glasgow Exhibition [Source 3] in the *Indian Magazine* describes the sweetmeat maker and jeweller as 'stolid' and 'passive' respectively, and although possessing unique skills they are also featured as exhibits rather than as independent artisans.

South Asian observers were as guilty of reverting to descriptions of certain 'types' when involved in these discourses of representation as British commentators. An Indian journalist, reporting on the 1886 Colonial and Indian Exhibition for the *Indian Mirror*, observed the Punjabi carpenters 'hammering away', the 102–year-old potter, and the 'Benares man, robed in a glittering "chapkan", with the gorgeous kinkhabs and other rich dress materials spread before him'.[7] T.N. Mukharji came to Britain as an assistant from the Indian government to catalogue the exhibition and answer questions from the public, having catalogued the 1883 Amsterdam colonial exhibition. His account of the 1886 exhibition [Source 4] portrays Indian artisans saluting the Queen as comic characters and 'essentialized' objects. Mukharji also invokes another stereotype, the jungle, which appears in other observations and displays of the subcontinent [Source 6]. These references to jungle or village life seemed to emphasize the quaint or exotic East, but also reinforced the ideological purpose of the imperial civilizing mission, especially as their presences in Britain were seen to differ from the perceived modernized and civilized West.

Art historians, anthropologists and other scholars have discussed the role of the space of the museum or imperial exhibition in discourses about India and South Asia. During the late nineteenth

6 S. Mathur, *India By Design: Colonial History and Cultural Display* (Berkeley: University of California Press, 2007), p. 29 on the 'cult of the craftsmen', and Chapter 1 (in Mathur) generally for more on the Liberty's village display.
7 *Indian Mirror*, 6 June 1886, quoted in Mathur, *India By Design*, p. 67.

and early twentieth centuries, the exhibition halls themselves were as much a spectacle as the objects inside. Tim Barringer has explained that the physical building and architecture of the South Kensington Museum in 1882 attracted more press coverage than the materials inside.[8] Mukharji talks at length about the entrance to the 1886 exhibition in his account [Source 4]. The guide to the 1908 Franco-British exhibition, held in Shepherd's Bush in London, [Source 6] is particularly proud of the Indian pavilion and in 1924, the artist Mukul Dey was employed to create the large façade for the Indian Court at Wembley [Source 10]. In Percival Phillips' account of the build-up to this British Empire exhibition, one can identify the resonance of Indian architecture in readers' minds (as with the Franco-British exhibition guide), here referring to the Taj Mahal and Jama Masjid; the Taj Mahal was certainly a familiar edifice to British audiences, often used in advertisements for Indian goods and services.

Exhibitions in this period were not always associated with imperial projects, and also refer to art displays in public and private galleries. Over the course of the twentieth century, acceptance of the validity of South Asian art and artists gradually grew and developed away from earlier stereotypes of the primitive nature of their artistic traditions. In 1910, George Birdwood's infamous lecture to the Royal Academy in which he professed that India had no 'fine' art, spurred various sympathizers of India to found the India Society in London. South Asian art needed interventionist support unlike other artistic traditions, notably Japanese art and wood-printing, or African sculptures, which had a more direct and popular influence on major European artists such as Claude Monet, Paul Gauguin and Pablo Picasso.[9] A key member of the India Society was Ananda Coomaraswamy, an art critic and graduate of University College London, of Sri Lankan and English heritage, who went on to become curator at the Boston Museum of Fine Arts. His article in the

8 T. Barringer, 'The South Kensington Museum and the Colonial Project', in T. Barringer and T. Flynn (eds), *Colonialism and the Object: Empire, Material Culture and the Museum* (London: Routledge, 1998), pp. 16–17.

9 See S. Wichmann, *Japonisme: The Japanese Influence on Western Art Since 1858* (London: Thames & Hudson, 1999) and W. Rubin (ed.), *Primitivism in 20th Century Art* (New York: Museum of Modern Art, 1984).

Burlington Magazine [Source 7] takes one of the criticisms of Indian art head-on, namely of the many-figured deities present in painting and sculpture. Yet, as Sarah Turner has explained, art critics such as Coomaraswamy and his India Society colleague E.B. Havell defended Indian art by referring to the spiritual and harking back to a mythic India of the past, further accentuating difference and division from European artistic practices.[10]

Individual artists from the subcontinent increasingly began to train at art schools in Britain such as Mukul Dey who studied at the Slade School of Art and the Royal College of Art (1920–22) and was involved with the 1924 Wembley Empire Exhibition [Source 10]. The 1934 art exhibition in the Burlington Galleries in London was a key turning point in the acknowledgement of modern Indian art as worthy of detailed attention, rather than as an imperial object. It attracted a great deal of publicity with a number of press notices and reviews, and an opening by the Duchess of York and the Maharajkumari of Burdwan.[11] This is particularly demonstrated by art critic John de laValette's commentary on the exhibition on the BBC [Source 12]. De la Valette's radio address to a wider public beyond the audience at the gallery validates an appreciation of Indian art. He describes the exhibits with care to explain the regional schools from which they were produced, marking an understanding of Indian art that was both 'national' and yet also heterogeneous, while also relying upon the recurring stereotype of the 'spiritual' India.

Clothing and appearance

The outward appearance of Indians became a marker of the ways in which they attempted to integrate into British society, but also as an identifiable means of difference. Clothing and hairstyle played

10 S.V. Turner, 'The "Essential Quality of Things": E.B. Havell, Ananda Coomaraswamy and Indian Sculpture in Britain', special issue on 'Nineteenth-Century Sculpture in its Global Contexts', ed. J. Edwards and M. Hatt, *Journal of Visual Culture in Britain* (Autumn 2010): 239–64.

11 P. Mitter, *The Triumph of Modernism: India's Artists and the Avant-garde 1922–1947* (London: Reaktion, 2007), p. 224.

important roles in identity construction, and were also easy forms by which the British could describe South Asian visitors. The description of clothes from the Indian subcontinent as 'costumes' implied that South Asians wore garments that should be put on for display and exhibition rather than everyday clothing which would not elicit such categorization. Such descriptions of South Asians as exhibits were also apparent in commentary on their public presence in Britain.[12]

Descriptions of South Asian women in Britain, in particular, emphasized the difference in garment style, such as saris, but also focused on the colours of these clothes. South Asian women's fashion preferences in terms of colour appeared to differ significantly from those of Victorian and Edwardian women, and were frequently noted. Where women in Britain tended to favour pale colours, white for Hindu women was associated with widowhood. South Asian women also drew upon a wide range of colour dyes available in the Indian subcontinent and so wore much brighter clothes than their British counterparts, allowing them to stand out and invite comment.

Prominent South Asian women in Britain were noted for the clothes they wore. Cornelia Sorabji, for example, mentions in her autobiography *India Calling* (published in 1934) that she was often accosted in streets by British ladies (in the 1890s) trying to convert her to Christianity: 'Indian boys and men had long been coming in respectable numbers. But their clothes had not the same allure or suggestion of foreignness. Dear old ladies were always trying to convert me – for instance – the heathen at their gates.'[13] Sorabji was bemused that by wearing a sari on the streets of London she was automatically assumed by people to be a 'heathen' when she was actually of Christian faith. Antoinette Burton has asserted that Sorabji used her dress as part of defiant kind of Indian womanhood rather than to submit to the kind of anglicization encouraged by various British groups.[14] In this way, clothes became important signi-

12 E. Tarlo, *Clothing Matters: Dress and Identity in India* (London: Hurst & Co., 1996).
13 C. Sorabji, *India Calling* (London: Nisbet, 1934), p. 52.
14 A. Burton, *At the Heart of the Empire* (Berkeley: University of California Press, 1999), p. 60.

fiers of identity for many South Asians. Indira Gandhi, née Nehru, for example, tended to wear tweed suits when she was a student at Somerville College, Oxford in the 1930s, but would wear 'vibrantly-coloured silk saris' when she attended India League or Majlis meetings in London, where the sari became a political statement of her 'nationality' within Britain, and thus she moved between two dress styles to match the expectations of her audiences.[15]

Descriptions of lower-class women from the Indian subcontinent were also littered with similar emphasis on colours and jewellery. The ayahs in [Source 9], for example, were described in terms of their colourful shawls, nose-rings and wide smiles. Such descriptions reduced these ayahs to objects and further infantilized them in the eyes of the reader. This article shows that they certainly appeared to occupy only one small space within London and Britain, despite their important role for families in India. Ayahs did seem to attract fascination and were sometimes portrayed in nineteenth-century paintings and literature, but their roles as significant carers and educators were rarely recognized.[16]

It should be noted that Muslim women who wore veils or the hijab were not particularly commonplace sights in Britain during this period and so there was little discourse about the levels of veiling and seclusion that were more prevalent in late twentieth-century Europe.[17] There were secluded women, however, as part of the entourage of the Awadh delegation to Britain in 1856, as Michael Fisher has noted.[18] The presence of this particular delegation high-

15 K. Frank, *Indira: The Life of Indira Nehru Gandhi* (London: HarperCollins, 2001), p. 129. See also Chapter 1's discussion of Savitri Chowdhary wearing Western clothes at her husband's prompting to avoid looking conspicuous in their Essex village but Indian clothes for Indian social occasions in London, in S. Chowdhary, *I Made My Home in England* (Laindon: Grant Best, 1962).

16 R. Visram, *Asians in Britain: 400 Years of History* (London: Pluto, 2002), p. 53.

17 The elite Muslim woman, Atiya Fyzee, who visited Britain first in 1906, was actively discouraged from wearing the veil by her family. See S. Lambert-Hurley and S. Sharma, *Atiya's Journeys: A Muslim Woman from Colonial Bombay to Edwardian Britain* (Delhi: Oxford University Press, 2010). See also R. Lewis, *Rethinking Orientalism: Women, Travel and the Ottoman Empire* (London: IB Tauris, 2004).

18 M.H. Fisher, 'Multiple Meanings of 1857 for Indians in Britain', *Economic and Political Weekly*, 42(19) (12 May 2007): 1703–9.

lights the tropes about the exotic that were used about Indian royalty, but also clarify different approaches to South Asians from lower-class backgrounds. Unlike Joseph Salter's description of the poor lascars in the East End of London [Source 1], which though patronizing was sympathetic to their race, *The Times* was quick to criticize: 'Although the appearance of the Princesses and principal attendants is most superb by reason of the elaborate and costly dresses with which they are attired, the mass of the inferior servants present an unusually filthy and unsightly group.'[19] The newspapers emphasized the unpleasant smells radiating from these lower-class Indians, conflating foul smell with their race and class.

The clothes that men from the Indian subcontinent wore when they stayed in Britain took on political significance over the period. Although the British had encouraged Indian princes to appear in full regalia at durbars and when visiting court in Britain, as we have seen, other upper classes of South Asian men were expected to wear European-style suits. The dhoti was taken by the British as further indication of the effeminacy of Indian men,[20] and so many South Asian men were happy to adopt the suit, especially in the colder climate of Britain. The gender politics of clothing are evident in the ways in which South Asian men were encouraged to anglicize, and therefore masculinize, their appearance, but women were generally encouraged to wear South Asian dress, thus further feminizing and infantilizing their position within society. However, these attempts at anglicization by men were not always appreciated by the British or Indians in India, and were interpreted and criticized as mimicry. Some embellished their suits with shawls, Punjabi shirts or turbans to emphasize 'cultural' difference [Sources 2 & 5].

Note the following description of the Annual Indian Social Conference in Swanwick, Derbyshire, a three-day forum founded by and for Indian students in 1917,[21] and the emphasis on how dress provided authenticity:

19 *The Times*, 28 August 1856, quoted in ibid., 1705.
20 T.R. Metcalf, *Ideologies of the Raj* (Cambridge: Cambridge University Press, 1998), p. 105.
21 S. Mukherjee, *Nationalism, Education and Migrant Identities: The England-Returned* (London: Routledge, 2010), p. 85.

The evenings were devoted to social entertainments, which included amongst other items, music, *mushaira*, i.e. verse competition and drama. In the *mushaira* impromptu poems were composed in English and in almost all the Indian vernaculars, but the chief feature was its original get up, most of the delegates being attired in Indian costume giving the proceedings an entirely Eastern effect.[22]

Gandhi, for example, recalls in his autobiography the task of becoming an 'English gentleman' that entailed buying newly cut suits, a chimney-pot hat (top hat) and wearing a gold double watch-chain when he was studying for the Bar in the 1880s; Saifuddin Kitchlew, a prominent member of the Indian National Congress, would wear silk gloves and a monocle when he was a student at Cambridge.[23] Were these attempts at mimicry or merely necessary for assimilation and disguise? Mortified by his white flannel suit when he landed in Britain, Gandhi hoped to be inconspicuous by wearing Western clothes but actually stood out even more by wearing a colour not commonly worn by British men in winter. Gandhi later famously rejected Western clothes in India and favoured the simple *khadi* (homespun) dhoti; his insistence on *khadi* became a central part of a political movement that boycotted foreign goods, favouring Indian business, where adopting this cloth could be easily followed by the masses. He wore the dhoti in his visit to London in 1931 for the Round Table conference and in meeting with workers in the East End and Lancashire; the images of which became powerful for the Indian nationalist cause within Britain, while also eliciting criticism from Winston Churchill who infamously described Gandhi as a half-naked 'fakir'.

Wearing long flowing robes, another example of a South Asian fashion for men, became associated with an alternative theme of difference that recurred, namely Eastern spirituality. Rabindranath Tagore visited and addressed audiences in London in 1913 in a long robe (and a long beard), which to British audiences emphasized his authenticity as 'Indian' and a 'spiritual' voice. Francis Yeats-Brown

22 *Britain and India,* 1(6) (June, 1920): 212–13.
23 M.K. Gandhi, *An Autobiography, or, the Story of My Experiments with Truth* (London: Penguin, 2001), p. 61; F.Z. Kitchlew, *Freedom Fighter: The Story of Dr Saifuddin Kitchlew* (Bognor Regis: New Horizon, 1979), p. 10.

describes the Buddhist teacher Anagarika Dharmapala, who met audiences in the 1920s, in terms of his stature and 'saffron robe' [Source 11]. Hair style also became linked with ideas of Eastern religions, as seen in Emily Lutyens' description of the theosophist Jiddu Krishnamurti (here Krishna) and his brother in London in 1911 as they watched the coronation of George V together:

> It was also something of a torture to Krishna, with his shy and retiring nature, to be obliged to face crowds, especially as his long hair, with European clothes, always provoked such comments as 'Get yer 'air cut'. The reason for this peculiar style of hair-dressing was that traditionally the Buddha, when as Prince Siddartha he had left home to seek enlightenment, had cut off his long locks to the shoulders with his sword ...

As he walked away from the Admiralty through the dense crowds, constant jeers were hurled at poor Krishna. There was one notable exception: as we passed through Seven Dials one woman standing at her door exclaimed as we passed, 'God bless his beautiful face!'[24]

The spectacle of appearance also became important in practical situations, for example Sikh soldiers who had problems wearing helmets, as described by Puji [Source 12 in Chapter 2]. Another example where hair, tunics and turbans provide relevant descriptions of South Asians in Europe can be seen in Douglas Crawford's article in the *Daily Mail* on the Indian soldiers in Marseilles during the First World War:

> Old women fought with men for the honour of shaking hands with the bronzed soldiers whom they impartially names 'Anglais' and 'Hindous', and young women and girls threw sweet-smelling flowers in their path or pinned pink roses in their tunics, in their turbans and even stuck them into the Indians' long hair. In response the dark Eastern eyes beamed a great content, and rows of marvellously white teeth flashed from laughing mouths.[25]

It was not only class and wealth that elicited different responses, but also purpose and occupation. The descriptions of South Asian men and women in Britain differed according to context, but we have

24 E. Lutyens, *Candles in the Sun* (London: Rupert Hart-Davis, 1957), p. 33.
25 'The Arrival of the Indian Troops', *The Indian Magazine and Review*, 527 (November 1914): 265–6.

seen that the clothes and other accessories worn by these individuals were extremely important ways in which they could represent themselves and be represented in this period.

The stage

Much of this chapter so far has explained how South Asians were portrayed as exhibits or objects in Britain, often against their will or knowledge. There were some South Asians, however, who were deliberately putting themselves on the stage to be viewed, although they too were reacting to audience expectations. Actors, dancers and musicians from the Indian subcontinent travelled to Britain in troupes or as individuals in order to entertain British audiences. Once again, we can observe ways in which clothing and appearance became easily identifiable tropes of difference, but exoticism was also accentuated through facial expressions, hand movements and voice.

As noted above (p. 209), there were a number of imperial events in London during this period that were a form of drama in themselves, where Indian princes appearing in traditional dress played an important role in romanticizing empire.[26] The 1911 Festival of Empire in London was celebrated with various historical re-enactments of the glory of the 'English nation' from the 'dawn of British History', with a scene from 'primitive' London, to the high point of the British Raj, with a re-enactment of the Delhi Durbar that crowned Victoria Queen-Empress in 1877. The pomp and pageantry of imperial performance was translated to other productions on the public stage. In the late nineteenth century, there were a number of stage plays with South Asian themes put on by British producers. Indian princes were common themes with plays such as the *The Nabob's Fortune*, *The Nabob*, *The Nabob's Pickle* and *The Saucy Nabob* all performed in Britain at this time.[27] They were also represented at Madame Tussaud's, which had a group of wax figures of the

26 D. Swallow, 'Colonial Architecture, International Exhibitions and Official Patronage of the Indian Artisan: The Case of a Gateway from Gwalior in the Victoria and Albert Museum' in Barringer and Flynn, *Colonialism and the Object*, pp. 52–67 at p. 53.

27 J.M. Mackenzie, *Propaganda and Empire* (Manchester: Manchester University Press, 1984), p. 49.

Maharaja of Kashmir, the Guikwar of Baroda, the Nawab of Dera Ismail Khan and the Begum of Bhopal.[28]

Yet, South Asian performers and producers were increasingly taking to the stage independently – for example, various plays written by Rabindranath Tagore were staged after 1912, Kedar Nath Das Gupta formed a dramatic company, the Union of East and West, in London in 1914. Niranjan Pal's play *The Goddess* was performed in London in 1922, and then Sabu made his break in cinema with the lead role in *The Elephant Boy* in 1937.[29] Although Sabu found success in film roles where he played an elephant driver, a boy brought up in the jungle or an Indian prince, there were no major South Asian stars of the stage in this period. However, African-American Paul Robeson gained critical acclaim from British critics for his portrayal of Othello in London in 1930 which he took to Broadway, and for his performance with Elizabeth Welch in the film *The Song of Freedom* in 1936 which tackled issues of race and class, both of which were more successful than Sabu's roles in challenging the traditional typecasting of film and theatre.[30]

Reviews of South Asians on the stage did not merely concentrate

28 J. Ram, *My Trip to Europe* (Lahore: Mufd-i-am Press, 1893), p. 51. Siobhan Lambert Hurley has discussed the Begum of Bhopal and veiling in Britain in 'Out of India: The Journey of Begum of Bhopal, 1901–1930', in T. Ballantyne and A. Burton (eds), *Bodies in Contact: Rethinking Colonial Encounters in World History* (London: Duke University Press, 2005), pp. 293–309.

29 See K. Kundu, S. Bhattacharya and K. Sircar, *Imagining Tagore: Rabindranath and the British Press (1912–1941)* (Calcutta: Sahitya Samsad, 2000) for an appendix of Tagore plays performed in Britain, 1912–41. Kedar Nath Das Gupta, a Bengali playwright, had moved to Britain in the early twentieth century and collaborated with Laurence Binyon on a production of *Sakuntala* in 1919. Niranjan Pal (1889–1959) had studied in London and became a successful film director, producer and screen-writer for the Bombay film industry. Sabu (1924–1963) became a major film star, appearing in productions such as *The Drum* (1938), *The Thief of Bagdad* (1940), *The Jungle Book* (1942), *The End of the River* (1947), and *The Black Narcissus* (1947).

30 S.A. Nollen, *Paul Robeson: Film Pioneer* (Jefferson: McFarland, 2010). See also C. Chambers, 'Images on Stage: A Historical Survey of South Asians in British Theatre before 1975' in G. Ley and S. Dadswell (eds), *British South Asian Theatres: A Documented History* (Exeter: University of Exeter Press, 2010) for more on the history of South Asian performers in British theatre.

on the aesthetics of the costumes and scenery; they also remarked upon the manner of the dramatic performance, movement and music, as we can see in Stanley Rice's review in 1922 [Source 8]. Compare Rice's review to that in the *Spectator* in the same year, reviewing a production of *The Goddess* at the Ambassadors Theatre. Having remarked upon the author's 'imperfect command' of English, the *Spectator* reviewer explains that the actors had 'not acquired the naturalistic Western style'.[31] Or another review of the same production in the *Stage*, which mentions the draperies on the stage, 'in front of which characteristically plaintive Eastern music (with semi-haunting ditty seemingly contrasted with a dirge) is played by a couple of performers in native costumes, an Indian lady wielding an instrument uniting the attributes of harp and double bass'.[32] Here, the term 'costume' is appropriate for performance, but another form of South Asian artistic output – music – is being remarked upon with negative overtones.

Britain and India describes Victoria Drummond's dance performance in December 1919 at the rooms of the Anglo-French Society at Scala House in London:

> Every gesture and position and each movement of the arms and fingers and pose in the Hindu dance is full of symbolical meaning of a religious basis, and perhaps it is this characteristic of the art, ignored in Western dances, which specially appeals to Miss Drummond. To appreciate fully Hindu dancing its symbolic nature must be understood, otherwise it tends to become meaningless to the Western observer who, thus thrown back on the Western standard of criticism, will probably find it lacking in spontaneity, in freedom of movement, and possibly in grace.[33]

British men and women, therefore, were also taking up South Asian art forms as in the case of Alice Richardson, married to the art-critic Ananda Coomaraswamy, who gave recitals of Indian music in 'Indian dress' under the name of 'Ratan Devi'.[34] Facial expressions and hand movements, which are integral for all dance forms, were

31 *Spectator*, 22 July 1922.
32 *Stage*, 22 June 1922.
33 *Britain and India*, 1(1) (January 1920): 56.
34 Alice Richardson, Making Britain Database www.open.ac.uk/makingbritain/content/alice-richardson (accessed 18 October 2010).

particularly pounced upon when describing or picturing Indian dances (Figures 4.2 and 4.3). But, as Judith Walkowitz has explained, public dance performance in the nineteenth century had been seen as a foreign import, alien to British culture,[35] and so the comparison above between Eastern and Western dance was a relatively new construct, further 'othering' a form that was already seen as not British, here emphasizing the influence of spiritual Hinduism upon cultural outputs.

Uday Shankar (1900–77) initially travelled to London to study art under William Rothenstein at the Royal College of Art, but was persuaded by Anna Pavlova, the Russian ballerina, to turn to dance. They created a sensation when they performed together in September 1923 at the Royal Opera House, and he then performed at the British Empire Exhibition in 1924. Shankar is credited for fusing various forms of dance to create a modern 'Indian' dance form and for popularizing Indian dance on the international stage. Although a close relationship between ballet and Indian classical dance was fostered in this period, the image of Indian dance as exemplified by Shankar was exoticized. The graceful forms of Shankar and Ram Gopal, who performed in Britain in 1939 and then after 1947, highlighted South Asian masculinity within a feminine art form, but admiration was also associated with their striking appearance in terms of costuming and gestures within the dance.[36] Shankar capitalized upon the interest in his alien expressions, pursuing them in his career path and establishing these particular movements as a 'norm' for British ideas of 'Indian' dance. It is possible that Shankar deliberately mocked Western expectations of Indian dance by exaggerating his expressions and movements to cater to British demands.

The audiences for Uday Shankar or Ram Gopal would have

35 J.R. Walkowitz, 'The Vision of 'Salome': Cosmopolitanism and Erotic Dancing in Central London, 1908–1918', *American Historical Review* 108(2) (2003), www.historycooperative.org/journals/ahr/108.2/walkowitz.html (accessed 18 October 2010).

36 Ram Gopal (1917–2003) has been described as a more 'traditional' and 'classical' Indian dancer than Uday Shankar. Gopal too collaborated with ballet dancers and helped increase Western interest in Indian dance forms in the middle of the twentieth century.

differed in composition from that at the performance of *The Goddess*. Equally, the audiences at imperial exhibitions would have been varied but also much larger. (There were approximately five and a half million visitors at the 1886 Colonial and Indian Exhibition and 1888 Glasgow Exhibition, and twenty-seven million attended the 1924 British Empire Exhibition.)[37] It was audience participation and reaction that moulded the discourse around South Asians in Britain – they too held power to shape public opinion. The different forms in which South Asians could be seen and gazed upon in Britain informed each other – the forms of paintings and sculpture could be seen in dance, the costumes of drama and dance performance were influenced by imperial spectacles, music and literature were in dialogue and building up a layered image of the different poses of South Asians. During the inter-war period, South Asians had a more independent presence within Britain, directing their own dramatic ventures, wearing their choice of clothes, painting their own subjects, but despite their increased involvement in shaping their image, there continued to be a fascination for a culture that remained unfamiliar.

Conclusions: a representation of South Asian culture?

All the depictions and descriptions of South Asians in Britain from 1870 to 1950 could not do full justice to the range of social groups and cultural traditions of the Indian subcontinent. Certain aspects and tropes about South Asians became over-emphasized by British commentators, but South Asians deployed them as well. Homi Bhabha has explained how the stereotype within colonial discourse deliberately described difference in excess and was used to exert power.[38] The encounter and dialogue on British soil, where the colonial relationship exerted itself differently from that in the subcontinent, allowed British ideas of South Asians to develop. We can see the ways in which categorizing South Asians did reduce them, but South Asians were also using these common tropes to establish their own identities and impressions upon the British public mind.

37 Mackenzie, *Propaganda and Empire*, p. 101.
38 H. Bhabha, 'The Other Question: Homi K. Bhabha Reconsiders the Stereotype and Colonial Discourse', *Screen* 24(6) (1983): 18–36.

British commentary on South Asian difference as evident by their presence in Britain itself should not always be dismissed as Orientalist or even racist. The meeting of cultures within the British space would always elicit interest and remarks upon the novelty of products brought over from a different climate. What would be more interesting and remarkable, in further studies, would be to trace the ways in which the presence of South Asians and their material and cultural outputs in Britain may have directly influenced British culture – in terms of a broadening introduction of colour into the clothes worn by females, in the headwear of men, in artistic methods, or in dance and drama, if at all.

The most noticeable effect of the meeting of these cultures appears to be a further British homogenization of the idea of South Asian or 'Indian' cultural properties. By the 1930s, commentators were keen to identify art or dance that was specifically 'Indian' and therefore 'national', positioning the Indian subcontinent within the narrative of modern progress. As political debates about Indian independence became more reasoned and attracted more international support, attitudes towards the subcontinent were developing to appreciate the calibre of South Asian cultural outputs. However, the terminology and approach to understanding South Asia did not alter much. Expressions of South Asian culture that did not fit into the common categories of the spiritual, exotic and Oriental were hardly remarked upon. Greater familiarity led to less amazement at the presence of South Asians within British towns and cities, but the number of South Asians was still proportionately small and so they continued to elicit attraction with emphasis on the novel or quintessentially 'Indian' up until the end of the 1940s.

When talking about the discourses of representation and Orientalism it is difficult not to get caught up in using the same essentialized categories in describing South Asians as earlier commentators have been criticized for. We must remember that the representation of South Asians in Britain was not static and was not controlled by a 'British' or 'colonial' eye. Just as South Asians were varied so were British voices and pens. It is important to note that much of the representation of South Asians, particularly in the earlier part of this period, was intimately affected and influenced by imperial relations and agendas. These imperial legacies continued to shape the way South Asians were represented in Britain after the independence of India and Pakistan in 1947; the 1951 Festival of Britain, for example, used the rhetoric of the Commonwealth to justify continued categorization of South Asians as 'spectacles'.[39] The imperial relationship was also not just a linear relationship between London and India, but South Asians were operating within a wider imperial network and were part of a global discourse that extended beyond the British Empire. American, European, Asian and African voices and perceptions were all also influencing the ways in which South Asians were seen and how they wished to represent themselves to the world and on the world stage. These displays were constantly changing and they varied depending from which standpoint you were viewing these global South Asian players.

39 J. Littler, '"Festering Britain": the 1951 Festival of Britain, Decolonisation and the Representation of the Commonwealth', in S. Faulkner and A. Ramamurthy (eds), *Visual Culture and Decolonisation in Britain* (Aldershot: Ashgate, 2006), pp. 21–42.

Source material for Chapter 4

1 Joseph Salter,[40] *The Asiatic in England* (London: Seeley, Jackson, and Halliday, 1872), Chapter 1, pp. 19–23.
[British Library shelfmark T8683]

'Found dead!' Who? Where? Has he no friends? How did he die? To these very natural questions, prompted by the common generosity of an English heart, we reply, 'We don't know.' But, gazing on the haggard face of the departed stranger, we conclude he has died in a land in which he was a foreigner for his tattered clothes and swarthy features suggest that his birth-place cannot be far from the banks of the Ganges. The coroner and his jury, however, have just come to the unsatisfactory verdict, 'Found dead;' after having put off the inquest to the present day, hoping to gain some information of the deceased; but all that is known is, a policeman found him, on a frosty winter night, dead on the pavement in one of the many avenues in High-street, Shadwell.[41] This child of the sunny land must have been dead some time, for he was quite cold. Nothing was found upon him to tell who he was, or what were the hard circumstances that led to his

40 Joseph Salter was a missionary who worked for the London City Mission in the East End of London. He was the first and resident missionary at the Strangers' Home for Asiatics, Asians and South Sea Islanders, founded in 1857. The Maharaja Duleep Singh (1838–93), the exiled and deposed former prince of the Punjab, was one of the benefactors of this home and Salter dedicated *The Asiatic in England* to him. Salter wrote one other book relating to his work with Asiatics in London: *The East in the West* (London: S.W. Partridge & Co., 1896).
41 Shadwell is a district in the East End of London.

death. There was a knife at his side, and his horny hands bore evidence of honest labour and hard toil. He must be one of the many Lascars who are engaged in bringing the produce of Hindustan to our isle. Poor fellow, he could have found neither help nor sympathy in this land of gold and philanthropy! Strange, indeed, in the midst of so many merchant princes made rich with Indian gold, that the stranger who brought us the precious things of the torrid zone, should die uncared for on a winter night in one of our London streets. But, perhaps, it is a solitary case, and has never occurred before, and may never occur again. What did the coroner say? Alas! he says, that no less than eight human beings of the same class have perished with cold and hunger in our streets during the present winter, and he has held nearly forty inquests on the same class of miserable beings during the last few years! Nearly forty sons of India have perished in our London streets with cold and hunger within a limited time, and no good Samaritan to pour in the oil and the wine, to soothe their dying moments with the good news of the sinner's Friends, and point the dying one to the better land, where

Sickness and sorrow, pain and death,
Are felt and fear'd no more.[42]

And this is all the Christian public know of a numerous class of our fellow-creatures who are living in our very midst, and constantly arriving on our coast with the produce of their own land. Tens of thousands of pounds are annually and rightly spent to ameliorate the temporal and spiritual condition of the heathen in their own distant land, but here, in the Christians' home, they only attract our notice when the coroner places the verdict of the jury on record: 'Found dead,' or 'Died of cold and starvation.'

These forty Asiatics, starved as much by the frost and snow of an English winter night as by want of food, are but a sample of a much larger class of the same race of beings who suffer, perhaps, more protracted misery, if not so acute, and are the prey of numerous hardships and injuries which never come under human ken; bearing, too, their prostrating misfortunes without the hope of ever making a

42 Couplet from a Christian spiritual song.

sympathetic Christian public sensible of their desperate condition, and the remedy most needed for their relief, from the want of a language with which to tell their gloomy tale ...

But we must know a little more about these Mohammedans and Hindoos residing somewhere in this great city of London, before we suggest a remedy, or make any effort for their temporal or spiritual welfare. How do they get here? Where are they to be found? How came they to be in this fearful condition? There are no idle vagrants, so many of whom prowl through the length of our island, preferring rather to beg than work. These are all sons of honest toil, and each one has worked his way to our shores and has landed in our midst with a bright eye and a merry heart, because he had Queen Victoria's golden coins hidden in a corner of his gaudy puggree;[43] enough in his own estimation and ours too, should he fall into right hands, to supply all the scanty wants of Oriental life, till he finds another ship that will take him back again to his family and friends rejoicing. One of these men stepped on shore gay in his apparel, reflecting the colours of the rainbow, firm in his tread, erect in his stature, with evident consciousness of self-sufficiency, for he carried £60 with him, the result of many months' toil on various seas; but we saw him, a few days afterwards, destitute in the streets; the bright beam of his eye had given place to an anxious look, and his gay colours displaced by dirty rags. He was reduced in so short a time to the level of his wretched countrymen, seeking the beggar's pittance from passers-by. Like him many have fallen with terrible rapidity, fallen so as to become familiar, and, perhaps, even satisfied, with the degraded level they have reached.

43 Small turban.

2 'India in London', *Pall Mall Gazette*, 6 Feb. 1888.[44]
[British Newspaper Library shelfmark LD28]

It is one of the objects of the National Indian Association to give Indian students in London an opportunity of obtaining 'an intimate knowledge of the best side of English home life and manners'.[45] One way in which this is done is by bringing educated Indians living in London into social contact with Europeans at the soirées which the association holds every two or three months in Chandos-street, Cavendish square.[46] For picturesqueness and for their pleasant tone these gatherings, where cultured England meets cultured India on an equal footing, are perhaps unique in the social life of London. If Miss Mary Carpenter,[47] who devoted a lifetime to the establishment of the association, could today come back and see the fruits of her labours at one of the soirées, she would rejoice in the work which unweariedly she carried on for fifty years. The last of the soirées was held a few days ago, and up to midnight the rooms were thronged with men and women representing in striking contrast the fair Saxon and the dusky Indian, but all bent on showing that they regarded each other as equal, and that there was no thought of the superiority of one race over the other. One group quietly stationed not far from the entrance of the room attracted at once the attention of every newcomer. A charming Indian lady draped fantastically in brilliant robes, with

44 The author is anonymous. The *Pall Mall Gazette* was a daily evening paper published in London, edited by William Thomas Stead (1849–1912) from 1883 to 1889, who pioneered a new emphasis in British journalism by introducing the 'interview' and for his investigative journalism.

45 The National Indian Association was founded in 1870 by Mary Carpenter (mentioned a few lines later: see n. 47) and Keshub Chunder Sen (1838–84), a Brahmo Samaj reformer, in Bristol, and then moved to its London headquarters in 1877. The Association was set up to provide a meeting place for Indians and the British.

46 Chandos Street, just off Regent Street, in Westminster, London.

47 Mary Carpenter (1807–77) was the daughter of the Unitarian Minister, Lant Carpenter, who had welcomed the Bengali Brahmo Samaj reformer, Ram Mohun Roy (1772–1833), into his home in Bristol in 1833. This sparked an interest in India for Mary Carpenter who visited India four times between 1866 and 1871. She was particularly concerned about promoting social reform in India, including female education.

dark eyes and snowy teeth more dazzling than the tinsel of her garments, held by her side a tiny girl of perfect Eastern beauty, whose great lovely eyes looked somewhat disdainfully on the crowd of admirers. With her little hands she tightly clutched the lace-like garment which was thrown over her curly deep-black hair, and came down to her feet, allowing her gaily embroidered dress only imperfectly to appear. Further on in the room the gorgeous robes of a young bar student attract attention. Wherever Abdul Majid has pursued his studies he has distinguished himself, and his keen intellect shines in his handsome face. How pleasantly he talks, with that natural ease and refinement which to acquire is in our Western world considered the acme of culture, on every subject that may be started! Talk to him of his sunny home and its history, and the names of eminent Indian princes and the great deities of the Hindoos throng each other in his animated discourse; start the theme of English politics, and the enthusiastic Home-Ruler is as conversant with every phase of our political life as if he had been born and bred to it. Go on to a lighter subject and ask him why he does not wear the regulation turban instead of a small black cap embroidered in gold with exquisite taste. Lightly he takes off the much admired head-gear to hand it over for inspection, and says with his frank, pleasant smile, "I'm flighty tonight; the turban is the headdress for serious men. It is the greatest ambition of an Indian boy to attain the age when he may leave off wearing the cap, and exchange it for the turban which means that he has become a man. But now and then even a man wears a cap, as you see tonight, only it does not command as much respect as the turban.'

Politely bowing, as he is introduced to the Lord Mayor by a stately lady, another young Indian is conspicuous in his purple satin gown and dark red turban. 'Dalpatram Bhagranji Shukla, otherwise Mr Shukla of the Inner Temple, a very learned man,' is the young Mahommedan's introduction to the Lord of the City, who shakes hands and converses most amicably with the clever law student.

'Your turban seems heavy, Mr Shukla?' 'Yes, it is a heavy thing, but it is ten yards long; no wonder it presses a little on the head. Fashions in turbans? Yes, there are. When I left home the dark red and gold which I wear was fashionable; in summer we wear pink turbans, and for deep mourning white ones. When the mourning is less deep, black turbans are worn –' but no continued conversation is possible in the ever-thickening crowd, and presently he is laughing at one of Thackeray's humorous characters, citing Macaulay, or conducting some fair lady to the refreshment-room.[48] Everywhere his frank, open face wins him friends, and his tutor, Mr Algernon Brown, who is appointed by the association to take young students under his care on their arrival in England, in order to guard them from the dangers which beset inexperienced Indian on coming to this country, looks with paternal pride at his promising protégé.

'We are the voices of the restless winds,' quotes somebody, pointing towards the room where a hundred voices are conversing.[49] Perhaps the sight of Lady Arnold, in a queenly white plush train, in which pink lights play at every movement, suggest the quotation. The author of 'The Light of Asia' is not present tonight, but the stars and Orders of India sparkle on many a black coat, and here is Sir Peter Lumsden, entering the room with a cheery word in Hindustani to his old friend and colleague Lieut.-General Pollard. Mr and Mrs Ilbert, Sir Donald and Lady Stewart, Lord and Lady Chelmsford, and innumerable other friends of India are present.[50] Miss Buss, who is always in the front rank where the advance of education is concerned, defends with the enthusiasm of youth, in spite of her venerable white hair, the Home Rule movement; young female medical students stand chatting about; there is life and interest and amusement in every one of the groups. But now one tall, dark man in a long caftan-like coat and curious high cap draws many eyes towards himself and

48 William Makepeace Thackeray (1811–63), novelist, born in Calcutta; Thomas Babington Macaulay (1800–59), historian and essayist worked in Indian administration 1834–38, producing the famous Minute on Education (1835) and reforming the Indian penal codes.

49 'We are the voices of the wandering wind' is from Sir Edwin Arnold's *Light of Asia* (1879) – a poem as told in verse by an Indian Buddhist on the life and teaching of Prince Gautama, the Buddha.

50 Sir Peter Lumsden worked for the Afghan Border Commission; Lieutenant General Charles Pollard; Sir Courtenay Peregrine Ilbert (1841–1924), married to Jessie, parliamentary draftsman, legal writer and administrator in India, 1880–86; Field Marshall Sir Donald Martin Stewart (1824–1900); Frederic Augustus Thesiger (1827–1905) and wife Adria Fanning were the parents of the future Viceroy of India.

his friends. He laughs and talks and gesticulates, and all who are near join in the fun. He is a Parsee and a fire worshipper, explains the old Anglo-Indian, one of the sect who never extinguish fire, and in whose houses there is always a fire burning. Many of the Indians present are in European evening dress. 'We like it better in England', they say, 'because in it we attract less attention.' Most curious of all the strange figures at the soirée are those who over the European garments wear some gorgeous gold-embroidered coat of coloured silk and a towering turban, to show, as they laughingly say, their sympathy with England without denying their preference of their home in the East. Nearly all the Indians address each other in English, for, as on the day of Pentecost, they are 'out of every nation' under the Eastern heaven.[51]

---

51 From the New Testament on Pentecost, Acts 2:5; 'Now there were dwelling at Jerusalem Jews, devout men, out of every nation under heaven.'

3 *'A Lady's Day at the Glasgow Exhibition', Indian Magazine*[52], 214
(*October 1888*): 540–6 [*by M. M'G*].[53]
[British Library shelfmark ST182]

The Hulwai (sweetmeat maker) happening to turn round his head as
we approached, we addressed him in the common colloquial of his
home. A beam of pleased recognition shot through his beady black eyes
as the magic sound of his own tongue released him from his national
appearance of stolidity. Although seated *on a chair* before a fire,
watching the melting of a large flat pot of butter, he complained of the
cold. We tried to palliate the fact of the unusually rigorous summer
with hopes of a warm autumn. The Hindu hugged himself doubtfully,
saying he must make the best of it, as he was in very good employment,
and getting better pay than he would in his own country.

The only kind of sweetmeat he made in the Exhibition was 'Goja'
– little pastry cakes – sold in the next stall by a young Asian, wearing
a funeral suit of black, not at all becoming to his swarthy skin. He,
however, smilingly informed us that he drove a roaring trade, and
that the situation was not half-bad. Part of this stall is occupied by
the Indian sonar (jeweller) placidly melting and moulding his metal
into varieties of ornaments peculiar to India, and which have become
fashionable of late years in this country.

Proceeding through the Indian courts, the sweet scent of khus-
khus[54] and sandal was delicious. Among the spices lay samples of the
pretty-looking nux vomica,[55] and the uninitiated would scarcely
think that the small silvery pods of the Mysore and Ceylon
cardamoms were closely packed inside with layers of tiny black seeds
of a highly appreciable flavour; these little seeds are much used in
Indian fine cookery. They are also greatly valued by the natives as a
tonic; mixed with betel-nut, and other spices, and wrapped in an
aromatic pan leaf. The Mohammedan, particularly, finds it a most
enjoyable quid in the pungent little packet.

52 *Indian Magazine* was the monthly journal produced by the National Indian
    Association from 1871 in London. It was renamed the *Indian Magazine and
    Review* in 1891 and ceased publication in 1933.
53 This is the pseudonym given by the author.
54 Poppy seeds.
55 Strychnine plant.

... We came next to the Jubilee Presents of our well-beloved Sovereign. India has been lavish to its Empress. Bewildering is the plethora of gold and silver articles in caskets, salvers, inlaid valuables, and all manner of things from the four points of the compass. The great pair of elephants' tusks, mounted on two ebony heads, and surmounted with a gold image of the goddess Durgā – in her two upper hands she holds emblematic flowers; with one lower hand she appears to bless, while with the other she seems to deprecate – the tusks, festooned in fine gold, with tendrils of the pepper vine, are a pretty sight to see. The berry of this tropical plant has a resemblance to the mulberry. The mass of beautiful white ostrich feathers, fashioned into fans large enough for the use of Gog and Magog,[56] give one a sense of the exquisite covering the Almighty Father bestows on His creatures.

The silver palanquin from Allahabad shows the kind of conveyance once in general use in Hindostan; and who but an Indian could devise such a hampering, harassing, magnificent, utterly unnecessary set of horse-trappings as has been sent to Her Majesty by one of her loyal subjects of the East?

Nothing could better demonstrate, nothing better illustrate, the luxurious, lavish display of an Eastern court. The poor horse, paraded in the agony of such cumbrous finery, cannot move his feet with freedom. The left fetlock has a heavy gold bangle round it, so heavy it has a pad under it. His head is covered, and hung with gold brocade. An upright feather ornament is on his head, from which suspends an emerald pendant. The monstrous fluffy silk tassels hanging round the shackled brute would act as instruments of torture if he ventured on a trot or canter. He is only suffered to proceed at a measured amble or stalking walk, led on each side of his head with a red or yellow rope.

---

56 Gog and Magog appear in the Qu'ran, and Old and New Testaments. In Britain they are depicted as giants, and are guardians of the City of London.

4 T.N. Mukharji[57], *A Visit to Europe* (Calcutta: W. Newman, 1889), pp. 66–70.
[British Library shelfmark 10108.de.9.]

The Procession started from the main entrance and proceeded through the vestibule where the clay figures representing the various races of the Indian soldiery were arranged in a row. Passing under the carved wood-work on which the Jaipur motto 'Where Virtue is, there is Victory' was emblazoned, it entered the Indian Court glittering with the richest workmanship of our skilled artisans, and finally it arrived before the 'Indian Palace' where we waited. His Royal Highness, the Prince of Wales here presented us individually to Her Majesty.[58] The Indian artisans who stood in the opposite row were instructed to receive the Queen with the salutation of 'Rám, Rám.'[59] Among them were some devout Muhammadans, who cried 'Rám, Rám,' but being unaccustomed to such a strange mode of salutation they added to it the words 'Al-Ahmad-ul-illah'. So they continually said – 'Rám, Rám, Al Ahmad-ul-illah, Rám, Rám, Al-Ahmad-ul-illah.' After this was over an address was read, and the procession then moved on. Not knowing what to do next we followed and passing through the Australian and the Canada courts, we arrived at the Albert Hall. As we were pushing our way, Sir Phillip Cunliffe-Owen came running to us and with a face full of concern said 'What are you doing!'[60] Then we realised our actual position. As soon as the address was read we followed Her Majesty and went on along with the Royal Family. We felt somewhat nervous and asked him, 'Shall we go back?'

57 Trilokya Nath Mukharji (1847–1919) from Calcutta worked as an exhibition assistant for the Indian Government and came to London in 1886 to assist in cataloguing, lecturing and answering questions at the exhibition. He was involved in the production of catalogues for the 1883 Amsterdam Exhibition and the 1888 Glasgow International Exhibition as well, but also wrote a range of humorous and satirical works in Bengali. This travelogue was also published in London by Edward Stanford.
58 The Prince of Wales, Edward Albert (King Edward VII, 1901–1910) had commissioned the 1886 exhibition to celebrate Queen Victoria's Golden Jubilee.
59 Invocations of the Hindu God King Rama.
60 Cunliffe-Owen was executive commissioner of the exhibition.

He said, 'No, stay where you are.' We were very sorry for the mistake, but there was no help for it; we could not go back even if we would, for the passage behind was entirely blocked up. So we were obliged to stand where we were. The Royal Albert Hall where the ceremony of opening the Exhibition was held is an immense circular building covered by a glass dome, and capable of holding 10,000 persons. It was built by a Company in 1868–71 at a cost of more than 30 lakhs of rupees (£200,000) ...

India formed by far the most interesting section of the Colonial and Indian Exhibition. Passing the vestibule at the main entrance, the visitor would stand before the clay models of the military races which uphold the power of England in the East. He would then be led to that gorgeous display of costly jewellery, gold and silver plate, brass and copper vessels with tasteful designs, minute wood carving, inlay work on metal, stone and wood, lacquered ware of ruby, emerald and golden hues, costly fabrics woven by patient hands unrivalled in the world, and various other articles which from time immemorial excited the wonder and commanded the admiration of the western nations. As the visitor stood facing this vast panorama of India's artistic wealth, he could watch on his right the multitude crowding to the spot where the jungle life in India was illustrated in a rather over-drawn vividness. Within a narrow compass was pressed the sloping section of a low rugged hill, high trees with arms spreading in all directions, bushy undergrowths, clumps of feathery bamboo, the wild date with stumps of their petioles sticking on all sides of the stem, rank grass, and other accessories of a sub-Himalayan scenery. This miniature representation of the happiest of hunting grounds in India was densely packed with all sorts of big and small game, the sight of which often elicited a sigh from the superannuated sportsmen, as the pleasant days of his youthful life rushed into his mind, when regardless of all danger from his ferocious enemy of the forest and the more deadly jungle fever of the Tafai,[61] he defiantly strode through hills and swamps dealing death and destruction wherever he went.

---

61 Lowland area in Nepal border region.

**5 Jhinda Ram, *My Trip to Europe* (Lahore: Mufd-i-am Press, 1893),
pp. 79–80.**[62]
[British Library shelfmark T38525]

On several occasions, I saw an Anglo-Indian coming out of a crowd
and rushing towards me to exchange a few words in Hindustani.[63] He
met me so enthusiastically as if I was his long departed friend or
relation. Hindustani was a sufficient attraction to the by-standers,
ladies as well as gentlemen, who looked upon it as jargon. Of course,
the Anglo-Indian, talking with me in Hindustani was considered a
hero amongst them, who could talk and understand the jargon. We
must all be thankful to Miss Manning, the Secretary of the National
Indian Association, who takes a great deal of interest in Indians
visiting England.[64] This energetic and noble lady holds a *soirée* every
three months in which Indian ladies and gentlemen living in London
are invited to join. I had the honour to attend one *soirée* in which
about 50 Indian ladies and gentlemen and about 250 Anglo-Indian
ladies and gentlemen attended. There were several lords, baronets,
knights and companions amongst them who have been rewarded for
the service they have done in India. Lord Napier of Magdala, the
veteran soldier, with a star on his breast, was conspicuous amongst
them.[65] I cannot sufficiently describe the grandeur of the scene which
presented to my eyes in the *soirée*. Oh! how splendid it looked to see
the English ladies dressed in most charming and elegant attires; with
their shining hair bandaged in a most fantastic manner over which

62 Ram's account of his visit to Europe in the 1880s were published as letters in
　Lahore's *Tribune* in 1887 and then published in book form in 1893. This
　extract is from a chapter titled 'General Treatment I Received from the Hands
　of English People'.
63 The term 'Anglo-Indian' used here denotes a British person who works or had
　worked in India. In the late nineteenth century, however, this term became
　synonymous with those of mixed descent, formerly known as Eurasians, and
　was enshrined as this definition in the 1911 Indian Census.
64 Elizabeth Adelaide Manning (1828–1905), Honorary Secretary of the
　National Indian Association 1877–1905.
65 Robert Cornelius Napier (1810–90) had a distinguished military career in
　India and Abyssinia. He was Commander-in-Chief in India 1870–76. In 1886
　was appointed to the office of Constable of the Tower of London.

were moving beautiful plumes, and sparkling costly diamonds; and the Indian ladies wearing their precious gold bordered *saris* and *dopattas*[66] covering their dark coloured hair bandaged plainly over which could be seen coarse golden ornaments. Oh! how magnificent it was to look at those attractive striking figures swimming along the hall amongst the English gentlemen wearing gorgeous costumes. Was it not curious enough to look at shy Indian ladies mixing freely with Europeans and the big Anglo-Indian ladies and gentlemen receiving their Indian fellow-subjects on an equal footing with and brotherly feeling? I had the honour of being introduced to several great and distinguished men by the noble lady, Miss Manning.

66 Scarf or shawl.

6 *Franco-British Exhibition, London, 1908. Official Guide* (London: Bemrose & Sons Limited, 1908), pp. 93–6.
[British Library shelfmark 7957.de.33]

Close to this building stands the Ceylon[67] tea-house (No. 121), and then comes a pavilion built in the severe style of Mohammedan architecture by the Government of India. Its dazing white façades, capped by many a graceful minaret, form a pleasing contrast to the green lawns and gay flower beds by which it is surrounded.

On entering the Indian pavilion the visitor is at once in the midst of a profusion of the best examples of the renowned sumptuary artistic wares of our great Asiatic possessions. The most striking object in the main hall is the magnificent carved wood show-case, a unique example of the combined skill of native carvers from all parts of India, and in every kind of indigenous wood, and the delicacy and intricacy of its lace-like carvings will excite wonder and admiration. In the hexagonal show-cases will be found specimens of silk and other fabrics. The beautiful and varied collections contributed by the Schools of Art of Bombay, Calcutta, Madras, Lahore, and Burma are exhibited in the side bays as well as in the great trophy. The valuable silk exhibit of the Kashmir State, the unique sandal-wood carvings of the Mysore State, the Jaipur pottery, Gwalior muslins, and art objects from Bikanir, Hyderabad, and other native states invite careful inspection. Many choice carpets and rugs from the celebrated looms of Kashmir, Vellore, Amritsar, Bikanir, the Punjab, and other parts of the Peninsula are hung on the walls of the building.

The Indian Tea Association show numerous samples of teas and other exhibits connected with this great industry; but what will be most popular is the realistic tableau of a typical Indian tea garden. A Bengal village scene forms a suitable background for the Jute section, of which the collection of Jute manufactures of Messrs. Thomas Duff & Co., of Calcutta, form an important item. The other great staple exports of India, such as wheat, grain, cotton, hides, skins, and seeds, are represented. The leather and textile manufactures of the Madras Presidency are shown in considerable completeness. The motor-car bodies exhibited by Mr Press, of Bombay, indicate that India does not

67 Ceylon is the former colonial name for Sri Lanka.

intend to be backward in this newest of industries; and the surgical instruments of Messrs. Powell, of the same Presidency, provide another example of the skill of the native worker. Among noteworthy exhibits in the industrial section are Messrs. Hattersley's working installation of hand-power looms adapted for domestic use in India; the sporting goods of Messrs. Uberoi, of Sialkot; the biscuits of Messrs. Pinto, of Mangalore; the Burma cheroots of Messrs. Scott; the Madras cigars of Messrs. Spencer; and the imposing exhibit of Indian condiment of Messrs. J.A. Sharwood.

In the grounds of the Indian section is a fine log of Bombay blackwood, imported by Messrs. D. Witt & Co.; also logs of padauk and teak, and a tent shown by the Elgin Mills of Cawnpur.

Twin towers guard the richly carved entrance to the native village (No. 122) that lies behind the Ceylon Tea-house. It is composed of a cluster of gaily coloured houses and huts in the style familiar to tourists who visit Colombo, the Gate of the Far East. The Bazaars are full of life, with their many brown artisans chatting, laughing and quarrelling, but intent all the while upon their handiwork. In the background a huge Pagoda towers over the village, and dark passages lead to the temple in the rocks, accessible only to the priests. Cingalee dancers, musicians, jugglers, and beautiful nautch-girls will entertain the visitors, and many of the mysterious tricks which have hitherto baffled explanation will be performed before the eyes of the astounded onlooker. After dusk a clever scheme of illumination will transform the Ceylon village into a perfect fairy-land.

The gardens behind the Indian Government building are dedicated to Eastern sports and pastimes (No. 123). A large circular track has been laid out, and on it numerous elephants, camels, and zebus[68] patiently await the pleasure of children who delight to ride, or rather to say they have ridden, on the back of such strange animals. They will also have an opportunity here of driving in quaint little Indian carts.

The huge white building close by is the Indian Arena. Erected in the pompous style of the East, and covering nearly 40,000 square feet, it holds seating accommodation for over 3,000 people, and is, we believe, the first open-air theatre ever constructed in England. Here,

---

68 Zebus are domestic cattle originating in South Asia.

under the title of 'our Indian Empire', a spectacular performance will be enacted two or three times a day. And, indeed, the whole of the Indian Empire has been ransacked from north to south, and from east to west, to collect the cleverest of Indian performers – over a hundred in number, who will perform their astonishing feats in the large ring. The scene depicts a feast-day at the Court of a mighty Rajah. Acrobats, tight-rope walkers, sorcerers, wrestlers, snake-charmers, and fakirs, have gathered together from all parts. A herd of working elephants is shown lifting and carrying enormous trunks of trees. Races are run by men and animals, and at the conclusion of the first part of the entertainment a procession is formed by all natives, augmented by some fifty gorgeously arrayed animals, and showing the various kinds of locomotion common in India. In the second part of the *spectacle* a realistic and exciting Tiger Hunt is presented, in the course of which a dozen fully grown elephants with their riders will slide down a precipice from a height of 40 feet into the lake below.

7 *Ananda K. Coomaraswamy,*[69] *'Indian Images with Many Arms',* *Burlington Magazine for Connoisseurs,* 22(118) (January 1913): 189–91, 194–6.
[British Library shelfmark P.P.1931.pcs]

Not a few writers, in speaking of the many-armed images of Indian art, have treated this peculiarity as an unpardonable defect. 'After 300 A.D.', says Mr Vincent Smith, 'Indian sculpture properly so called hardly deserves to be reckoned as art. The figures both of men and animals become stiff and formal, and the idea of power is clumsily expressed by the multiplication of members. The many-headed, many-armed gods and goddesses whose images crowd the walls and roofs of mediaeval temples have no pretensions to beauty, and are frequently hideous and grotesque'.[70] Mr Maskell speaks of 'these hideous deities with animals' heads and innumerable arms'.[71] Sir G. Birdwood considers that 'the monstrous shapes of the Puranic deities are unsuitable for the higher forms of artistic representation; and this is possibly why sculpture and painting are unknown as fine arts in India'.[72] Quotations of this kind could be multiplied; but enough has been said to show that for a certain class of critics there exists the underlying assumption that in Indian art the multiplication of limbs or heads, in addition of animal attributes, is in itself a very grave

69 Ananda Kentish Coomaraswamy (1877–1947) was an art-critic and curator. Born in Sri Lanka to a Sri Lankan father and English mother, he was brought up in England from the age of one. He was one of the original members of the India Society, founded in London in 1910. Coomaraswamy wrote a number of articles for the *Burlington Magazine* on Indian Art, and a variety of books. Some of the ideas in this article can be found in his most influential work, *The Dance of Siva* (New York: Simpkin, Marshall, 1924).

70 *Imperial Gazetteer of India, 1910,* Vol. II [original footnote]. Vincent Arthur Smith (1843–1920) was a historian who had worked for the Indian Civil Service.

71 *Ivories,* 1905, p. 332 [original footnote]. Alfred Maskell was an art historian who had worked for the South Kensington Museum.

72 *Industrial Arts of India,* 1880, p. 125 [original footnote]. George Birdwood (1832–1917) had been Sheriff of Bombay, curator of the Bombay government art museum and keeper of the India Museum in South Kensington. He retired in 1905 from a position in the India Office.

defect, and fatal to any claim for high merit on behalf of the works concerned.

We need not cite in defence examples of Greek art such as the Victory of Samothrace or the head of Hypnos; of Egyptian, such as the noble figures of Sekhet or other animal gods; or of Byzantine or mediaeval angels; or of modern works such as some of M. Rodin's; for it is clear that all these must, if the critics be consistent, equally suffer condemnation. On the contrary, leaving all other precedents alone, I maintain that Indian figures with many arms or heads, so far from being bad art, or needing any apology, are in themselves unanswerable evidence of the wonderful creative energy of the Indian genius.

Every serious student of art must agree that it is quite impossible to lay down rules about the material with which an artist may work. There are no 'laws of art' admitting one form and forbidding another. Beauty disappears when she is most sought and appears again where she is least expected. One can only demand of the artist that he should succeed; the more complex or seemingly irreconcilable the materials which he chooses, the greater the honour if he proves himself their master. In all art which is not merely representative we have always to bear in mind the analogies with music. There are symphonies as well as sonatinas. Unity is essential to both; but the unity of a short lyric is not the same as the unity of a larger work or of a drama. The first unity consists in having only one motif; the second in the clear expression of one master-motif connecting a variety of episodes. We cannot say that this difference makes one kind of art greater or less than another; but still less ought we to say that the second kind is inferior because of its complexity.

In criticizing Indian or any sculpture, then, let us recognize that the single figure of unique intention is a short poem: a group of figures or a many-armed and many-headed figure is a whole drama. We have no business to inquire whether the single or the complex figure transgresses the actual or imaginary canons of some other art; what we want to know is whether it is alive. If any Indian many-armed figure lacks the quality of life, it is to be condemned for that reason, and not because it has more heads or arms than we see on every man in the street.

... It should have been clear, from *à priori* considerations along, that the excellence or defect of a work of art can no more be attributed to its human or super – or semi-human form, than it can be judged by any other special convention. Every art tradition is a language. To say that Indian is bad, because some of its form are many-armed, is equivalent to saying, for example, that Chinese poetry is bad because it is not written in the English language. It is, in fact, what we do when we describe a foreigner's speech as a lingo or a gibberish. All such criticisms based on peculiarities, and ignoring the fundamental questions of rhythm, significance and vitality are valueless, and are properly to be described as insular. Indeed probably all depreciatory generalizations about any race or any art may be dismissed as confessions of incompetence. Every art must be judged, first in accordance with such universal standards as we have above accepted, and secondly in accordance with its own special canons and conventions: never by the special canons of another art.

This is a matter distinct from the question of personal likes and dislikes. But the first principle of criticism, as Blake tells us, is enthusiasm; and those who dislike a thing are very unlikely to have anything of value to say about it. If circumstances compel any such person to classify the extant materials for the study of Indian art, his studies will be the more valuable the more strictly confined they are to archaeology. Blind guides in art are worse than none. Amongst those who should not air their views on Oriental art are those who, when they speak of art, mean illustration; for in the Oriental world they will rarely meet with that they seek, and the expression of their disappointment is apt to become wearisome. Perhaps we shall hear no more of criticisms of Oriental art based solely on personal objections to special physical peculiarities, or other particular conventions. May it be so: otherwise there will inevitably arise two schools of students of Oriental art, those who like it, and those who dislike it. This will not carry us very far: it would be better to unite in an endeavour to learn something about it.

8 *Stanley Rice,*[73] *'Indian Plays in London'*, *Asiatic Review*, XVIII(53)
(Jan 1922): 129.
[British Library shelfmark ST243]

Under the auspices of the Maharaja of Jhalawar,[74] Pandit Shyam
Shankar has given a series of Indian performances at the Court
Theatre.[75] The courage of his experiment is worthy of the highest
praise, for art can snap its fingers at politics, and to learn to appreciate Indian art is to unlock the innermost chamber of Indian
personality. It is true that the house was by no means full, yet the
public are not to blame, because at present Indian music and Indian
dancing are 'caviare to the general'.[76] The peculiar excellence of both
have not yet been grasped; until we become more accustomed to
strange scales and strange movements, an audience in England must
be rather interested than enthusiastic.

The bill was varied. Undoubtedly the most artistic part of it was
the 'Water Carrier's' song and dance and the performance of Indian
music on the sitar, diruba, and the flute (the latter a European
imitation in metal of the Indian wooden flute), accompanied, of
course, by the tabla, or double drum.[77] But this part was, for the
reasons already given, the least popular. The audience were more
familiar with the illusion scene which followed, because the art of the
Indian conjuror is so thoroughly well known in England that good
folk have been known to mutter in all sincerity their conviction of
Satanic co-operation.

The two plays offered were not so successful. The 'Princes of
Chitor' was set in obviously Saracenic surroundings, and the play
suffers dramatically and artistically from being written almost
entirely in monologue. The queen monopolizes quite five-sixths of
the whole speaking part. Finally, the 'Sleeper Awakened' was handicapped by its description as a 'screaming farce'. It was, in fact, mildly

73 Stanley Rice wrote regular reviews for the *Asiatic Review*, a journal published
in London (1885–1952) on South Asian affairs.
74 Jhalawar was a princely state in South-East Rajasthan.
75 The Court Theatre, Sloane Square, London, had produced many George
Bernard Shaw plays at the beginning of the twentieth century.
76 William Shakespeare, *Hamlet*, Act 2, Scene 2.
77 The sitar and diruba are Indian string instruments.

funny comedy, in which the humour chiefly consisted of 'stage business'. It was very noticeable that the principal male singer was utterly at sea in European times and rhythms. The orchestra tried in vain to follow him, but it was nearly always in front or behind – an interesting compliment to the English difficulty of mastering Indian time and rhythm.

But no Indian production can fail to please the eye. Not only was there a revel of colour, but the innate Indian artistic sense was prominent in the blends and contrasts to be noticed in the same costume. To an audience, however, accustomed to the finished productions of the English stage, there was somewhat of an amateur flavour in the performance, and one may hope that a more careful study of technique will lead to improved productions in the future.

9 A.C. Marshall, 'Nurses of our Ocean Highways: The Fascinating Story of the Ayahs and Amahs who sail the Seven Seas', *Quiver*,[78] 57 (August 1922): 923–6.
[British Library shelfmark P.P.268.CB]

She was very brown and wrinkled like an apple that has been laid aside far into the spring. Upon her head were scanty, greying locks that plainly told of what once had been lustrous, sheeny hair, black as a crow's tail. Her bony wrists carried silver bangles, and attenuated fingers toyed with ear-rings of quaint native workmanship.

She was a travelling Indian ayah, smiling and complacent, gentle and maternal, soft-spoken and plainly self-reliant, with small dark eyes alight with keen intelligence.

... That the Home forges another link in the chain that binds India to the Motherland there can be no doubt. It is within the care and administration of the London City Mission, which carries on its good work in so many unimagined directions in the mighty Metropolis, and has been in existence many years.[79] In the Home there is accommodation for thirty of these ocean nurses, and not one of them is asked for payment in any form, however long they may be in securing employment.

The chief amusement of the ayahs is to dip deeply into the folios of an ordinary scrapbook, in which are neatly pasted pictures from our illustrated magazines and weeklies. They play for hours among themselves a native game named *pachis*, with an embroidered board not unlike that used for ludo. Sitting impassively tailorwise on rugs, they throw up cowrie shells and tiny wooden tops or acorns, and score according to the manner in which the pieces fall. A little tobacco, more or less surreptitiously, and the chewing of the betel nut sums up the total of their petty weaknesses.

From the point of view of religions, there are among the ayahs many converts to Christ's teachings, followers of Mahomet, Buddhists, Confucians, and others. Almost all attend daily the purely

78 The original title for the *Quiver*, when it was started in 1861, was *The Quiver, Designed for the Defence of Biblical Truth and the Advancement of Religion in the Homes of the People.*

79 The London City Mission (LCM) took over management of the Ayahs' Home in 1900, locating it in King Edward's Road, Hackney.

optional Christian service that is held at the Home and which must
be the means eventually of spreading our beliefs among the heathen.
In private, in the bedrooms, the devotees of certain faiths burn their
candles and worship after the manner of their fathers.

Caste enters somewhat embarrassingly into the internal relationships of some of these birds of passage. A few of the ayahs belong to
the submerged strata and may not even pass at table, let alone touch,
the food of those of better rank.

On the whole, however, the family is a thoroughly happy one, and
there is nothing worse to be feared than an occasionally trifling
argument, when for a short time the blunt words may be selected
from three or four languages and tossed about, till some passing
incident brings a sudden peace.

There are other points that I am tempted to touch upon – the
riddle of the golden jewellery that some ayahs wear in their very
nostrils, for instance. These curious ornaments are puzzles in themselves to white folk, yet they give joy to those who wear them. There
are wiseacres who declare that these decorations are the tribal
punishment for losing caste, but the matter is too delicate to permit
inquiry, and must remain another unsolved mystery of the East.

Then there is that salaam, with both hands shielding their eyes,
and the low, graceful bow that accompanies the action – the
passports with their smudgy thumb impressions for identifications –
the gaily coloured shawl and wrappers – the picture of an amah in
her very masculine native pantaloons – the kits and bedding in neat
barrack-room array round the walls of the common room.

I remember, too, hearing of an ayah who was shipwrecked; of
another who was twice torpedoed in the Great War; of a third who
left the Home, was saved from a liner sunk by enemy action, and
turned up again at Hackney before the news of the disaster became
public property.

And as I conclude these reminiscences of a strange group of
clannish women that a far-flung Empire and our innate lust for
wandering have brought into being as a class, I seem to see in the
back of my mind's eye a cabin in a great ocean-going steamship. In a
bunk is a soft, but restless, bundle. Bending over the bundle, keeping
the little white arms and hands still, is Antony – or is it Lee Ah Su? –
or Mariambai? – or Gangoo? – or Agida the Cingalese? – crooning

out that low, rhythmic lullaby that soothes to slumber the babies of all the universe, white or black, brown or yellow, the song that forms the melody and grand march-past of ever-faithful mother-love.

10 *Daily Mail,* 2 April 1924, p. 13.[80]
[British Newspaper Library shelfmark MLD6]

ARTIST-HERMIT OF WEMBLEY
85 Ft. PAINTING SINGLE-HANDED
GORGEOUS DISPLAY IN INDIAN PAVILION
By Sir Percival Phillips[81]

There is one man in the great army of workers at Wembley Park whose desperate eagerness to finish his share of the British Empire Exhibition within the allotted time is an example to others. His name is Mukel Dey.[82] You will find him leading an almost hermit-like existence in the great domed pavilion, half mosque and half palace in appearance, which is India's contribution to the new Imperial City.

He is labouring night and day, heedless of overtime or trade unions, snatching a little sleep at intervals in a hut only a few feet away from his work, pausing reluctantly for food and intent only on completing the task in hand.

Needless to say, Mukel Dey is an artist. He has come from the famous Tagore art school in Bengal to paint single-handed a mural decoration 85ft. long in the Bengal Court. It promises to be one of the many artistic marvels of Wembley. Mukel Dey says modestly that Europe has never seen anything like it.

PANELS IN VIVID COLOURS

He is covering the wall with a freehand design in white on chocolate ground, inset with large panels containing gay figures in bold and vivid colours. The pattern of the main design is one that Mukel Dey has seen the village women of Bengal draw with their fingers in the loose earth. The panelled figures show the influence of his long study

80 The *Daily Mail* was owned by Harold Harmsworth, Lord Rothermere (1868–1940), from 1922 and was essentially conservative-leaning.
81 Percival Phillips (1877–1937) was a well-known journalist and war correspondent.
82 Mukul Dey (1895–1989) was a Bengali artist who specialized in dry-point etching. He studied and worked in London from 1920 to 1927. His name is spelt Mukel throughout this article by Phillips.

of the famous Ajanta caves in Hyderabad, which are decorated with early Buddhist frescoes, the earliest examples of Indian mural paintings.[83]

Other native artists are beautifying the courts and galleries of the pavilion which is to be the exhibition home of the Indian Empire, but Mukel Dey seems to over-shadow them all as he toils away with set face and burning eyes, building up his masterpiece with the sure hand of a craftsman. 'I must be ready', murmurs Mukel Dey when people try to talk to him.

The pavilion of the Indian Empire will be very beautiful when it is finished. Visitors who know India will recognise in its graceful lines a strong suggestion of the Taj Mahal and the Jama Masjid harmoniously blended in an original design which still preserves its originality. A great cloistered court surrounds the main building, and opening from it are lesser courts and galleries where the arts and industries of the Eastern Empire will be displayed in appropriate settings.

There will be alligators, snakes, goats, oxen, and water buffalo among the offerings of the Indian provinces. Many of the exhibits have arrived. The Madras section is complete. Bengal and the Punjab still await the majority of their collections. The intricate model exhibit of the Calcutta Improvement Trust lies unpacked in one corner. A model of the docks has been sent by the Port Commissioners. The Victoria Memorial at Calcutta, which has been described as a modern Taj Mahal, will be shown in miniature.

Bengal is contributing a varied display of products by its inhabitants, ranging from ivory, brass, bell-metal, and copper goods of exquisite design and workmanship to jute, leather tanned and treated in native fashion, and embroideries from the Kalimpong Industrial School. There will be an exhibit showing the progress made in treating leprosy; a collection of chemicals, including Indian crude drugs, and examples of agricultural progress in Bengal.

Madras and the Punjab have sections not less comprehensive.

In the Punjab Court the decorations are being done by pupils from the Mayo art school at Lahore (founded by Mr Lockwood Kipling, father of Mr Rudyard Kipling), under the supervision of

83 The Ajanta caves had been 'rediscovered' in 1819 by a British hunting party.

Mr Lionel Heath, principal of the school, and Mr H.M. Quadri, head teacher.[84] Their wall designs are based upon 17th-century Punjabi tile work.

Although the effect obtained is very brilliant, the artists regret that they have not been able to use their own native colours, which, they say, 'glitter like jewels'. Unfortunately it takes too long to make them. One colour may require a month's preparation.

84 Lionel Heath (1871–1938) was appointed Principal of Mayo School of Arts and Crafts at Lahore in 1913.

11 F. *Yeats-Brown,*[85] *'A Buddhist in Bayswater', Spectator (30 January 1926), pp. 160–1*[86].
[British Library shelfmark ZC.9.d.558]

Last month I heard a tall priest, dressed in the saffron robes of an Oriental ascetic, attempt to convert an American audience to Buddism [*sic*]. A few days ago I saw him again in London and learned of his object in coming here. His project is to establish a Buddhist missionary centre in England.

Before taking my seat in the Town Hall, New York, I had looked round the hall and observed that the gathering was comprised chiefly of that curious type of citizen, with lofty brow but vacant eye, who seems to emerge from nowhere to form the clientele of Eastern cults. Some distinguished persons, however, were supporting the speaker on the platform, amongst them Mr Ralph Waldo Trine, author of *In Tune with the Infinite.*[87]

Had any of us, I asked myself, really attained to inward harmony? Judged by outward appearance one person only in that audience of a thousand stood out as having learned the secrets of poise and peace, and that was the Anagàrika Dharmapàla who was to address us.[88] Certainly he looked delicate, but he seemed to hold an inner light within him, a latent fire of purpose.

'Our friend is most infirm', said the chairman, 'and you must excuse him if he speaks sitting down.' But when our Buddhist came to speak, he rose to the full six feet of him and brandished a walking

85 Francis Yeats-Brown (1866–1944) was author of *The Lives of a Bengal Lancer* in 1930. He had been an officer in the British Indian Army and an assistant editor for the *Spectator* for whom he often wrote reviews on books about or written by Indians. In 1937, Yeats-Brown wrote a book on yoga and lectured in the United States and Europe on India, religion and yoga.
86 The *Spectator*'s editor from 1925 to 1932 was Evelyn Wrench (1882–1966) and although generally sympathetic to the Conservative party also had Liberal contributors.
87 Ralph Waldo Trine (1866–1958) wrote a number of books on philosophy and religion.
88 Anagarika Dharmapala (1864–1933) was a Sri Lankan Buddhist who toured Asia, America and Europe and is credited with reviving South Asian Buddhism.

stick at the audience. 'I learned of your faith in a mission school in Ceylon,' he said 'and one day the missionary took his gun and shot some little birds – so – and so! That made me revert to the faith of my fathers. But I have studied the Bible and revere its teachings. Your Master was poor and homeless. In all humility I claim to follow in His footsteps. I also have no money and nowhere to lay my head. But I have work to do in bringing the peace of the Buddha westward, and friends have provided funds for me to establish a church in London. On my way, I have stopped to tell you of the Lord Buddha, who was born a Prince and renounced his Kingdom to find, if may be, a solution to life's mysteries. For six years he studied the Ancient Wisdom, to find at last, in the words of your Teacher, that the Kingdom of Heaven is within Man himself. There is no heaven or hell but of your own making. Discover, then, the paradise here in this body pent – the heaven here and now of which Lord Buddha tells.'

And so on for an hour. Not a move or a cough from the audience. Not a tremble in those lips that thundered the denunciations of an Isaiah against our spiritual sloth, nor any hint of exhaustion in that frail frame. Here was a man with a message. He delivered it erect, composed, master of himself and his hearers, with the art of an orator and the dignity of a priest to whom the world is nothing. When he sat down there was a dead silence, followed by a burst of applause. We were moved – but not converted.

How will his audiences take him in England? Can the austere, bloodless precepts of Buddism [*sic*] gain a foothold in this land of beef and beer? In order to find out, I made a pilgrimage to 52 Lancaster Gate where the Anagàrika Dharmapàla is now living. He is a handsome man of sixty, with aquiline features, and a shock of white hair. He was sitting over a gas fire, his saffron robe looking rather *dépaysé* in the gloom of a London winter.

Buddha, he argues, came to India at a time when that country was in a bloom of its glory. His message can be understood only by a highly-developed people. So now that Great Britain and America are in the flower of their prosperity the Angàrika Dharmapàla claims – and doubtless will receive – as fair a hearing for his preaching as our missionaries get in India and Ceylon. As a young man, the Anagàrika Dharmapàla was the guest of Sir Edwin Arnold in London, and went from there to Chicago to attend the World's Parliament of Religions, as spokesman for Buddhism.[89] Since then he has been working in Calcutta and Buddh-Gaya. During the War he was imprisoned as a pacifist. No matter; that is over. As an undoubted authority on Southern Buddhism he is to be welcomed. The East has something very real to give the West, although the West, in its workshop of *nama rupa* (names and forms) is inclined to believe with Lord Chesterfield that ten minutes of concrete thinking is worth a lifetime of the 'inane meditation of India.'

Is meditation inane? If we practiced peace as we practice golf might not our asylums and hospitals be emptier? Meditation has certainly not done the Anagàrika Dharmapàla any harm. He is serene, alert, perceptive, versatile in no common degree. When his time comes to die, he tells me, he will do it with open eyes. 'It is all over – snap – in a second,' he says, '– one of the easiest actions in this beautiful life of ours. We priests who try to teach you of life would consider it a humiliation to die haphazard, struggling. We learn to meet death as it should be met. As to sleep, you can almost dispense with it if your mind and body are pure. Two hours is enough for me. Happiness? You win it through meditation and your mind you conquer through right management of breath. I see you have the lotus seat – ' (half unconsciously, as I listened, I had crossed my legs in the ancient posture of the Buddhist statues) '– and that will help your breath. Breathing, as your doctors tell you, is directly linked with brain processes.'

But to report him thus is scarcely fair. A philosophy which reaches from the bowels of man to cosmic spaces cannot be condensed into a few paragraphs. One thing, however, should be said. Buddhism has been misinterpreted as annihilation, instead of being translated as bliss. Buddhists, like Christian Scientists, affirm happiness as a law. The Buddhist heaven is 'closer than hands or breathing', and is to be won in this life, not in the hereafter.

The Angàrika Dharmapàla will create few eddies in the spiritual life of this country, for his teaching is too alien to our mental habits. But he should be heard by those interested in Eastern faiths, for as a teacher of them he is as authentic as he is eloquent.

F. Yeats-Brown

89 The World's Parliament of Religions in Chicago took place in 1893.

12 'India Society's Exhibition of Modern Art', *Indian Art and Letters,*
VIII(2) (1934): 98–9: Address by John de la Valette[90] broadcast from the
London studios of the BBC, 18 December 1934 at 4.30.[91]
[British Library shelfmark SV13]

The New Burlington Galleries are only a stone's throw off Bond
Street, and therefore in the heart of the West End. On the well-lit top
floor have been brought together in adjoining rooms some of the
best work of present-day Indian artists. From Western India, where
the Bombay School of Art has exercised such a marked influence,
outstanding works have come, and from Bengal, where Calcutta has
been the centre of the modern artistic revival. From Madras in the
south, from Delhi, Lucknow, and Lahore in the north, beautiful
pictures have been sent, whilst interesting pieces have been lent by
the Maharajas of Patiala, Indore, and Jaipur, and the State Schools of
Art in Baroda, Kashmir, and Indore.

In the first gallery the effect of Mr Gladstone Solomon's teaching
at the Bombay School of Art is clearly visible in the excellence of the
drawing and the frequent use of European technique.[92] Nevertheless,
the graceful treatment of individual figures, the ease with which large
groups are composed, and the general tendency of aims and ideals
remain essentially Indian. Of historical interest is a big portrait in oils
of Sir Jamsetji Jeejebhoy, who was not only the first Indian to be
created a baronet, but also the founder of the Bombay School of
Art.[93]

The second gallery has on its north wall a very representative
collection of water colours from Northern India, prominent among

90 John de la Valette was secretary of the Royal Society of Arts in the 1930s.
91 *Indian Art and Letters* was the journal of the India Society published from
   1925.
92 William Ewart Gladstone Solomon (1880–1965), born in South Africa,
   became Principal of the Bombay School of Art in 1918.
93 Jamsetji Jeejebhoy (1783–1859) was born in Bombay and began his career
   trading cotton and opium with China. He soon established a large mercan-
   tile firm in Bombay and pursued philanthropic interests that included
   founding the Bombay School of Art in 1857. He was knighted in 1842 and
   awarded a baronetcy in 1858.

which are the works of the three brothers Ukil.[94] In some cases we notice a tendency to exaggerate the wash-process of water-colour painting, which modern Indian artists have derived from Japanese rather than from Indian sources.

Further on are three exquisite water-colour figures by that brilliant artist Chugtai, which cannot fail to appeal.[95] The Lucknow collection is rich in small paintings, some of them on silk, in which the line work is as delicate as the blending of the colours.

The south and part of the east walls are taken up by the Bengal school. The works here shown of the Tagore brothers explain why they exercised so great an influence on their contemporaries as to account for the modern renaissance of art in Bengal.

Dr Abanindranath Tagore's set of illustrations for the Arabian Nights tales deserves to be used for its intended purpose, while Goganendranath Tagore's sepia drawings have many of the qualities which European modernists strive after.[96] The younger exponents of this school show that they are versed in their native traditions, and yet not insensitive to modern artistic conceptions.

Madras sent only a few pictures, but every one of them perfect in quality. Perhaps the dismal crow on a dripping branch, entitled 'After the Storm', by Mr Roy Chowdhuri, Principal of the Madras School of Art, deserves to be singled out for praise.[97] The black-and-white room includes a masterly large-size cartoon for 'Asoka's Last Gift,' by Mr A.K. Haldar, the head of the Lucknow School of Art,[98] excellent

94 Sarada Ukil (1889–1940), Ranada Ukil and Barada Ukil (1892–1967). The Ukil brothers were born in Bengal but Sarada Ukil set up the Ukil School of Art in Delhi in 1926. Ranada was one of the painters of the mural in India House in Aldgate in 1931.
95 Abdur Rahman Chughtai (1899–1975) was an artist inspired by the Persian and Moghul traditions. His works were exhibited in the 1924 Wembley Exhibition. After partition, Chughtai became known as the national artist of Pakistan.
96 Abanindranath Tagore (1871–1951) was a leading member of the Bengal School of Art. Gaganendranath Tagore (1867–1938), elder brother of Abanindranath and modernist painter, was the first Indian to use Cubism.
97 Devi Prasad Roy Chowdhury (1899–1975) was appointed the first Indian Principal of the Madras School of Art in 1929.
98 Asit Kumar Haldar (1890–1964) was the son and grandson of painters and the grand-nephew of Rabindranath Tagore. He was the first Indian to be elected to the Royal Society of Arts in London in 1934.

etchings by Mr Mukul Dey, Principal of the Calcutta School of Oriental Art, and a vigorous mezzotint by Mr Gupta, who leads the art movement in Lahore.[99]

The progress of architecture in Western India is demonstrated in the long corridor, and there are interesting sculptures from Bombay and Lucknow.

For the British visitor the most irresistible, and perhaps the most surprising, impression is that of the underlying unity of aims and ideals which this all-India Exhibition demonstrates. This seems a most valuable lesson to learn at this particular moment, when it is more than ever important that the peoples of India and of this country should understand one another.

We have so often been told to think of the peoples of India as cut up into numberless races, creeds, and castes with mutually exclusive aims and ideals, that it can only be helpful to be made to realize beyond the need for words how great is the fundamental similarity of thought and aspiration which links the King's subjects in all parts of his great Indian Empire.

Through modern Indian art we become aware of a spiritual unity among Indians which transcends whatever political differences may ruffle the surface of Indian thought. For nowhere are Indian thought and Indian outlook upon life more faithfully reflected than in the art of that great country.

99 Samarendranath Gupta was a former pupil of Abanindranath Tagore and Principal of the Mayo School of Art in Lahore.

Afterword

Rozina Visram

It is now over a quarter of a century since Pluto Press published my *Ayahs, Lascars and Princes: Indians in Britain 1700–1947* in 1986. Here I reflect on how I came to write the book.

If the truth were told, I did not set out to write a book. It arose out of my schoolteaching experiences. In 1972 I began teaching history and politics in a large comprehensive school in South East London. All local authority schools in London at the time came under the Inner London Education Authority (ILEA). Coming as I did with teaching experience in post-independence Zanzibar, the history curriculum in London schools with its prevailing Euro-centric bias and interpretations seemed to provide a limited world view. It is not possible now to remember every detail of the curriculum or all the available textbooks. But I do recall teaching the First World War to a group of fourth-year examination pupils. It was then, while browsing through A.J.P. Taylor's *The First World War: An Illustrated History* (Penguin Books, 1972 edn) in a library, that I came across one particular photograph. This was perhaps for me a defining moment: the beginning of what would become my research passion and which would set me eventually on the path of my pioneering study. Among a group of European soldiers in the photograph were three wounded Indians, one of them on a stretcher. It was the caption that arrested me. It read, 'Wounded Indians far from home'.

Now it must have been my colonial education. But neither at school in Zanzibar nor at college in Kenya nor at university in Uganda had I learnt that Indian soldiers had fought on the Western Front during the First World War. I knew Indian soldiers were deployed in Britain's colonial wars of conquest. I knew of Senegalese soldiers with the French army fighting on the Western Front. I also knew of African porters, the Carrier Corps, employed by the British army in East Africa during the First World War. (Tanganyika was then a German colony; hence the Great War had come to East Africa.) In fact, my maternal grandparents lived in Dar es Salaam in the district called *Kariako* and it was my grandfather who had told me of the origin of the name – an area associated with the Carrier Corps. But an Indian soldier fighting in a white man's war in Europe? It made nonsense of the ideology of the Raj. The photograph stayed in my memory. Much later, in the archives of the Imperial War Museum, I would come across albums of photographs of Indians in the trenches of the Western Front and discover extracts of their letters – the Censored Mails – in the India Office Library and Records.

Racism experienced by many black and South Asian people in the 1970s and 1980s, and the various initiatives to combat racism in the education service, provide another backdrop to *Ayahs, Lascars and Princes*. Perceived as recent arrivals and as economic migrants, they were seen as intruders into British society who had contributed nothing, and as such had no place in Britain. Seen as scroungers, their lives were disfigured by discrimination, marginalization and even racial violence. Schools reflected similar societal attitudes. My own personal experiences of the parents and the pupils I taught in a mixed, largely white school were on the whole very positive. There were few overt incidents of racism, but I vividly recall one distressing incident when I found under a pile of worksheets on my table a swastika and 'wogs out' scrawled in black ink. I recall too the deep embarrassment of the (white) cleaner who insisted that she would remove the offensive graffiti for me. For black and South Asian students racist taunts and abuse in the playground were not an uncommon experience. White teachers too could have low expectations of their pupils.

Black and South Asian parents and educationalists on the other hand, increasingly concerned at the treatment of their children by the British school system and the effect on their children's achievement, began to campaign for change. Another issue of concern to them was the impact of a Eurocentric curriculum on the self-image of their children. There is much literature on all this and I need not dwell on it here. Suffice it to say that the history curriculum became one arena for change as teachers began to examine the kind of history being taught and the way it was being taught.

Attempts to reflect the 'multi-cultural' nature of British society, and to counter Eurocentric perspectives and interpretations of the history curriculum, led to a spate of initiatives, but mainly in those schools with a visible presence of 'immigrant children' and then usually as special units bolted on to the existing curriculum. These initiatives took a variety of forms and paralleled trends in women's history, also at the time an issue of concern in education.

One of the methods adopted by some history teachers was to include the teaching of ancestral homelands, either separately as free-standing units on Africa, the Caribbean or India – lasting about half a term each – or as part of the 'contact and encounters' approach instead of the traditional theme of European voyages of exploration and 'discovery'.

Another approach was that of teaching the lives of 'great men and women', for instance in science, the arts or politics. Apart from Mary Seacole, the Jamaican-born Crimean nurse, these lives tended to be those of famous African-Americans.

A further alternative was a more issue-based approach, focusing on the social, political and economic contexts of slavery, conquest and colonialism.

Simultaneously these approaches were accompanied by an examination of standard texts for racist interpretations and exclusions.

Rarely was any attempt made to study the history of black people as part of British history. If studied at all, it was only as a separate unit.

By this time, following its initial Multi-Ethnic Policy Statement issued in 1977, the ILEA, after a period of consultation with various community groups, parents, teachers and heads of schools, issued an Anti-Racist Statement and Guidelines for all the ILEA establishments to show the Authority's commitment to eradicating racial discrimination. Then in 1979, as a result of joint collaboration and funding from the ILEA and the University of London Institute of Education, the Centre for Multicultural Education (CME, now the Centre for Inter-cultural Education) was set up as a cross-departmental and Institute-wide Centre with Dr Jagdish Gundara as its head. Such an

initiative by a local education authority and a higher education insti-
tution was a major innovation at the time. A Teacher-Fellowship
Scheme was also instituted allowing practising teachers from all
disciplines time to research and produce materials in their chosen
field for use in the classroom. After two years the CME came directly
under the control of the Institute, but the Fellowship Scheme and in-
service courses for teachers remained part of the continuing
collaboration. And it was the Teacher Fellowship Scheme – my lucky
break – that would give me the opportunity, space and time to
research and reflect on the process of migration, British History and
the school curriculum.

Before that, in 1981 the first International Conference on the
history of black peoples in Britain was held at the University of
London Institute of Education. (The papers were later published in
1992 by Avebury under the title *Essays on the History of Blacks in
Britain from Roman Times to the Mid-twentieth Century*, edited by
J.S. Gundara and I. Duffield.) There were no papers on South Asians
at the Conference and some discussion unsurprisingly centred on
this omission as at the time the term 'black' was used politically to
denote African, Caribbean and South Asian peoples. In many ways
the Conference marked a breakthrough for the serious study of
blacks and South Asians in Britain.

I was awarded a Fellowship for the academic year 1983/84 and my
brief was to produce a resource pack of photographs, documents and
text for use by teachers in the classroom. Indians in Britain from the
eighteenth century to the mid-twentieth century was my chosen
topic. I must admit I knew precious little. I had some vague
knowledge of servants derived from the novels of Dickens and
Thackeray; of sailors as part of the imperial maritime labour force;
of one Indian MP; and, of course, the Indian soldiers. How and
where was I to begin? Jagdish Gundara, the head of the Centre, was
encouraging and supportive throughout and gave me much valuable
advice. It was a busy year. At this distance in time, however, it is
difficult to convey the hours of work, the excitement, the frustra-
tions, the difficulties and the very many moments of doubt of
embarking on such a major project of research. Here I can only
provide a flavour.

Locating the elite, for instance Dadabhai Naoroji, the Liberal MP,

Maharajah Duleep Singh, Krishna Menon, Labour councillor for St Pancras, or Sake Dean Mahomed, the Brighton shampooing surgeon proved relatively easy. I could find entries under their names in the British Library printed books catalogues, and with help from archivists could seek out official documents or correspondence in the India Office Library and Records or in local archives. But finding the working class who not only left no records behind of their own but could also easily slip through official records proved a much harder task. People I consulted, however, were generous with their advice. For instance, Jatinder Verma of Tara Arts Theatre and Chris Power, joint author with Nigel File of *Black Settlers in Britain 1555–1958* (Heinemann Educational Books, 1981), readily shared their research and pointed me to the eighteenth-century newspapers. Searching for Indian servants through the reels of microfilms of Burney Papers was akin to looking for the proverbial needle in a haystack. The ever-helpful archivists at the India Office suggested that the Public and Judicial files might yield entries on the working class. Searching through the catalogue hand lists I unearthed some entries, but under categories such as 'natives of India abroad', 'the poor', 'destitute' and even 'lunatics'.

We now forget how much easier the task of a researcher is made by the very many electronic search aids and by having such sources as newspapers, census material or the Old Bailey Papers available on-line. When I began, even Martin Moir's excellent *A General Guide to the India Office Records* (London: British Library, 1988) was not available to guide me through the labyrinth of the classifications of records as the British Library only published it in 1988, two years after the publication of *Ayahs, Lascars and Princes*. As for academic studies, these all too often focused on the arrival of Indians and Pakistanis as economic migrants during the second half of the twentieth century, with only a brief mention of a few sailors, Sikh pedlars and adventurous individuals in the pre-Second World War period. These studies also suggested there was a discernible pattern of migration and community formation in the post-war period beginning with the arrival of single men planning to stay a few years and later, in response to the tightening immigration laws, being joined by families. These studies further suggested that it was only at this stage that the infrastructure usually associated with community life, such as ethnic shops, places of worship, social, political and cultural organizations, were established by South Asians in Britain. All these I would find in earlier times.

As I found my way around the various archives and dug deeper, I realized that although South Asians had been largely written out of the standard history books, they were very much present in various official records, in paintings and photographs, in newspapers, in memorials around us and in contemporary writings. I further realized that there *was* a South Asian history in Britain and that what I had managed to unearth was merely a small sample of this history. The long interaction between Britain and the Indian subcontinent begun in 1600 through trade, conquest, colonialism, and empire and the movement of peoples in *both* directions had brought not only goods, ideas and influences, but also South Asians to Britain long before the 1950s. And the influence of this interrelationship and interchange on the development of British society and culture, and the contributions of South Asians, were manifest in many areas of British life and formed one important strand of British history. This then would guide my thinking for the Resource Pack for schools – i.e., to integrate the history of South Asians into British history, enabling students to ask questions, widen their understanding and to move away from the traditional version of the 'island story' of Britain.

But the school pack was not to see the light of day. Instead it was suggested by the Inspectorate team that I think in terms of a school-book and approach national publishers. Of the five publishers – two of whom had published books on black history for schools already – none considered another book on 'black history' to be a worthwhile commercial proposition. They thought the subject, and the wealth and range of sources available, interesting but the general feeling remained: schools around the country would not find it relevant. So much then for my view that this was British history for all children and not only 'immigrant history'.

It was on the advice of Peter Fryer, author of *Staying Power: History of Blacks in Britain* (Pluto Press, 1984), that I wrote to Pluto Press. Although committed to publishing such a book, the problem for Pluto Press was that they did not have a school list. Could I turn this into a book of interest to the general reader that could become a companion volume to *Staying Power*? This was indeed a daunting – if not terrifying – prospect. I had never written a book. I had no confidence in my ability as I considered my writing experience to be limited. There was my Edinburgh M.Litt. thesis, *David Livingstone and India* (1971), and a published article on the same subject read at a conference to mark the centenary of David Livingstone's death, held at the Centre of African Studies, University of Edinburgh in 1973. During the Fellowship year in 1984 I had two small pieces for young readers published in *Dragon's Teeth*; a piece on 'Indian "Labour Migration" to Britain, 18th–19th century'; written jointly with Ian Duffield and Jagdish Gundara as part of a paper on 'Imperialism, Migration and the Indian Ocean' prepared for the Second International Conference on Indian Ocean Studies in Perth, Australia, December 1984; and another, 'The First World War and Indian Soldiers', presented at the Conference on the History of Black Peoples in London, held at the University of London Institute of Education in November 1984. And that was about it. But writing such a book had become a matter of honour to me as part of my Fellowship project. And it became a challenge I could not walk away from. Friends and colleagues were encouraging and offered to read my draft manuscript. The process of writing was a lonely and even at times painful but interesting experience. And *Ayahs, Lascars and Princes: Indians in Britain 1700–1947* came out in 1986.

Ayahs, Lascars and Princes was very much a first book and, as I wrote in the preface at the time, 'more a study of a few individuals than of communities'. Working as a researcher for the Museum of London in the early 1990s for their project and exhibition, 'The Peopling of London', deepened and widened my knowledge and understanding of the process of migration and the many layers of British history. My passion for research continued and, as I came across more material, a different and fuller picture of Asian life in Britain emerged. Three books for schools and several articles (including on history in the National curriculum) followed, and then in 2002 came *Asians in Britain: 400 Years of History* (Pluto Press). Other scholars, notably Bashir Maan and Shompa Lahiri in Britain and Antoinette Burton and Michael Fisher in the USA, have further added to our knowledge and understanding of this earlier period. All this has gone a long way to recovering South Asian history, and to challenging the accepted notions of the nature of their migration and community formation, and to highlighting the manifold contributions made by South Asians to British life and culture in the period before the arrival of the post-1950s generation. The interdisciplinary project *Making Britain: South Asian Visions of Home and Abroad 1870–1950*, which expands on my work and with which I have been involved as an adviser, has further revealed the wide range of voices, their networks and connections and the source material available.

Select bibliography

Manuscripts and records

All manuscripts, records and series details are fully cited in the footnotes. Here are lists of the main collections and archives.

Oriental and India Office Collections, The British Library, London (IOR)
Economic and Overseas Department: L/E/7 and L/E/9 Series
European Manuscripts: MSS Eur Series
Information Department: L/I/1 Series
Military Department: L/MIL/17 Series
Public and Judicial Department: L/PJ/6 and L/PJ/12 Series
Political and Secret Department: L/PS/11 Series
War Staff Papers: L/WS/1 Series

National Archives, Kew, London
Colonial Office: CO 323
Home Office: HO 45
War Office: WO 32; WO 95

The British Library, London
BM Add. 50524, f.109

Other repositories
The British Library Newspaper Library Colindale, London
Columbia University Rare Book and Manuscript Library (Ms. Coll.
   Poetry London-New York Records, 1943–1968)

Tower Hamlets Local History Library and Archives
The University of Reading Special Collection MS2750

Unpublished interviews

S. Banfield and R. Ahmed, 'Interview with Shakun Banfield', 17 March 2008.

Pujji, M. S., Stadtler, F. and Visram, R., 'Interview with M. S. Pujji', 18 February 2009.

Ram, A., 'This is my Home Now: Reminiscences of a Panjabi migrant in Coventry', no date.

Books, chapters, articles and reports

Adams, C. (ed.), *Across Seven Seas and Thirteen Rivers: Life Stories of Pioneer Sylheti Settlers in Britain* (London: THAP, 1987).

Ahmed, R., 'Networks of Resistance: Krishna Menon and Working-Class South Asians in Interwar Britain', in R. Ahmed and S. Mukherjee (eds), *South Asian Resistances in Britain, 1858–1947* (London: Continuum, 2011).

Ali, A., Singh, I.N., Shelvankar, K. and Subramaniam, A. (eds), 'Editorial', *Indian Writing*, 1(1) (Spring 1940): 3–4.

Ameer Ali, Syed, 'Anomalies of Civilisation: A Peril to India', *The Nineteenth Century and After* (April 1908): 568–81.

Anand, M.R., *Curries and Other Indian Dishes* (London: Desmond Hamsworth, 1932).

——, 'Review of Ali's *Twilight in Delhi* and Bromfield's *Nights in Bombay*', *Indian Writing* 1(3) (March 1941): 175–7.

——, 'The Place of India', in H. Ould (ed.), *Writers in Freedom* (London: Hutchinson, 1942), pp. 127–32.

Anon., 'Review of Toru Dutt', *The Examiner* (26 August 1876), p. 967.

Anon., 'Various Versifiers', *The Graphic* (4 November 1876), n.p.

Anon., 'Review of Toru Dutt', *The Examiner* (4 January 1879), p. 25.

Anon., 'Review of Arnold's *Light of Asia*', *The Examiner* (30 August 1879), pp. 1127–8.

Anon., "Review of Müller's *Upanishads*', *The Saturday Review*, 48(1) (13 September 1879), p. 335.

Anon., 'Review of Toru Dutt', *Guardian* (17 August 1881), p. 7.

Anon., 'A Hindoo Poetess', *Pall Mall Gazette* (21 April 1882), n.p.

Anon., 'India in London', *Pall Mall Gazette* (6 February 1888), n.p.

Anon., 'A Lady's Day at the Glasgow Exhibition', *Indian Magazine*, 214 (October 1888), n.p.

Anon., 'Review of *The Indian Eye on English Life*', *Saturday Review*, 76(1) (11 November, 1893): 548.

Anon.,'Review of *The Indian Eye on English Life*', *Calcutta Review*, 105(209) (July 1897): 107–20.

Anon., 'Review of *The Indian Eye on English Life*', *Athenaeum*, No. 4220 (30 January 1909): 129.

Anon., 'Dinner for Mr Tagore', *The Times* (13 July 1912), p. 5.

Anon., 'Review of *Gitanjali*', *Athenaeum*, No. 4438 (16 November 1912), n.p.

Anon., 'Review of *Gitanjali*', *Athenaeum*, No. 4458 (5 April 1913), n.p.

Anon., 'A Princess Fined: Refusal to Pay Taxes', *The Times* (30 December 1913), p. 2.

Anon., 'It's the Man that Matters', *Daily Graphic* (30 October 1924), n.p.

Anon., 'The Mark of their Caste', *Daily News* (23 July 1927), n.p.

Anon., 'Review of Cornelia Sorabji's *India Calling: The Memories of Cornelia Sorabji*', *Times Literary Supplement* (29 November 1934), p. 851.

Anon., 'Review of Cornelia Sorabji's *India Calling*', *The Times* (4 December 1934), p. 20.

Anon., 'Review of Karaka's *Oh you English!*', *Times Literary Supplement* (18 July 1935), p. 468.

Anon., 'Review: Nehru's Autobiography', *The Times* (28 April 1936), p. 10.

Anon., 'Review of Nehru's *India and the World*', *The Times* (14 July 1936), p. 11.

Anon., 'Mr. Wells and Mohammed', *Manchester Guardian* (13 August 1938), p. 10.

Anon., 'Indian Students: Eager Volunteers in London', *The Times* (3 September 1939), p. 3.

Anon., 'Immigration Points System Begins', BBC News, 29 February 2008 http://bbc.co.uk/1/hi/7269790.stm.

Ansari, H., *'The Infidel Within': Muslims in Britain since 1800*

(London: Hurst, 2004).

Ansari, H., 'Mapping the Colonial: South Asians in Britain', in N. Ali, V.S. Kalra and S. Sayyid (eds), *A Postcolonial People: South Asians in Britain* (London: Hurst, 2006), pp. 143–56.

Appignanesi, L. and Maitland, S. (eds), *The Rushdie File* (London: Fourth Estate, 1989).

Bagguley, P. and Hussain, Y., 'Flying the Flag for England: Citizenship, Religion and Cultural Identity among British Pakistani Muslims', in T. Abbas (ed.), *Muslim Britain: Communities under Pressure* (London and New York: Zed Books, 2005), pp. 208–21.

Balachandran, G., 'Cultures of Protest in Transnational Contexts: Indian Seamen Abroad, 1886–1945', *Transforming Cultures* e-journal, 3(2) (2008), http://epress.lib.uts.edu.au.ojs/index.php /TFC (accessed 20 December 2010).

Bance, P., *The Duleep Singhs: The Photograph Album of Queen Victoria's Maharajah* (Stroud: Sutton Publishing Ltd, 2004).

Barringer, T. and Flynn, T. (eds), *Colonialism and the Object: Empire, Material Culture and the Museum* (London: Routledge, 1998).

Benjamin, W., 'Theses on the Philosophy of History', in *Illuminations*, ed. and intro. Hannah Arendt, transl. Harry Zohn (London: Fontana 1992 [1973]), pp. 245–55.

Bhabha, H.K., 'The Other Question . . .: Homi K. Bhabha Reconsiders the Stereotype and Colonial Discourse', *Screen*, 24(6) (1983): 18–36.

Bickley, F., 'Review of Naidu's *The Broken Wing*', *Bookman*, 52(308) (May 1917): 51.

Blunt, E., 'Discordant Voices', *Times Literary Supplement* (10 May 1941), p. 220.

Boehmer, E., '"Immeasurable Strangeness" in Imperial Times: Leonard Woolf and W.B. Yeats', in N. Rigby and H.J. Booth (eds), *Modernism and Empire* (Manchester: Manchester University Press, 2000).

——, *Empire, the National and the Postcolonial, 1890–1920* (Oxford: Oxford University Press, 2002).

Booth, H.J. and Rigby, N. (eds), *Modernism and Empire* (Manchester: Manchester University Press, 2000).

Brah, A., *Cartographies of Diaspora: Contesting Identities* (London: Routledge, 1996).

Brock, A.C., 'Mr Tagore's Poems', *Times Literary Supplement* (7 November 1912), p. 492.

Brown, F.H., 'The Women of India and the West', *Times Literary Supplement* (12 October 1911), p 384.

——, 'Review of Cornelia Sorabji, *India Calling*', *The Observer* (27 January 1935), p. 7.

Brown, H., 'Review of *The Village*', *Times Literary Supplement* (15 April 1941), p. 215.

Burnell, A., 'The Sacred Books of the East', *The Academy* (9 August 1879), p. 95.

Burton, A., Making a Spectacle of Empire: Indian Travellers in Fin-de-Siècle London', *History Workshop Journal*, 42 (1996): 127–46.

——, *At the Heart of the Empire: Indians and the Colonial Encounter in Late-Victorian Britain* (Berkeley: University of California Press, 1998).

—— (ed.), *Politics and Empire in Victorian Britain: A Reader* (Basingstoke: Palgrave, 2001).

——, *Dwelling in the Archive: Women Writing House, Home and History in Late Colonial India*, Oxford: Oxford University Press, 2003).

Calder-Marshall, A., 'Review of Anand's *Across the Black Waters*', *Life and Letters Today* 28(4) (1941): 83–8.

Cannadine, D., *Ornamentalism: How the British Saw Their Empire* (London: Allen Lane, 2001).

Chambers, C., 'Images on Stage: A Historical Survey of South Asians in British Theatre Before 1975', in G. Ley and S. Dadswell (eds), *British South Asian Theatres: A Documented History* (Exeter: University of Exeter Press, 2010).

Charques, R.D., 'Tales of Indians: Review of Ahmed Ali's *Twilight in Delhi* and Mulk Raj Anand's *Across the Black Waters*', *Times Literary Supplement* (7 December, 1940), p. 619.

Chaudhuri, N., Katz, S.J. and Perry, M.E. (eds), *Contesting Archives: Finding Women in the Sources* (Urbana, IL: University of Illinois Press, 2010).

Chaudhuri, R., 'The Dutt Family Album', in A. Mehotra (ed.), *A History of Indian Literature in English* (London: Hurst, 2003), pp. 53–69.

Chitale, V., An Interview with Kingsley Martin in 'The Man in the

Street', broadcast May 15th, 1942, Contributors Talks File 1, BBC WAC, transcript, pp. 1–12.

Chowdhary, S., *Indian Cookery* (London: André Deutsch, 1954).

——, *I Made My Home in England* (Laindon: Grant-Best Ltd, n.d. [c. 1957])

Coomaraswamy, A.K., 'Indian Images with Many Arms', *Burlington Magazine for Connoisseurs*, 22(118) (January 1913): 189–91, 194–6.

——, *The Dance of Siva* (New York: Simpkin, Marshall, 1924).

Coombes, A., *Reinventing Africa: Museums, Material Culture and the Popular Imagination in Late Victorian and Edwardian England* (New Haven: Yale University Press, 2001).

Corrigan, G., *Sepoys in the Trenches: The Indian Corps on the Western Front 1914–15* (Stroud: Spellmount, 2006).

Das, S., 'Sepoys, Sahibs and Babus: India, the Great War and Two Colonial Journals', in M. Hammond and S. Towheed (eds), *Publishing in the First World War: Essays in Book History* (Houndmills, Basingstoke: Palgrave Macmillan, 2007), pp. 61–77.

—— 'India and the First World War', in M. Howard (ed.), *A Part of History: Aspect of the British experience of the First World War* (London: Continuum, 2008).

—— (ed.), *Race Empire and First World War Writing* (Cambridge: Cambridge University Press, 2011).

de Certeau, M., *The Practice of Everyday Life*, transl. Steven Rendall (Berkeley: University of California Press, 1987).

De La Valette, J., 'India Society's Exhibition of Modern Art', *Indian Art and Letters*, VIII(2) (1934): 98–9.

Dendooven, D. and Chielens, P. (eds), *World War I: Five Continents in Flanders* (Tielt: Lannoo, 2008).

Derrida, J., *Acts of Literature*, ed. Derek Attridge (London: Routledge, 1992).

Devee, S., *Autobiography of an Indian Princess* (London: John Murray, 1921).

Douds, G.J., 'The Men who Never Were: Indian POWs in the Second World War', *South Asia: Journal of South Asian Studies*, 27(2) (August 2004): 183–216.

Dover, C., *Brown Phoenix* (London: College Press, 1950).

Driver, F. and Gilbert, D. (eds), *Imperial Cities* (Manchester: Manchester University Press, 1999).

Fisher, M.H., *Counterflows of Colonialism: Indian Travellers and Settlers in Britain, 1600–1857* (New Delhi: Permanent Black, 2004).

——, 'Multiple Meanings of 1857 for Indians in Britain', *Economic and Political Weekly*, 42(19) (12 May 2007): 1703–9.

——, Lahiri, S. and Thandi, S., *A South Asian History of Britain* (Oxford: Greenwood World, 2007).

Forster, E.M., *Two Cheers for Democracy* (London: Penguin, 1945).

Frances, H., '"Pay the Piper, Call the tune!": The Women's Tax Resistance League', in M. Joannou and J. Purvis (eds), *The Women's Suffrage Movement* (Manchester: Manchester University Press, 1998).

Franco-British Exhibition, London, 1908. Official Guide (London: Bemrose & Sons Limited, 1908).

Frank, K., *Indira: The Life of Indira Nehru Gandhi* (London: HarperCollins, 2001).

Fryer, P., *Staying Power: History of Blacks in Britain* (London: Pluto, 1984).

Gandhi, M.K., *An Autobiography, or The Story of my Experiments with Truth*, transl. M. Desai (London: Penguin, 2001).

George, T.S.G., *Krishna Menon: A Biography* (London: Jonathan Cape, 1964).

Gerzina, G.H. (ed.), *Black Victorians/Black Victoriana* (New Brunswick, NJ: Rutgers University Press, 2003).

Ghosh, A., *In an Antique Land* (New Delhi: Seagull Press, 1992).

Gorrell-Barnes, R., 'An Indian Prince in Europe', *Times Literary Supplement* (5 December 1912), p. 561.

Government of India, *India's Contribution to the Great War* (Calcutta: Government of India, 1923).

Government of India, *Our Merchant Seamen* (New Delhi: Government of India 1947).

Green, J., *Black Edwardians: Black People in Britain, 1901–1914* (London: Frank Cass, 1998).

Greenhalgh, P., *Ephemeral Vistas: The Expositions Universelles, Great Exhibitions and World's Fairs, 1851–1939* (Manchester: Manchester University Press, 1988).

Greenhut, J., 'The Imperial Reserve: The Indian Corps on the Western Front, 1914–15', *Journal of Imperial and Commonwealth*

History, 12(1) (1983): 54–73.

Hobhouse, M., 'Review of *Primavera*', *The India Magazine*, No. 238 (October 1890): 512.

Hoffenberg, P.H., *An Empire on Display: English, Indian, and Australian Exhibitions from the Crystal Palace to the Great War* (Berkeley: University of California Press, 2001).

Home Office, Life in the UK Test: www.lifeintheuktest.gov.uk.

Hosain, A., 'Of Memories and Meals', in Antonia Till (ed.), *Loaves and Wishes: Writers Writing on Food* (London: Virago, 1992), pp. 141–6.

Huggan, G., *The Postcolonial Exotic: Marketing the Margins* (London: Routledge, 2001).

Hughes, D.L., 'Kenya, India and the British Empire Exhibition of 1924', *Race and Class*, 47(4) (April–June 2006): 66–85.

Indian Comforts Fund, *War Record of the Indian Comforts Fund: A Record and Review, 1939–1945* (London: Indian High Commission, 1946).

India Office, *India and the War 1939–1945, The Facts* (London: Information Department, India Office, 1946).

Innes, C.L., *A History of Black and Asian Writing in Britain, 1700–2000* (Cambridge: Cambridge University Press, 2000).

Jack, G.M., 'The Indian Army on the Western Front, 1914–1915: A Portrait of Collaboration', *War in History*, 13(3) (2006): 329–62.

Jenkinson, J., *Black 1919: Riots, Racism and Resistance in Imperial Britain* (Liverpool: Liverpool University Press, 2009).

—— 'On the Margins? South Asians in Britain during the 1919 Seaport Riots', unpublished paper presented at the 'Making Britain: South Asian Resistances, 1870–1950' Inter-University Postcolonial Seminar Series, spring 2009.

Kapurthala, R.J.S., *My Travels in Europe and America 1893* (London: Routledge and Sons, 1895).

Karaka, D.F., *With the 14th Army* (Bombay: Thacker, 1944; London: D Crisp, 1945).

——, *Then Came Hazrat Ali: Autobiography 1972* (Bombay: D.F. Karaka, 1973).

Khilnani, S. 'Gandhi and Nehru', in A. Mehrotra (ed.), *A History of Indian Literature in English* (London: Hurst, 2003), pp. 135–56.

Kitchlew, F.Z., *Freedom Fighter: The Story of Dr Saifuddin Kitchlew*

(Bognor Regis: New Horizon, 1979).

Klug, F., 'In the Footsteps of H.G. Wells', *New Statesman*, 9 October 2000, www.newstatesman.com/200010090006.

Kundu, K., S. Bhattacharya and K. Sircar, *Imagining Tagore: Rabindranath and the British Press (1912–1941)*(Calcutta: Sahitya Samsad, 2000).

Kureishi, H., *Dreaming and Scheming: Reflections on Writing and Politics* (London: Faber, 2002).

Lahiri, S., *Indians in Britain: Anglo-Indian Encounters, Race, and Identity, 1880–1930* (London: Frank Cass, 2000).

——, *Indian Mobilities in the West, 1900–1947: Gender, Performance, Embodiment* (New York: Palgrave Macmillan, 2010).

Lambert-Hurley, S., 'Out of India: The Journey of Begum of Bhopal, 1901–1930', in T. Ballantyne and A. Burton (eds), *Bodies in Contact: Rethinking Colonial Encounters in World History* (Durham: Duke University Press, 2005), pp. 293–309.

Lambert-Hurley, S. and Sharma, S., *Atiya's Journeys: A Muslim Woman from Colonial Bombay to Edwardian Britain* (Delhi: Oxford University Press, forthcoming).

Lawrence, D.H., *The Collected Letters* (London: Heinemann, 1970).

Lewis, R., *Rethinking Orientalism: Women, Travel and the Ottoman Empire* (London: IB Tauris, 2004).

Littler, J., '"Festering Britain": the 1951 Festival of Britain, Decolonisation and the Representation of the Commonwealth', in S. Faulkner and A. Ramamurthy (eds), *Visual Culture and Decolonisation in Britain* (Aldershot: Ashgate, 2006), pp. 21–42.

Lloyd, D., *Anomalous States* (Dublin: Lilliput Press, 1993).

Lutyens, E., *Candles in the Sun* (London: Rupert Hart-Davis, 1957).

Maan, B., *The New Scots: The Story of Asians in Scotland* (Edinburgh: Donald, 1992).

MacKenzie, J., *Propaganda and Empire: The Manipulation of British Public Opinion 1880–1960* (Manchester: Manchester University Press, 1984).

MacMunn, G., *The Martial Races of India* (London: Sampson Low, Marston & Co., 1930).

Majeed, J., *Autobiography, Travel and Postnational Identity: Gandhi, Nehru and Iqbal* (Basingstoke: Palgrave, 2007).

Malabari, B.M., *The Indian Eye on English life or Rambles of a Pilgrim*

Reformer (London: Archibald Constable & Co., 1893).

Marr, A., *The Making of Modern Britain* (Basingstoke: Palgrave, 2009).

Marshall, A.C., 'Nurses of our Ocean Highways: The Fascinating Story of the Ayahs and Amahs who sail the Seven Seas', *Quiver*, 57 (August 1922).

Mathur, S., *India by Design: Colonial History and Cultural Display* (Berkeley: University of California Press, 2007).

McCartney, W. and 'Poy', *Evening News* (6 July 1923), n.p.

McKeich, C., 'Botanical Fortunes: T.N. Mukharji, International Exhibitions, and Trade between India and Australia', *reCollections: Journal of the National Museum of Australia*, 3(1) (March 2008): 1–12.

McLynn, F., *The Burma Campaign: Disaster into Triumph 1942–45* (London: Bodley Head, 2010).

Menezes, S.L., *Fidelity and Honour: The Indian Army from the Seventeenth to the Twenty-First Century* (New Delhi: Oxford University Press, 1999).

Merewether, J.W.B. and Smith, F., *The Indian Corps in France* (London: John Murray, 1917).

Metcalf, T.R., *Ideologies of the Raj* (Cambridge: Cambridge University Press, 1998).

Mitchell, T., 'The World as Exhibition', *Comparative Studies in Society and History*, 31(2) (1989): 217–36.

Maharani of Baroda, the, and S.M. Mitra, *The Position of Women in Indian Life* (Longmans Green and Co, 1911).

Mitter, P., *The Triumph of Modernism: India's Artists and the Avant-garde 1922–1947* (London: Reaktion, 2007).

Modood, T., *Multicultural Politics: Racism, Ethnicity and Muslims in Britain* (Edinburgh: Edinburgh University Press, 2005).

Mukharji, T.N., *A Visit to Europe* (Calcutta: W. Newman, 1889).

Mukherjee, S., 'Herabai Tata and Sophia Duleep Singh: Suffragette Resistances for India and Britain, 1910–1920', in R. Ahmed and S. Mukherjee (eds), *South Asian Resistances in Britain, 1858–1947* (London: Continuum, 2011).

——, *Nationalism, Education and Migrant Identities: The England-Returned* (London: Routledge, 2010).

Naidu, S., *The Golden Threshold* (London: Heinemann, 1905).

Nasta, S., *Home Truths: Fictions of the South Asian Diaspora in Britain* (Basingstoke: Palgrave, 2002).

Natesan, G.E. (ed.), *All About the War: the Indian Review War Book* (Madras: G.A. Matesan & Co, 1915).

Nollen, S.A., *Paul Robeson: Film Pioneer* (Jefferson: McFarland, 2010).

O'Malley, K., *Ireland, India and Empire: Indo-Irish Radical Connections, 1919–64* (Manchester: Manchester University Press, 2008).

Omissi, D., *The Sepoy and the Raj: the Indian Army, 1860–1940* (Basingstoke and London: Macmillan/King's College, London, 1994).

——, (ed.), *Indian Voices of the Great War: Soldiers' Letters, 1914–18* (Basingstoke: Palgrave Macmillan, 1999).

Orwell, G., Memo, 1 Feb. 1942, in P. Davison (ed.), *The Complete Works of George Orwell: All Propaganda is Lies* (London: Secker & Warburg, 2001).

——, Letter to the Editor, *Times Literary Supplement* (23 May 1942), p. 259.

Owen, N., *The British Left and India: Metropolitan Anti-Imperialism 1885–1947* (Oxford: Oxford University Press, 2007).

Parekh, B., *Rethinking Multiculturalism: Cultural Diversity and Political Theory* (Basingstoke: Macmillan 2006 [2000]).

Parsons, T., *British Imperial Century, 1815–1914* (Oxford: Rowman & Littlefield, 1999).

Perry, F.W., *The Commonwealth Armies: Manpower and Organisation in two World Wars* (Manchester: Manchester University Press, 1988).

Phillips, P., 'Artist-Hermit of Wembley', *Daily Mail* (2 April 1924), p. 13.

Phillips, S., Binyon, L., Ghose, M. and Cripps, A.S., *Poems, by Four Authors* (Oxford: B.H. Blackwell, 1890).

Prasad, B. (ed.), *Official History of the Indian Armed Forces in the Second World War, 1939–45*, 23 vols (Combined Inter-Services Historical Section (India & Pakistan), 1952–1963).

Radhakrishnan, S., *The Philosophy of Tagore* (Basingstoke: Macmillan, 1918).

Raine, K., *India Seen Afar* (Devon: Green Books, 1990).

Ralph, O., *Naoroji, the First Asian MP: A Biography of Dadabhai Naoroji* (Antigua: Hansib, 1997).

Ram, J., *My Trip to Europe* (Lahore: Mufd-i-am Press, 1893).

Rama Rau, D., *An Inheritance: The Memoirs of Dhanvanthi Rama Rau* (London: Heinemann, 1977).

Ranasinha, R., *South Asian Writers in Twentieth-century Britain: Culture in Translation* (Oxford: Oxford University Press, 2007).

——, 'South Asian Writers and the BBC', *Journal of South Asian Diaspora* (March 2010): 57–71.

Ray, S., 'The Spirit of Tagore', *The Quest* (October 1913): 40–57.

Rice, S., 'Indian Plays in London', *Asiatic Review*, XVIII(53) (January 1922): 129.

——, 'Indian Writers of English Verse and Prose', *Indian Art and Letters*, xiv(2) (1940): 94–104.

Rubin, W. (ed.), *Primitivism in 20th Century Art* (New York: Museum of Modern Art, 1984).

Russell, G., *For King & Another Country* (Ilfracombe: Stockwell, 2010).

Ruthven, M., *A Satanic Affair: Salman Rushdie and the Rage of Islam* (London: Chatto & Windus, 1990).

Saklatvala, S., *The Fifth Commandment: Biography of Shapurji Saklatvala* (Salford: Miranda Press, 1991).

Saklatvala, Shapurji, maiden speech to House of Commons, 23 November 1922 (HC Deb 23 November 1922, Vol 159 cols 115–17).

Salter, J., *The Asiatic in England* (London: Seeley, Jackson and Halliday, 1872).

——, *The East in the West* (London: S.W. Partridge & Co., 1896).

Sandhu, S., *London Calling: How Black and Asian Writers Imagined a City* (London: HarperPerennial, 2004).

Schneer, J., *London 1900: The Imperial Metropolis* (London: Yale University Press, 1999).

Sen, S., *Migrant Races: Empire Identity and K.S. Ranjitsinhji* (Manchester: Manchester University Press, 2004).

——, *Travels to Europe: Self and Other in Bengali Travel Narratives 1870–1910* (New Delhi: Orient Longman, 2005).

Sengupta, P., *Sarojini Naidu: A Biography* (London: Asia Publishing House, 1966).

Shah, S.I.A., 'Review Essay', *The Bookman* (October 1931): 7–8.

Shahani, R.G., 'Review of Anand's *The Sword and the Sickle*', *Times Literary Supplement* (2 April 1942), p. 221.

Shepherd, S.T., 'Review of *The Coolie*', *Times Literary Supplement* (20 June 1936), p. 520.

Singh, I., 'Indian Art at the Imperial Institute', *Indian Writing*, 1(3) (March 1941): 151–5.

Sivanandan, A., *A Different Hunger: Writings on Black Resistance* (London: Pluto Press, 1982).

Smith, T., *Asians in Britain* (London: Dewi Lewis, 2003).

Snaith, A., 'Sarojini Naidu in London', Postcolonial Seminar, King's College London, 19 March 2010.

Sokoloff, B., *Edith Ramsay: The Life of Edith Ramsey* (London: Stepney Books Publications, 1987).

Sorabji, C., *India Calling: The Memories of Cornelia Sorabji* (London: Nisbet, 1934).

Squires, M., *Saklatvala: A Political Biography* (London: Lawrence & Wishart, 1990).

Sturgeon, M., *Studies in Contemporary Poets* (London: George C. Harrap 1916).

Tabili, L., *'We Ask for British Justice': Workers and Racial Difference in Late Imperial Britain* (Ithaca, NY: Cornell University Press, 1994).

Tambimuttu, M.J., *Poetry London*, First Letter, February 1939.

——, *Out of this War: A Poem* (London: The Fortune Press, 1941).

Tarlo, E., *Clothing Matters: Dress and Identity in India* (London: Hurst and Co., 1996).

Thomas, N., *Colonialism's Culture: Anthropology, Travel and Government* (Cambridge: Polity Press, 1994).

Thompson, E.J., *Rabindranath Tagore* (Oxford: Oxford University Press, 1926).

Thomson, M.M., 'A Pilgrimage to Battersea', *British Weekly* (11 December 1924), n. p.

Tomlinson, P., 'Rev. of Nehru's *Unity of India*', *Times Literary Supplement* (6 September 1941), p. 446.

Trouillot, M.R., *Silencing the Past: Power and the Production of History* (Boston: Beacon Press, 1995).

Turner, S.V., 'The "Essential Quality of Things": E.B. Havell, Ananda Coomaraswamy and Indian Sculpture in Britain', special issue on 'Nineteenth-Century Sculpture in its Global Contexts', ed. J.

Edwards and M. Hatt, *Journal of Visual Culture in Britain* (Autumn 2010): 239–64.

Visram, R., *Ayahs, Lascars and Princes: Indians in Britain 1700–1947* (London: Pluto, 1986).

——, *Asians in Britain: 400 Years of History* (London: Pluto, 2002).

Wadia, A., *The Light is Ours: Memoirs and Movements* (International Planned Parenthood Federation, 2001).

Wadsworth, M., *Comrade Sak. Shapurji Saklatvala MP: A Political Biography* (Leeds: Peepal Tree, 1998).

Wainwright, A.M., *'The Better Class' of Indians: Social Rank, Imperial Identity, and South Asians in Britain, 1858–1914* (Manchester: Manchester University Press, 2008).

Walkowitz, J.R., 'The Indian Woman, the Flower Girl, and the Jew: Photojournalism in Edwardian London', *Victorian Studies*, 42(1) (October 1998): 3–46.

——, '"The Vision of 'Salome'": Cosmopolitanism and Erotic Dancing in Central London, 1908–1918', *American Historical Review* 108(2) (2003): www.historycooperative.org/journals/ahr /108.2/walkowitz.html (accessed 18 October 2010).

War Office, *Statistics of the Military Effort of the British Empire During the Great War, 1914–1920* (London: His Majesty's Stationary Office, 1922).

Wells, H.G., *Crux Ansata: An Indictment of the Roman Catholic Church* (2nd edn, Book Tree, 2000).

Wemyss, G., *The Invisible Empire: White Discourse, Tolerance and Belonging* (Farnham: Ashgate, 2009).

Wichmann, S., *Japonisme: The Japanese Influence on Western Art Since 1858* (London: Thames & Hudson, 1999).

Wilde, O., 'Review of *Primavera: Poems, by Four Authors*', *Pall Mall Gazette* (24 May 1890), p. 3.

Willcocks, J., *With the Indians in France* (London: Constable, 1920).

Yeats, W.B., Introduction, Rabindranath Tagore, *Gitanjali* (London: Macmillan, 1916).

Yeats-Brown, F., 'A Buddhist in Bayswater', *Spectator* (30 January 1926), pp. 160–1.

Young, P., *Report on Investigation into Conditions of the Coloured Population in a Stepney Area*, printed by 'The Hornsey Journal' Ltd, 1944.

Web resources

Making Britain Database: www.open.ac.uk/makingbritain
Oxford Dictionary of National Biography: www.oxforddnb.com

Index

Note: 'n.' After a page number indicated the number of a note on that page. Numbers in italic refer to figures on that page.